DIABETIC
LIVING®

EAT SMART
LOSE WEIGHT™

Houghton Mifflin Harcourt

Boston New York

2018

hmhco.com

Library of Congress Cataloging-in-Publication Data is available.

ISBN 978-1-328-73996-4 (paperback)
ISBN 978-1-328-73903-2 (ebook)

Printed in China

SCP 10 9 8 7 6 5 4 3 2 1

Meredith Corporation
Diabetic Living® Eat Smart Lose Weight™

EXECUTIVE EDITOR: Jennifer Wilson

CREATIVE DIRECTOR: Michael Belknap

CONTRIBUTING PROJECT MANAGER:
Shelli McConnell, Purple Pear Publishing, Inc.

DESIGN AND LAYOUT: Ananda Spadt, Super Panda Co.

COPY EDITOR: Gretchen Kauffman

COVER ART DIRECTOR: Nikki Sanders

COVER PHOTOGRAPHER: Blaine Moats

COVER FOOD STYLIST: Jennifer Peterson

DIABETIC LIVING® TEST KITCHEN DIRECTOR: Lynn Blanchard

DIABETIC LIVING® TEST KITCHEN CHEF: Carla Christian, RD, LD

Houghton Mifflin Harcourt

EXECUTIVE EDITOR: Anne Ficklen

MANAGING EDITOR: Marina Padakis Lowry

PRODUCTION EDITOR: Helen Seachrist

ART DIRECTOR: Tai Blanche

PRODUCTION DIRECTOR: Tom Hyland

FROM *the* EDITORS

Losing weight doesn't just happen by eating less. *What* you eat is actually more important than *how much*. Healthy living also means eating well.

Eat Smart Lose Weight will show you how. After you identify the steps for losing weight, you'll set goals and uncover ways to avoid the hazards that may prevent you from reaching them.

Next you'll learn to fuel your body with nutritious choices and discover the roles carbohydrate and protein play in a good diet. Our recipes are balanced and carb-aware, as well as low in fat.

Throughout this book, you'll find delicious meals, including family dinners and restaurant remakes.

We'll also teach you some specifics. To add health-smart vegetables to your diet, turn to "Veggie-Packed" *(p. 102)*. For examples of eating healthfully every day (it can be tricky), check out "5 Days of Meal Plans" *(p. 196)*. "Build a Healthy Plate" *(p. 124)* provides 10 complete meals that show you how to dish out portions in a healthy way.

The final piece to the losing-weight puzzle is exercise. In "Move More" *(p. 202)*, you'll find ways to exercise every day without going to the gym. It's full of tips and motivation and features five 30-minute at-home workouts.

You've made the commitment to lose weight. Nice work. This book will support you every step of the way.

Now it's time to get started on a healthier you!

1/4 Teaspoon   1 Teaspoon

EAT SMART
LOSE WEIGHT™
CONTENTS

WHAT IT TAKES *to*

LOSE WEIGHT

Determination and perseverance are key to weight loss success. These tips can help you lose weight and keep it off as you strive to meet your overall health goals.

YOUR CHECKLIST

Set goals with a focus on making healthy lifestyle changes that can lead to improvements in your overall health.

☑ Start Each Day with Breakfast

Kick-starting your day with a healthy breakfast can reinforce your resolve to eat healthfully the remainder of the day. Data from the National Weight Control Registry show that people who successfully keep pounds off eat breakfast.

☑ Pick Better Beverages

Calorie-loaded soft drinks, coffee drinks, fruit juice, and alcoholic beverages can pack on pounds. Opt for water and sugar-free beverages most of the time and sweeten coffee and tea with a low-calorie sweetener instead of sugar. Give plain water some punch with a sparkling water maker to add fizz or slices of fresh citrus and/or sprigs of fresh herbs for flavor.

☑ Fill Up on Water

You may be able to satisfy your hunger by quenching your thirst. Keep water with you to drink between meals and during meals. When a hunger craving hits, take a big drink. Foods that are high in water content, such as nonstarchy vegetables, can help you feel full as well.

☑ Plan Your Meals

Here's the weekly drill: plan your meals, inspect your pantry, stick to your shopping list, prepare your meals, eat, and repeat. Research suggests the fewer decisions you need to make about what and how much to eat, the more successful you'll be with weight control.

☑ Get to Know Portions

Restaurant portions skew how we view "normal" portions of food because more food on the plate is seen as a better value. Use a scale and measuring spoons and cups to learn what a healthy portion of food actually is and retrain your thinking.

☑ Eat More Veggies and Fruits

Vegetables and fruits, whether fresh, canned, or frozen, are nutrient-packed and low in calories. Fill at least half the plate with vegetables. Consume fruit, but remember to count the carbs.

☑ Keep Track

People who write down the foods they eat tend to lose twice as much weight as people who don't account for what they eat. Use an app on your phone or a simple pad of paper to keep track of everything you eat and how much. You can even use an app that tracks calories, fat, protein, and carbs, too.

☑ Snack Smart

Snacking can be dangerous— if you wait until you are hungry, you may overeat. Snack at regular times to ward off hunger and keep your blood sugar in check. If you crave a snack, drink a glass of water first. If you're still hungry, choose a healthy snack. Check your blood sugar before snacking to help choose the best type of snack (are you experiencing low blood sugar and need a fast-acting carb snack?), and take your medications as prescribed by your doctor.

☑ Move More and Stress Less

Studies show that losing weight and being physically active at least 30 minutes most days of the week can be powerful medicine to slow the progression of diabetes. De-stressing doesn't have to be complicated: Try a yoga class, use deep breathing, walk in the woods, or listen to music.

SETTING GOALS

When you set goals to improve your overall health, losing weight will naturally follow. What motivates you—keeping up with your children or grandchildren, taking vacations, or running a 5K race? Make your journey less about weight loss and more about living life to the fullest.

DEVELOPING HEALTHY *HABITS*

Forming healthy habits takes time, effort, and courage. This is a marathon, not a sprint. Over time your successes will lead to more success; forming healthy habits gets easier. Instead of hard work, it will just be life, and a healthy one at that! Follow these steps to get started.

1. Select the weight loss tip on page 7 that will be the easiest for you to adopt, such as eating more veggies and fruits each day.

2. Assess your current behaviors related to this tip and set some goals. Ask yourself: How many vegetables and fruits do I eat now? Then look at the barriers in your life that may get in the way of making this a habit. Figure out a way past those barriers. If you think it's too much work to prepare fresh vegetables, consider purchasing cut-up broccoli and carrots. Or wash and prep produce when you get home from shopping before it goes into the refrigerator.

3. Make changes in small steps and incorporate the goals with actions you already practice. Add a banana or blueberries to your breakfast. Or, if you eat a lunch of a sandwich and side of chips, choose carrots or grape tomatoes instead of the chips.

4. Pat yourself on the back for each small success you attain. Small rewards give you a feeling of accomplishment—buy a bouquet of flowers, take an hour for yourself, or buy a lottery ticket. Do whatever makes you smile.

SET GOALS THE *SMART* WAY

You'll be closer to forming healthy habits when you set S-M-A-R-T goals to help you get there.

Specific
Be exact and detailed. Narrowly define your goal.

Measurable
Choose a frequency. Ask: how often will I do this?

Attainable
Make your goal challenging, but something you can accomplish.

Realistic
Set a goal that fits the realities of your lifestyle and schedule.

Timely
Stay motivated and on track by setting short-term goals.

SAMPLE GOALS
TO GET YOU STARTED

This week, I will take four 30-minute walks after dinner.

For three dinners this week, I will make sure half my plate is filled with nonstarchy vegetables.

I will keep a record of everything I eat for one week.

I will drink at least 64 ounces (8 cups) of water every day this week.

6

WEIGHT LOSS TRAPS

& How to Avoid Them

You journal, you plan meals, you even exercise,
but the scale won't budge. Don't give up!
See if you've stumbled into one of these common
roadblocks and learn how to get them out of the way.

1.
THE *WRONG* PERSPECTIVE

"Don't diet," says Samantha Heller, M.S., RD, CDN, author of *Get Smart* (Johns Hopkins University Press, 2010). "Dieting instills fear and loathing in people. Adopting healthy lifestyle choices that can be kept forever should be the primary goal." Monitoring portion sizes and regular exercise are much more effective. Focus on eating the right combination of carbohydrate, protein, and fat and exercise regularly so you lose fat, not muscle mass, says Osama Hamdy, M.D., Ph.D., director of the Joslin Diabetes Center Inpatient Diabetes Program. On average, half of all weight loss can be attributed to losing muscle, and people already are prone to losing one pound of muscle each year.

2.
LACK OF *MOTIVATION*— ESPECIALLY TO EXERCISE

Losing weight won't happen if you are not "100 percent dedicated and motivated," Heller says. You have to be all-in to reach your weight loss goals. "Saying, *I don't know how to start; I don't know what to do*, is not a get-out-of-jail-free card," she says. "Get up, put your shoes on, and go for a walk. Start with five to 10 minutes, and over time your ability to put in more time will increase."

3.
POOR FOOD CHOICES & *TOO MUCH FOOD*

We tend to eat too much and not just of the bad stuff—the good stuff, too. Measure portions of all foods, even fruits and vegetables. Eating a healthful food doesn't justify overeating it.

Follow the plate method. Start with a 9-inch plate and fill half of the plate with nonstarchy vegetables, such as green beans, cucumbers, or salad greens. Fill one quarter with lean protein and the remaining quarter with a starch or grain. People who use visual cues to control portions lose more weight than those who don't, Heller says.

4.
EMOTIONAL EATING

Turning to food in response to stress, depression, loneliness, boredom, and more is an all-too-common coping mechanism. When emotional eating becomes a habit, food is no longer fuel for the body, says Suzanne Pecoraro, RD, CDE, owner of Diabetes Education Support Services. She recommends identifying emotions associated with mindless snacking to break the cycle. "Behavior-modification techniques can be useful. For example, if you feel the need to eat,

set the timer for 10 minutes and do something else, like taking a walk around the house, until the timer goes off."

When the time is up, you may just have better control over what you eat.

It's important to identify what emotions are often tied to your eating or overeating. Keep a journal and record when you overeat, making note of how you are feeling and what happened during the day.

5.
SOME DIABETES *MEDICATIONS*

Some diabetes meds may cause weight gain. Hamdy recognizes the frustration experienced by patients who are told to lose weight while being prescribed medications that do just the opposite.

"There are medications that don't cause weight gain. Talk with your health care provider about switching to those," he says.

"They can be more expensive, but in the long term the cost is minimal compared to the potential complications of not switching."

6.
IMPATIENCE

Weight loss won't happen overnight. Any new behavior is a skill that needs to be practiced, Heller says. "Creating a step-by-step plan can make behavior and habit changes a lot easier." Set realistic goals, such as losing five pounds by the first of next month. To get there, set smaller, more specific goals, like eating breakfast every morning. Join a gym and choose a workout class to attend twice a week or arrange to walk four times a week with a friend. A healthy rate of weight loss is one to two pounds per week. If you lose weight more quickly, it scares your body into thinking it is starving. When your body is in starvation mode, it wants to hold on to every bit of energy it can, making weight loss more difficult.

IS **SUGAR** OKAY?

NO MORE CARBS?

WHAT ABOUT EGGS?

CAN I EAT POTATOES?

Diet Myths **BUSTED!**

There's a lot of bad diet advice out there. Don't fall for these nutrition myths.

When you were first diagnosed with diabetes, your doctor may have taken only a few minutes and explained just a few things about the disease to you. It was hardly everything you need to know about your new way of eating.

You may have heard mostly what *not* to eat rather than what you *should* eat.

"The don't-eat list is shorter," says Michele Chynoweth, RD, CDE, California nutrition and diabetes consultant.

The full story is that there are many foods you can still eat, though nutrition guidelines can be confusing. Doctors only provide simplified and sometimes outdated dietary advice:

No sugar.
No pasta.
No potatoes.
No red meat and eggs.
Sound familiar?

Most people think diabetes means giving up their favorite foods and that they will be stuck eating the same things over and over.

Not so, says Susan Yake, RDN, CDE, and 2016 chair of the Academy of Nutrition and Dietetics Diabetes Care and Education Practice Group. "Dietitians can help people work some of those favorite foods into their meal plan."

A registered dietitian (RD or RDN) will give you a diet plan and help you navigate the grocery aisles. (You'll get a referral when you're diagnosed. If you don't, ask your doctor for one.) RDs won't tell you to eliminate certain foods, but rather to eat them less often.

"Food shouldn't be a bad guy," Chynoweth says.

Read on to bust four common diabetes food myths.

MYTH 1
CARBS ARE THE ENEMY

Many people think a high-carb diet caused their type 2 diabetes. But other factors, such as excess weight, genetics, and age, contribute to the disease.

Drastically cutting carbs won't necessarily treat diabetes. But it could cause starvation ketosis, which is different than diabetic ketoacidosis, and can result in headache, nausea, bad breath, and confusion, as well as nutrient deficiencies.

"Carbs are our energy system—that's our fuel; that's our gas in the car. Our brain works on carbohydrates, so we need them," Chynoweth says.

The U.S. Department of Agriculture (USDA) recommendation is that 45–65 percent of daily calories come from carbohydrate. Focus on complex carbs, such as fruit and whole grains that contain fiber and vitamins.

"I found when my patients changed to a more balanced program, where they were having the right amount of carbohydrate in their meals, they actually had more energy and felt better," Yake says.

MYTH 2
CUT OUT CHOLESTEROL & FAT

Health experts used to think dietary cholesterol, found in animal sources like red meats and eggs, sent blood cholesterol sky high. New research says otherwise.

"For most people, an egg a day is fine," Yake says.

Eggs provide protein as well as many nutrients, such as lutein, which contributes to good eye health.

Lean meat options, like chicken breast and pork tenderloin, and fish containing healthy fats, such as salmon, are typically recommended over beef.

If you do eat beef, choose lean cuts such as eye of round roast or steaks and top sirloin steaks and 95 percent lean ground beef. Enjoy lean beef in 3-ounce portions.

The USDA recommends that 20–35 percent of calories come from fat, but less than 10 percent should come from unhealthy saturated fats.

Fat contains more calories per gram than protein and carbohydrate, so it's important to keep portions in check to prevent excess calorie consumption that can lead to weight gain.

MYTH 3
NO WHITE FOODS

Don't cut out all white foods just yet. There are plenty of white foods that contain a wealth of nutrients. Whole grains like oatmeal and vegetables like mushrooms, cauliflower, and garlic contain disease-fighting antioxidants.

"Soluble fiber, especially in oatmeal, is helpful for both cholesterol as well as for blood sugars," Chynoweth says.

Even white potatoes can contribute to a healthful diet because they are a great source of potassium.

What makes potatoes unhealthy is how they're prepared and how much you eat. Calories and fat add up when potatoes are fried or topped with butter, salt, cheese, and sour cream. Instead, roast cubed potatoes in a little olive oil with herbs.

To keep portions in check, opt for a small baked potato (1¾- to 2½-inch diameter), which has up to 31 grams of carb, as your meal's starch source or choose ½ cup cubed potatoes, which contains 15 grams of carb.

MYTH 4
NO SUGAR

You don't have to cut sweets completely. Just don't make eating them an everyday occurrence.

"Most of us can't do never," Chynoweth says. "When we have a whole decade, two decades, or three decades forward to look at, to say, 'I will never have this again'—it tends to make a person feel punished."

Plus, because simple-carbohydrate foods, such as candy, raise blood sugar, they can benefit people with diabetes when hypoglycemia (low blood sugar) occurs.

Once carbohydrate has been digested and absorbed into the bloodstream—whether it came from an apple or candy—the body just sees it as glucose. But healthy options like fruits and whole grains offer nutrients, unlike the candy.

Enjoy sweets by working them into your daily carb allotment. If you want cake, skip your starch equivalent at dinner. Then you can have dessert without going over for the day. "You can still keep blood sugars in really good control," Yake says.

CALM *your* CRAVINGS

Food cravings happen anywhere, any time, and often when you least expect them. All foods can fit in a healthful diabetes meal plan. Simply acknowledge a craving and give yourself permission to give in sometimes. This lets you control the craving instead of it controlling you.

SMART WAYS
TO SATISFY CRAVINGS

Giving in to a craving is not "cheating" or "failure." Instead, learn how satisfy a craving without overdoing it.

Give in a Little

There are very few foods you can't have, although you do have to stay within your meal-plan allowance, especially for carbohydrate. If you love caramels, eat one and count it. But don't give in to something you won't really enjoy all that much.

Eat What You Truly Love

When you eat that food you love, enjoy it. Choose the best quality you can—it will create a better sense of well-being and satisfaction. Spend your chocolate craving on a gourmet chocolate instead of wasting it on a stale vending machine candy bar.

Get a Nutrition Boost
to Satisfy a Craving

Combine the sweet you crave with something that is a healthful food choice that provides satisfying protein, fiber, and other nutrients. For example, dip apples in a little high-quality caramel sauce or top bananas with a little natural peanut butter and drizzle with melted dark chocolate.

Calm the Craving,
but Keep It Small

Nibbling carrots, crackers, pretzels, and apples when you really want ice cream often backfires. Eating around your craving with all those "healthy" foods may cause you to consume more calories and carbs than if you'd just had ½ cup of ice cream to begin with. In fact, start with just a spoonful or bite—that may be enough.

CORNER THE CRAVING

Want to just shut a craving down? Try these tips. You may find one strategy works for you every time. Or maybe you need to mix it up to keep cravings at bay.

GO COLD TURKEY

Cutting out all added sugars works for some people. The first 28 to 72 hours is the toughest, but sugar cravings tend to diminish after a few days. If a sugar craving persists after that time, it should be easier to train your brain to be satisfied with less.

RECOGNIZE
EMOTIONAL EATING

When you are stressed or sad, it's possible to use food as a means to feel better. Learn skills to control these feelings, such as meditation or yoga, exercise, deep breathing, talking to a friend, listening to music, and even dancing. If necessary, see a professional to pinpoint strategies that will work for you.

LEAD A
BALANCED LIFE

Get enough sleep, exercise regularly, and eat healthful foods. Taking good care of yourself is the best way to fend off the sense of deprivation that triggers cravings and binge eating.

PAUSE A MOMENT

Cravings rise and fall like waves. When a craving hits, stop and think about it. Think, "I am stronger than my craving and can wait it out." Surf the urge, and it will pass.

MAKE LIST OF
DISTRACTIONS

Write down all the nonfood things you can do to distract yourself from eating. Take a bike ride, read a magazine, go to the library, visit a museum, go to the gym, go to the mall, do a craft, fold your laundry, clean your closet, or organize the junk drawer. When cravings annoy you, choose one activity and do it.

PREPARE *for* TEMPTATIONS

Food and drink is often at the center of family
and social gatherings. Use the following suggestions
to have a plan to help conquer temptations
and make smart choices in every situation.

TEMPTATIONS AT *SOCIAL EVENTS*

You won't have control over the food at a party or potluck. Before you go, exercise, eat, and take your medications as usual so you're in control. Don't go hungry—have a salad or some vegetables with yogurt before you go. Mentally prepare and plan to eat lightly.

If there is a buffet, scope out the food offerings before adding anything to your plate. Mentally choose the foods that fit your meal plan, then serve yourself exactly that and don't return to the food table. If you are feeling really hungry, have a big drink of water so you feel more full before you eat. Once you've eaten, distract yourself by chatting with others.

Meeting for happy hour? Alcohol has empty calories and can raise or lower your blood glucose as well as weaken your resolve, so sip carbonated water with lemon or lime. If you really want an alcoholic drink, choose a light beer or a short glass of wine.

TEMPTATIONS *AT WORK*

Sometimes you find yourself rushed for lunch before the next meeting. If you didn't pack a lunch (the best choice) and you have time to hit the drive-through at a nearby fast food joint, pick one that has a "light"

menu—salads, fruit parfaits, and grilled meat sandwiches can all be good choices. If your company has a cafeteria, go for the grilled and veggie-loaded items or build your own salad from the salad bar and choose fat-free dressing.

Celebrations at work often involve food. Is someone having a birthday? Take just a small piece of cake and/or leave the frosting on your plate. Is there a box of bagels or donuts set out in the morning? If you can't resist, take just a portion of one and forgo the cream cheese on the bagel. After that, change your route in the office so you don't keep walking past the box.

Meetings that last all day or are scheduled during lunch often come with a wide variety of traditional snacks and lunch offerings. If you can, talk to the meeting planner and ask if fruit and vegetables can be provided.

TEMPTATIONS FROM *FRIENDS/FAMILY*

If your mom makes all your childhood favorites when you visit or you're home for the holidays, it can be a minefield. Loudly proclaim how good it all is, then indulge in a just a bite or two of the richest dishes. Make yourself useful serving others and cleaning up to keep from overeating.

When a friend calls you to meet for coffee at a coffee shop, save calories, fat, and money by avoiding all the sugar-loaded drinks (remember, honey, syrups, and agave have carbohydrate). Enjoy a cup of black java or flavored unsweetened tea or get a blended drink "skinny." Just pass on the baked items.

Go ahead and take the kids out for ice cream. Opt for the junior-size scoop in a cup and nix the toppings.

TEMPTATION BUSTERS
Five quick tricks to keep yourself on track.
Chew sugar-free gum. **Brush your teeth.** Pop a sugar-free breath mint. **Drink a big glass of water.** Grab a mug of green tea.

EAT *SMART*

The first step to taking control of your
health is eating well. Focus on fresh
foods and smart cooking techniques
to feel better and trim weight.

SHOP SMART *for* BETTER HEALTH

Take the guesswork out of choosing the most healthful foods at the supermarket. With the right ingredients in your kitchen, you can create meals to manage your diabetes and to lose weight.

HAVE A PLAN

◆ *Plan your week's meals and snacks before you head to the market. Use this to generate your grocery list.*

◆ Maintain your pantry; replenish healthy staples as your supplies run low so you always have go-to items for quick meals and healthy snacks.

◆ Organize your list by the way your grocery store is laid out so you can avoid wandering around the store and walking by tempting treats.

◆ Use a grocery app on your phone or tablet to make preparing and updating your shopping list a snap.

STICK TO YOUR LIST

◆ Don't shop when you are hungry or stressed. You'll be less likely to grab indulgent comfort foods and treats if you shop after you've eaten and at a time when you are relaxed.

◆ *Focus on your list and buy only the foods you came for.*

◆ Shop without kids if possible. Supermarkets display foods with added sugars, refined carbohydrate, and high fat content at kids' eye level for a reason. You will meet your family's health and nutrition goals more easily without enduring pint-size protests.

DAIRY

◆ Avoid flavored milk products due to high carb content and added sugars.

◆ *Be selective with flavored yogurts. Many are sweetened with sugar and are higher in carbohydrate. Fat-free yogurts tend to be lower in carbohydrate; low-fat varieties may have twice the carbohydrate.*

◆ Almond milk and soymilk are dairy alternatives. Choose light or unsweetened varieties to cut calories, carbohydrate, and added sugars.

◆ When choosing spreads, opt for 60% vegetable oil spread in tub form.

◆ Choose reduced-fat cheese or smaller amounts of regular cheese. The fat-free versions lack flavor and produce undesirable results in recipes.

WHOLE GRAINS

◆ Choose 100 percent whole grain products when possible. Look at the ingredients list and make sure the first ingredient listed is a whole grain, such as whole wheat flour, brown rice, or barley.

◆ True whole grain contains all parts of the grain seed—the bran, endosperm, and germ—and typically takes a long time to cook. Pearled grains have been polished to remove the bran layer and cook much more quickly. These quick-cooking products have fewer nutrients, but they are still a healthful choice.

◆ *Opt for foods that contain 3 grams or more of dietary fiber per serving.*

◆ Packaged tortillas, wraps, breads, and buns often contain high amounts of sodium. Compare brands and choose a variety that is whole grain and lower in sodium.

◆ Don't seek out gluten-free items unless you have celiac disease. Many gluten-free grain products are higher in fat and calories and sometimes carbohydrate compared to the gluten-containing foods they emulate.

◆ Store whole grains in airtight containers in a cool, dark place. Most will last up to 4 months in the pantry or 8 to 12 months in the freezer.

VEGETABLES AND FRUITS

- For best quality and flavor, choose fresh vegetables and fruits that are in season. Plus, in-season produce costs less than out-of-season options.
- *Eat the rainbow. Select an assortment of colorful vegetables and fruits. Each color family offers a wealth of nutrients.*
- Precut vegetables and fruits are a good option when you're pressed for time—they require no prep. Plus, purchasing only as much as you will eat helps to avoid waste.
- Stock up on frozen vegetables and fruits; they are just as healthful and cost less than out-of-season fresh produce. Avoid frozen vegetables that contain added sauce, which is high in sodium and fat. Look for fruit that is unsweetened and frozen without juice or syrup.
- No-salt-added canned vegetables, no-sugar-added canned fruits, and fruits canned in their own juice are also nutritious alternatives to fresh vegetables and fruits.

MEAT AND SEAFOOD

- Choose fresh meats that haven't been enhanced with a salt solution, tenderizing solution, or marinade; these meats tend to be high in sodium. Check the labels.
- Select packaged meat with the latest freshness date, especially if you are planning on eating it later in the week. If you find meats with a close freshness date at a discount, buy and freeze those as soon as you get home.
- Buy lean, low-sodium varieties of turkey, chicken, beef, and ham deli meats rather than cured meats like salami and summer sausage. Watch portion sizes to avoid excessive sodium.
- Avoid breaded chicken and fish products. They are high in added sodium, and the breading is not made from whole grains. You're better off coating plain meat when you get home so you can control the content of the coating.
- *Many fish varieties provide heart-healthy fats. Avoid frozen fish with added sauce. Buy canned fish packed in water and choose a lower-sodium brand if possible.*
- Loin cuts from beef and pork and skinless chicken and turkey breast are the leanest options of all the cuts.

HOW TO READ PACKAGE LABELS

Learning to read food labels will help you make smarter food choices.
Labels are a great tool for counting calories and carb and fat grams.
Here's a look at an updated label.

1. Serving Size

All serving sizes are noted in common household measures (1 cup) or the number of items (8 crackers) as well as a weight. Be careful—some packages have more than one serving. You might have to do some math.

2. Calories

Calories are key to maintaining or losing weight. The calories noted are for the serving size listed. Pay attention to how much of the food you normally eat and translate it into the serving size to calculate how many calories you'll consume.

3. Total Fat

This is the sum of all types of fat. The total fat may also be broken out into different types (trans fat, saturated, monounsaturated, and polyunsaturated). Aim for 20–35 percent of daily calories from fat.

4. Sodium

The amount of sodium found in one serving of the food is listed on the label. Limit sodium intake to 2,300 milligrams total per day or to a level indicated by your health care provider. Sodium can vary among brands.

5. Total Carbohydrate

When counting carbs, it is more important to look at the "total carbohydrate" level than the amount of "sugars." The total carbohydrate is the sum of the sugar, sugar alcohols, starch, and fiber in the food, which may be listed under the total carbohydrate level.

6. Dietary Fiber

This is the sum of all fiber, insoluble and soluble. Insoluble fiber is not digestible. Soluble fiber is digested but remains gummy and thick, helping you feel full. For foods with more than 5 grams of fiber, subtract half the grams of fiber from the total carbs to get your carb count.

7. Sugars

The "sugars" on the label include all naturally occurring sugars plus added sugars. Sugars added during manufacturing, such as refined sugar, will appear on the label as "added sugars." Naturally occurring sugars, like sucrose in fruit and lactose in milk, are part of a well-balanced meal plan.

Nutrition Facts

8 servings per container

(1) Serving size   2/3 cup (55g)

Amount per serving

Calories (2)   **230**

	% Daily Value*
Total Fat 8g (3)	**10%**
Saturated Fat 1g	**5%**
Trans Fat 0g	
Cholesterol 0mg	**0%**
(4) Sodium 160mg	**7%**
Total Carbohydrate 37g (5)	**13%**
(6) Dietary Fiber 4g	**14%**
Total Sugars 12g (7)	
Includes 10g Added Sugars	**20%**
Protein 3g	
Vitamin D 2mcg	10%
Calcium 260mg	20%
Iron 8mg	45%
Potassium 235mg	6%

* The % Daily Value (DV) tells you how much a nutrient in a serving of food contributes to a daily diet. 2,000 calories a day is used for general nutrition advice.

PRODUCE
AT ITS BEST

Americans waste about 25 percent of the food and drink they buy. Think of that half-full bag of soggy spinach that's been hiding in the back of the fridge for weeks. You'll minimize throwaways by storing produce correctly. Here's how.

DISCOVER NEW PRODUCTS FOR KEEPING PRODUCE FRESH. PICK THOSE FOR YOUR FAVORITE FOODS.

SMALL FRUIT

*berries, cherries,
grapes, cut fruit*

Storage

Refrigerate, unwashed.

Make it last

Dry on a paper towel and freeze
in a resealable plastic bag in a flat,
single layer to extend shelf life.

FRUIT

*apples, pears, bananas,
tomatoes, and other seed-bearing fruit*

Storage

Allow to ripen at room
temperature if necessary.

Make it last

Once fruit is ripe,
refrigerate to extend
shelf life. (Cold temperatures
slow the ripening process.)

*PRODUCE LASTS
LONGER UNWASHED.
RINSE IT WITH
RUNNING WATER
WHEN YOU'RE
READY TO EAT IT.*

FRESH HERBS

Storage

Wrap a paper towel around herbs
and store in the refrigerator 10 to
14 days. *Exception:* Store basil at
room temp with stems in water. Don't
get the leaves wet—they turn black.

Helpful hint

To minimize herb waste, try Gourmet
Garden Stir-In Pastes, which last up to
3 months and don't compromise flavor.

ONIONS & POTATOES

Storage

Store in a cool, dry, dark place,
such as the back of the pantry.

Helpful hint

Keep onions away from other
produce. Many foods absorb
an onion's flavor.

VEGETABLES

*broccoli, cauliflower, green beans,
lettuces, carrots*

Storage

Refrigerate, unwashed.

How to wash

Before you hit the cutting board,
run produce under warm water for
10 seconds to get rid of bacteria.
Avoid adding extras—like bleach and
vinegar—to the cleaning process.

THE CASE FOR CANNED AND FROZEN PRODUCE

◆ Canned produce is usually the
least expensive option. You won't
lose fiber or minerals; just watch
for added sugar and sodium.
Buy fruit packed in 100 percent
juice—not syrup—and opt for
no-salt-added veggies.

◆ If a fruit or veggie is out of
season, it will likely be more
affordable in the frozen foods
section. The nutritional value of
frozen produce is also highly
comparable to fresh since it's
often frozen at peak ripeness.

◆ Buy frozen fruit with no sugar
added (avoid sweetened and
lightly sweetened).

◆ Buy frozen vegetables without
extra sauces, which can add
sodium and calories.

DITCH THE CRISPER DRAWER

◆ Fruits and veggies produce
ethylene gas, which is what
causes them to ripen. When
grouped together in the same
refrigerator bin, they ripen faster
because of the trapped ethylene.
Instead, place them throughout
the fridge.

SOURCES
◆ Robert Schueller, director of public
relations at Melissa's Produce
◆ Allison Kuhn, M.S., RDN, LD, director
of retail dietetics at Kroger

3 oz. cooked
shrimp
20 g protein

3 oz. cooked
chicken breast
26 g protein

BECOME *a* PROTEIN PRO

It may seem that everywhere you look, Americans are crazy for protein. Is this trend being fed by one of the many low-carbohydrate diets, such as Paleo, or by new research that suggests eating a bit more protein may increase satiety and assist with weight control? The jury is still out.

Yet food manufacturers have jumped on this protein craze and brought protein-padded products to market. But do you really need more protein, especially in your bars, cereal, and drinks? Hardly! According to the *Dietary Guidelines for Americans*, we eat more than enough protein, with too much of that protein being animal-based. That's not a wise plan when it comes to type 2 diabetes. Some

major studies have shown an association between eating less red meat and reducing the odds of developing type 2 diabetes.

To become a protein pro and learn about healthier protein choices, it's good to understand that protein and fat are generally paired together in protein foods (such as red meat, poultry, cheese, seafood, nuts, and eggs). There are some exceptions: Protein is also in some fat-free foods, such as beans and nonfat dairy.

Choose a variety of protein foods from all sources. Follow the tips on the next page and be smarter about eating protein.

3 oz. cooked salmon
22 g protein

1½ oz. cheese
10 g protein

1 oz.
almonds
6 g protein

1 cup milk
9 g protein

¾ cup
cottage
cheese
21 g protein

HOW MUCH
DO YOU NEED?

The amount of protein you need is based on how much you weigh.
Most adults need 0.4 gram of protein per pound. Multiply your weight
by 0.4 to calculate your Recommended Dietary Allowance of protein.

6'2", 215 lb.
86 g pro./day

5'7", 180 lb.
72 g pro./day

5'8", 190 lb.
76 g pro./day

5'4", 150 lb.
60 g pro./day

PROTEIN SAVVY

1. Eat protein in small servings. As a rule of thumb, don't let protein foods fill more than one quarter of your plate.

2. Choose lean and low-fat protein, especially sources also low in saturated fat and cholesterol (beans, nuts, low-fat dairy, tofu, and skinless chicken).

3. Cook protein in ways that don't add a lot of fat, such as grilling, roasting, and sautéing.

4. Get away from planning meals with proteincentric dishes. Use meat as a side dish or to stretch the protein in a main course.

3 oz. cooked
pork tenderloin
22 g protein

3 oz. cooked
beef steak
21 g protein

BASIC CARB COUNTS

Fuel your body with nutritious carbs from whole grains, fruits, vegetables, and low-fat dairy products. Read labels and learn some basic carb counts to make meal planning easy and to keep blood sugar in check.

GRAINS

	SERVING	CARB
Corn tortilla (6-inch)	1	12 g
Microwave popcorn (light, butter flavor)	3 cups	13 g
Whole wheat waffle (4-inch, frozen)	1	13 g
Whole wheat bread	1 slice	11 g
Oatmeal, cooked	½ cup	14 g
Tortilla chips	1 oz.	18 g
Lentils, cooked	½ cup	20 g
Black beans, cooked	½ cup	20 g
Quinoa, cooked	½ cup	20 g
Whole wheat penne pasta, cooked	½ cup	21 g
Brown rice, cooked	½ cup	25 g
Hard pretzels	1 oz.	23 g
Whole grain bagel	1	49 g

FRUITS

	SERVING	CARB
Raspberries	½ cup	7 g
Orange, small	1	15 g
Watermelon, diced	1 cup	11 g
Blueberries	½ cup	11 g
Strawberries, halved	1 cup	12 g
Green grapes	½ cup	14 g
Canned peaches (juice pack), drained	½ cup	14 g
Peach, medium	1	15 g
Raisins	2 Tbsp.	16 g
Banana, small	1	18 g
Apple, medium	1	25 g
Orange juice	8 oz.	26 g
Pear, medium	1	27 g
Banana, large	1	36 g

VEGETABLES

	SERVING	CARB
Button mushroom slices, raw	$1/2$ cup	2 g
Spinach leaves, raw	2 cups	2 g
Cucumber, raw	$1/2$ cup	2 g
Green beans, raw	$1/2$ cup	4 g
Cauliflower, raw	1 cup	5 g
Sweet pepper slices, raw	1 cup	6 g
Broccoli, raw	1 cup	6 g
Tomato slices, raw	1 cup	7 g
Kale, raw	1 cup	6 g
Peas, cooked	$1/2$ cup	11 g
Baby carrots, raw	1 cup	12 g
Corn, cooked	$1/2$ cup	18 g
Sweet potato, cooked	$1/2$ cup	21 g
Baked potato, small	1	31 g
Baked potato, large	1	51 g

SIZE MATTERS!

This is especially true for veggies and fruits. Next time you select piece of fruit or a potato, be mindful of size. Carb count will vary.

8–8 $7/8$ in. length
6–6 $7/8$ in. length
3–4 $1/2$ in. diam.
1 $3/4$–2 $1/2$ in. diam.

Large banana: 36 g carb   Large potato: 51–143 g carb
Small banana: 18 g carb   Small potato: up to 31 g carb

DAIRY

	SERVING	CARB
Cheddar cheese	1 $1/2$ oz.	1 g
Soymilk (light, original)	8 oz.	5 g
Almond milk	8 oz.	8 g
Fat-free milk	8 oz.	12 g
Whole milk	8 oz.	12 g
Vanilla ice cream	$1/2$ cup	17 g
Low-fat vanilla frozen yogurt	$1/2$ cup	18 g
Flavored fat-free Greek yogurt	5.3 oz.	18 g

GET COOKING

Eating healthfully is the first step toward weight loss and living well with diabetes. Cooking and eating meals at home gives you control over your diet. Proper planning, the right equipment, and thoughtfully chosen ingredients let you cook with less fat and fewer calories.

PLAN AHEAD

It's hard to cook a meal after a busy workday. Planning your meals is key to staying on track. For each meal, determine your carbohydrate, protein, fat, and nonstarchy veggie choices and stick to them. Prep as many ingredients in advance as you can, such as washing and cutting up vegetables, roasting vegetables, portioning meats, and making dressings.

USE HEALTHY FATS

Not all fat is bad. You can make smarter choices in the kitchen by swapping saturated fat such as butter with better-for-you unsaturated fats like canola oil and olive oil. But all fats are high in calories, so use them in moderation.

People who cook at home *consume about*

200
calories less per day
than those who don't.
—Johns Hopkins Bloomberg School of Public Health

BOOST FLAVOR

Low-sodium doesn't mean low-flavor. Fresh herbs, spices, citrus, and vinegar provide bold flavor, helping you feel satisfied. Adding chile peppers, garlic, small amounts of pungent cheeses (Parmesan, feta, blue cheese), and/or onion is another way to add flavor.

TRY HOMEMADE

If it's packaged, chances are you can make your own version at home. For example, instead of buying fruit-flavored yogurt, buy plain low-fat yogurt and add your favorite fruit. To control sodium, mix up your own seasoning blends. Make your own salad dressings in a jar or dressing shaker.

PICK A SKILLET

A nonstick skillet is an essential kitchen tool for cooking with less fat. Get a heavy skillet with a lid for the most versatility. Use wood or nylon utensils for cooking and hand-wash the skillet to extend its life. Most traditional nonstick surfaces will eventually scratch, and you will need a new one. If you want the latest in kitchen tools, try a ceramic nonstick skillet. It conducts heat well, and the nonreactive surface is easy to clean.

GO THIN

Thin sandwich buns can save you up to 5 grams of carbohydrate and 50 calories per serving compared with traditional buns. What's more, thinner buns let you enjoy the flavor of sandwich fillings more. You can also use thin bagels, very thinly sliced bread, and extra-thin corn tortillas.

LIMIT SUGAR

It's natural to want a sweet treat, but use sugar sensibly. Any form—white, brown, honey, syrup—adds calories and carbs with no nutritional value. Some people with diabetes prefer sugar substitutes to manage calories and carbs while satisfying sweet tooth.

DRESS LIGHTLY

An oil mister makes it easy to add just a spritz of flavor to salad greens. And a salad dressing shaker simplifies making and storing lower-fat, lower-sodium dressings at home.

START YOUR DAY *with*
BREAKFAST

Eating a good breakfast every day can help you lose weight.

Squash, Bacon, and Feta Breakfast Bake, *p. 34*

Black Bean-Corn Breakfast Burritos

29 g CARB

SERVES 6
TOTAL 25 min.

- 4 **eggs**
- ¼ **cup milk**
- ¼ **tsp. salt**
  Dash chili powder
  Dash black pepper
- ⅓ **cup chopped green sweet pepper**
- 2 **Tbsp. snipped fresh cilantro**
- 1 **Tbsp. olive oil**
- ½ **cup canned black beans, rinsed and drained**
- ½ **cup whole kernel corn or roasted corn**
- 6 **8-inch whole wheat flour tortillas or flour tortillas**
  Pico de gallo (optional)
- ½ **cup queso fresco or shredded Monterey Jack cheese (2 oz.)**

1. In a small bowl whisk together the first five ingredients (through black pepper). Stir in sweet pepper and cilantro. In a 10-inch skillet heat oil over medium; pour in egg mixture. Cook, without stirring, until mixture begins to set on the bottom and around edge. Using a spatula or large spoon, lift and fold the partially cooked egg mixture so the uncooked portion flows underneath. Continue cooking 2 to 3 minutes more or until egg mixture is cooked through but is still glossy and moist. Remove from heat.

2. In a bowl combine beans and corn. Microwave 1 minute, stirring after 30 seconds.

3. Meanwhile, heat tortillas according to package directions. Spoon egg mixture down the centers of the tortillas. Top with black bean-corn mixture. If desired, top with pico de gallo. Sprinkle with cheese. Fold bottom edges of tortillas up and over filling, fold in opposite sites, and roll up from the bottom. Serve immediately.

PER SERVING *(1 burrito each)* **CAL** 260, **FAT** 11 g (4 g sat. fat), **CHOL** 131 mg, **SODIUM** 585 mg, **CARB** 29 g (4 g fiber, 4 g sugars), **PRO** 12 g

Black Bean-Corn Breakfast Burritos

Squash, Bacon, and Feta Breakfast Bake

Recipe pictured on p. 32

16 g CARB

SERVES 6
HANDS ON 35 min.
TOTAL 2 hr.

- 1 3-lb. spaghetti squash
- ½ cup refrigerated or frozen egg product, thawed, or 2 eggs, lightly beaten
- ⅓ cup finely shredded Parmesan cheese
- 3 Tbsp. all-purpose flour
- 2 Tbsp. snipped fresh sage
- 6 slices lower-sodium, less-fat bacon, coarsely chopped
  Nonstick cooking spray
- 3 cups coarsely chopped, trimmed fresh Swiss chard, kale, or spinach
- 2 oz. reduced-fat feta cheese, crumbled (about ⅓ cup)
- 6 eggs
- ¼ tsp. salt
- ¼ tsp. black pepper

1. Preheat oven to 375°F. Line a small baking pan with parchment paper. Cut spaghetti squash in half crosswise. Use a spoon to scoop out and discard seeds and strings. Place squash halves, cut sides down, on prepared baking pan. Bake about 1 hour or until squash is tender when pierced with a sharp knife. Cool completely on a wire rack. Reduce oven temperature to 350°F.
2. For crust, in a large bowl combine the next four ingredients (through sage).

Using a fork, scrape squash pulp into the bowl with the egg mixture. Gently stir until well combined. Spread mixture in a greased 2-qt. rectangular baking dish. Bake, uncovered, about 20 minutes or until crust is set and edges are starting to brown.
3. Meanwhile, in a 10-inch nonstick skillet cook bacon over medium until just browned but not crisp. Transfer bacon to a bowl. Drain and discard bacon drippings. Spray skillet with cooking spray. Add chard to skillet; cook and stir 1 minute.
4. Top squash crust with chard, feta cheese, and bacon. Bake, uncovered, about 5 minutes more or until heated.
5. Coat the same skillet with cooking spray. Heat skillet over medium. Break three eggs into skillet, keeping eggs separate. Sprinkle with half of the salt and pepper. Reduce heat to low; cook eggs 3 to 4 minutes or until whites are completely set and yolks start to thicken. Remove from heat for sunny-side-up eggs. For fried eggs over-easy or over-hard, when the whites are completely set and yolks start to thicken, turn eggs and cook 30 seconds more (for over-easy) or 1 minute more (for over-hard). Remove eggs from the skillet; keep warm. Repeat with remaining three eggs and remaining salt and pepper.
6. To serve, cut baked casserole into six portions. Serve each portion with an egg.

PER SERVING *(1 portion casserole + 1 egg each)* **CAL** 218, **FAT** 11 g (4 g sat. fat), **CHOL** 199 mg, **SODIUM** 530 mg, **CARB** 16 g (3 g fiber, 5 g sugars), **PRO** 15 g

Moroccan Eggs

25 g CARB

SERVES 4
HANDS ON 12 min.
TOTAL 30 min.

- 1 15-oz. can garbanzo beans (chickpeas), rinsed and drained
- 1 tsp. paprika
- ½ tsp. ground cumin
- 2 tsp. olive oil
- 2 cups low-sodium tomato pasta sauce
- 2 to 3 Tbsp. water
- 4 eggs
- ¼ cup snipped fresh cilantro
- 2 Tbsp. finely chopped red onion

1. In a 10-inch nonstick skillet cook garbanzo beans, paprika, and cumin in hot oil over medium 10 minutes or until slightly toasted. Stir in pasta sauce and water; heat. Crack eggs into skillet with sauce. Reduce heat to medium-low. Cover and cook about 8 minutes or until egg whites are set and yolks are desired doneness. To serve, sprinkle with cilantro and onion.

PER SERVING *(1 egg + ¾ cup tomato mixture each)* **CAL** 240, **FAT** 10 g (2 g sat. fat), **CHOL** 189 mg, **SODIUM** 232 mg, **CARB** 25 g (3 g fiber, 8 g sugars), **PRO** 12 g

Moroccan Eggs

**Italian-Style
Salsa Omelet**

Zucchini Patty Egg Stacks

Italian-Style Salsa Omelet

16 g
CARB

SERVES 2

TOTAL 30 min.

- ½ cup quartered cherry tomatoes
- 2 Tbsp. coarsely chopped dried cherries
- 2 dried apricot halves, snipped
- 1 Tbsp. thinly slivered red onion
- 1 Tbsp. snipped fresh Italian parsley
- 1 Tbsp. snipped fresh basil
- 2 tsp. white balsamic vinegar
- 1 tsp. olive oil
- 2 eggs
- 2 egg whites
- ⅛ tsp. salt
  Nonstick cooking spray
  Freshly cracked black pepper

1. For salsa, in a small bowl combine the first eight ingredients (through oil). Toss to combine.

2. In a small bowl combine one of the eggs, one of the egg whites, and half of the salt. Using a fork, beat until mixture is combined but not frothy. Lightly coat an unheated 8-inch nonstick skillet with cooking spray. Preheat the skillet over medium-high. Add egg mixture to skillet. Reduce heat to medium. As egg starts to set, use a spatula to gently lift the edges of egg, tilting pan to allow liquid egg to run under set egg. Continue until egg is set but still shiny. Fold egg in half, then in half again. Remove from skillet; keep warm.

3. Repeat with remaining egg, egg white, and salt. Serve omelets topped with the salsa and cracked pepper.

PER SERVING (1 omelet + 6 Tbsp. salsa each) **CAL** 176, **FAT** 8 g (2 g sat. fat), **CHOL** 186 mg, **SODIUM** 277 mg, **CARB** 16 g (1 g fiber, 13 g sugars), **PRO** 11 g

Zucchini Patty Egg Stacks

6 g
CARB

SERVES 4

HANDS ON 20 min.

TOTAL 58 min.

- 1½ cups shredded zucchini
- ⅛ tsp. salt
- 1 egg white
- 2 Tbsp. whole grain saltine crackers, crushed
- 2 Tbsp. finely chopped onion
- 2 Tbsp. snipped fresh parsley
- 1 Tbsp. finely shredded Parmesan cheese
- ⅛ tsp. black pepper
  Nonstick cooking spray
- 4 tsp. olive oil
- 4 slices Canadian-style bacon (2 oz.)
- 4 cups water
- 1 Tbsp. vinegar
- 4 eggs
- 4 tsp. finely shredded Parmesan cheese

1. In a bowl toss together the zucchini and salt. Let stand 30 minutes. Using a clean kitchen towel or a double thickness of 100-percent-cotton cheesecloth, squeeze out excess liquid from zucchini (up to 1 cup).

2. In a large bowl whisk egg white until foamy. Stir in zucchini and the next five ingredients (through pepper).

3. Coat a 12-inch nonstick skillet with cooking spray. Add olive oil and heat over medium-high. Spoon zucchini mixture into skillet in four mounds. Press down lightly with the back of a spoon to flatten each mound into a patty about 3 inches in diameter. Cook 4 to 6 minutes or until golden brown, turning once. Remove patties from skillet. Keep warm.

4. In the same skillet heat Canadian bacon over medium 1 minute, turning once. Top each zucchini patty with a slice of Canadian bacon. Keep warm.

5. In a 10-inch skillet combine the water and vinegar. Bring to boiling; reduce heat to simmering. Break an egg into a cup and slip egg into the simmering water. Repeat with remaining eggs, allowing each egg an equal amount of space. Simmer eggs, uncovered, 3 to 5 minutes or until whites are completely set and yolks begin to thicken but are not hard. Remove eggs from water with a slotted spoon.

6. Place eggs on zucchini stacks. Sprinkle with the 4 tsp. Parmesan and, if desired, additional pepper.

PER SERVING (1 stack each) **CAL** 172, **FAT** 11 g (3 g sat. fat), **CHOL** 195 mg, **SODIUM** 396 mg, **CARB** 6 g (1 g fiber, 2 g sugars), **PRO** 12 g

Egg and Squash Boats

Egg and Squash Boats

17 g
CARB

SERVES 4
TOTAL 25 min.

- 2 8-oz. delicata squash
- 5 Tbsp. water
- 1 cup frozen loose-pack brown rice
- 4 links refrigerated fully cooked chicken breakfast sausage, chopped
- ¼ cup finely shredded Parmesan cheese
- ½ tsp. dried sage, crushed
- ⅛ tsp. black pepper
  Nonstick cooking spray
- 4 eggs
- 1 Tbsp. balsamic glaze

1. Cut squash in half lengthwise; remove and discard seeds and strings. In a 2-qt. square baking dish place two squash halves, cut sides down; add 2 Tbsp. of the water. Cover with vented plastic wrap. Microwave 4 to 6 minutes or until squash is just tender; keep warm. Repeat with the remaining squash halves.
2. In a microwave-safe bowl stir together the next five ingredients (through pepper). Cover and microwave about 1½ minutes or until heated.
3. Meanwhile, coat a 10-inch nonstick skillet with cooking spray; heat skillet over medium-low. Break eggs into skillet. Cook 3 to 4 minutes or until whites are firm. Add the remaining 1 Tbsp. water to skillet; cover and cook 4 to 5 minutes or until yolks begin to thicken but are not hard.
4. To serve, fill squash halves with rice mixture. Arrange a cooked egg on each. Drizzle with balsamic glaze and, if desired, sprinkle with additional pepper.

PER SERVING (1 egg and squash boat each) **CAL** 216, **FAT** 9 g (4 g sat. fat), **CHOL** 215 mg, **SODIUM** 327 mg, **CARB** 17 g (2 g fiber, 8 g sugars), **PRO** 17 g

Blueberry Buckwheat Pancakes

36 g
CARB

SERVES 4
TOTAL 30 min.

- ½ cup buckwheat flour
- ½ cup whole wheat flour
- 1 Tbsp. sugar*
- ½ tsp. baking powder
- ½ tsp. ground cinnamon
- ¼ tsp. baking soda
- ¼ tsp. salt
- ¼ cup refrigerated or frozen egg product, thawed, or 1 egg, lightly beaten
- 1¼ cups buttermilk or sour milk
- 1 Tbsp. canola oil
- ½ tsp. vanilla
- ¾ cup fresh or frozen blueberries, thawed
- ¼ cup sugar-free maple-flavor syrup
- 4 tsp. light butter with canola oil

1. In a medium bowl stir together the first seven ingredients (through salt). Make a well in the center of flour mixture.
2. In a small bowl combine egg, buttermilk, oil, and vanilla. Add buttermilk mixture all at once to flour mixture. Stir just until combined but still slightly lumpy. Stir in blueberries.
3. For each pancake, pour about ¼ cup batter onto a hot, lightly greased griddle or heavy skillet. Spread the batter into a circle about 4 inches in diameter. Cook over medium 1 to 2 minutes on each side or until pancakes are golden brown, turning over when pancakes have bubbly surfaces and edges are slightly dry. Serve warm with syrup and butter.

Tip To make sour milk, place 3¾ tsp. lemon juice or vinegar in a 2-cup glass measuring cup. Add enough milk to make 1¼ cups total liquid; stir. Let stand 5 minutes before using in recipe.

PER SERVING (3 pancakes + 1 Tbsp. syrup + 1 tsp. light butter each) **CAL** 237, **FAT** 8 g (2 g sat. fat), **CHOL** 8 mg, **SODIUM** 450 mg, **CARB** 36 g (4 g fiber, 10 g sugars), **PRO** 9 g

*Sugar Sub Choose Splenda Sugar Blend. Follow package directions for 1 Tbsp. equivalent.
PER SERVING WITH SUB Same as above, except **CAL** 232, **CARB** 35 g (9 g sugars)

SPRINKLE ON FRESH BERRIES FOR A POWER FOOD BOOST.

Blueberry
Buckwheat
Pancakes

**Poppy Seed Oat Waffles
with Citrus Syrup**

Poppy Seed Oat Waffles with Citrus Syrup

26 g **CARB** | **SERVES** 8
| **HANDS ON** 15 min.
| **TOTAL** 30 min.

- ⅔ cup all-purpose flour
- ½ cup oat bran
- ⅓ cup whole wheat flour
- 2 Tbsp. flaxseed meal
- 1 Tbsp. sugar*
- 2 tsp. poppy seeds
- 1½ tsp. baking powder
- ¼ tsp. salt
- ¾ cup fat-free milk
- ¼ cup refrigerated or frozen egg product, thawed, or 1 egg, lightly beaten
- ¼ cup water
- 3 Tbsp. canola oil
- 1 tsp. vanilla
- 1 recipe Citrus Syrup

1. In a medium bowl stir together the first eight ingredients (through salt). Make a well in center of flour mixture.
2. In a small bowl combine the next five ingredients (through vanilla). Add milk mixture all at once to flour mixture; stir just until moistened (batter should be slightly lumpy).
3. Lightly grease and preheat a standard waffle baker. Pour half of the batter (about 1 cup) onto grid, spreading to cover. Close lid quickly; do not open until done. Bake until golden and crisp. Using a fork, lift waffle off grid. Repeat with the remaining batter. Serve warm with Citrus Syrup and remaining orange slices.

Citrus Syrup Peel and slice **2 medium oranges** over a small saucepan to catch juice. Add **½ cup water** and **1 Tbsp. each cornstarch and honey** to orange juice in saucepan. Cook and stir over medium until thickened and bubbly. Add half of the orange slices (reserve the remaining slices until ready to serve). Cook and stir 2 minutes more. Remove from heat. Stir in **1 Tbsp. lemon juice.**

PER SERVING *(1 waffle section + 2 Tbsp. syrup each)* **CAL** 173, **FAT** 7 g (1 g sat. fat), **CHOL** 0 mg, **SODIUM** 190 mg, **CARB** 26 g (3 g fiber, 8 g sugars), **PRO** 5 g

***Sugar Sub** Choose Splenda Sugar Blend. Follow package directions to use 1 Tbsp. equivalent.
PER SERVING WITH SUB Same as above, except **CAL** 171, **SUGARS** 7 g

---

Pumpkin-Walnut Baked French Toast with Maple-Coffee Syrup

31 g **CARB** | **SERVES** 8
| **HANDS ON** 25 min.
| **TOTAL** 2 hr. 55 min.

- Nonstick cooking spray
- 6 cups cubed and dried reduced-calorie wheat bread (8 oz.)
- 1½ cups fat-free milk
- 1¼ cups refrigerated or frozen egg product, thawed, or 3 eggs, lightly beaten
- ¾ cup canned pumpkin
- ¼ cup packed brown sugar*
- 1 tsp. ground cinnamon
- ¼ tsp. ground nutmeg
- 1 cup chopped walnuts, toasted
- 2 Tbsp. granulated sugar*
- 1 Tbsp. cornstarch
- ⅔ cup water
- 1 tsp. instant coffee crystals
- ⅓ cup reduced-calorie maple-flavor syrup
- ½ tsp. vanilla
- Banana slices (optional)

1. Coat a 3-qt. rectangular baking dish with cooking spray. Arrange the dried bread cubes in the prepared baking dish.

Pumpkin-Walnut Baked French Toast with Maple-Coffee Syrup

2. In a bowl whisk together the next six ingredients (through nutmeg) until smooth. Gradually pour egg mixture over bread; press lightly with the back of a large spoon to moisten bread. Sprinkle walnuts over bread. Cover and chill 2 to 24 hours.
3. Preheat oven to 350°F. Bake, uncovered, 25 to 30 minutes or until a toothpick inserted in center comes out clean. Let stand 10 minutes before serving.
4. For maple-coffee syrup, in a small saucepan combine granulated sugar and cornstarch. Whisk in water. Cook and stir over medium until thickened and bubbly. Cook and stir 2 minutes more. Remove from heat and stir in instant coffee crystals, syrup, and vanilla.
5. Cut French toast into eight pieces. If desired, top each serving with banana slices. Drizzle with warm syrup and serve warm.

PER SERVING *(1 piece French toast + about 2 Tbsp. syrup each)* **CAL** 257, **FAT** 10 g (1 g sat. fat), **CHOL** 1 mg, **SODIUM** 230 mg, **CARB** 31 g (5 g fiber, 19 g sugars), **PRO** 12 g

***Sugar Sub** We do not recommend using sugar subs for this recipe.

Overnight Peach-Raspberry French Toast

49 g
CARB

SERVES 4
HANDS ON 20 min.
TOTAL 9 hr. 10 min.

Nonstick cooking spray
4   oz. fat-free or reduced-fat cream cheese (neufchatel), softened
1   fresh peach, pitted and finely chopped
8   slices reduced-calorie multigrain bread
1   cup refrigerated or frozen egg product, thawed, or 4 eggs, lightly beaten
1   cup fat-free milk
2   tsp. granulated sugar*
1   tsp. vanilla
¼   tsp. ground cinnamon
1   fresh peach, pitted and sliced
1   recipe Raspberry Sauce
1   Tbsp. powdered sugar* (optional)

1. Coat a 2-qt. rectangular baking dish with cooking spray. In a bowl stir together cream cheese and chopped peach.

Spread mixture on four of the bread slices. Top with the remaining bread slices to make sandwiches. Arrange the four sandwiches in the prepared baking dish.
2. In another bowl stir together egg, milk, sugar, vanilla, and cinnamon. Slowly pour egg mixture over sandwiches in baking dish. Use the back of a wide spatula to press the bread into egg mixture. Cover with foil and refrigerate overnight.
3. Preheat oven to 375°F. Bake 25 minutes. Remove foil and bake 10 to 15 minutes more or until sandwiches puff up and the liquid is absorbed. Remove from oven and place on a wire rack. Let stand 15 minutes.
4. To serve, top French toast sandwiches with peach slices and Raspberry Sauce. If desired, sprinkle with powdered sugar.

Raspberry Sauce Thaw **2 cups frozen unsweetened raspberries.** Do not drain. In a food processor or blender process or blend berries until smooth. Press berries

through a fine-mesh sieve; discard seeds. In a small saucepan stir together **3 Tbsp. sugar*** and **1 tsp. cornstarch.** Add raspberry puree. Cook and stir over medium until thickened. Cook and stir 1 minute more. Transfer to a bowl. Serve warm or cover and chill until ready to use.

PER SERVING (1 French toast sandwich + 2 Tbsp. sauce each) **CAL** 266, **FAT** 2 g (0 g sat. fat), **CHOL** 5 mg, **SODIUM** 461 mg, **CARB** 49 g (11 g fiber, 28 g sugars), **PRO** 18 g

*Sugar Sub Choose Splenda Granular for the granulated sugar. Follow package directions for 2 tsp. and 3 Tbsp. equivalents. We do not recommend a sub for the powdered sugar.
PER SERVING WITH SUB Same as above, except **CAL** 227 cal., **CARB** 39 g (18 g sugars)

Pumpkin- and Fruit-Topped Bagels

27 g
CARB

SERVES 4
TOTAL 15 min.

½   cup canned pumpkin
½   cup plain fat-free Greek yogurt
2   whole wheat bagel thins, split and lightly toasted
1   medium apple or pear, cored and chopped or thinly sliced
4   slices lower-sodium, less-fat bacon, crisp-cooked and crumbled
⅔   cup fresh blueberries
2   Tbsp. chopped pecans, toasted
1   to 2 tsp. honey (optional)

1. In a bowl stir together the pumpkin and yogurt. Spread over bagel thins. Top with the next four ingredients (through pecans). If desired, drizzle with honey.

PER SERVING (1 bagel half each) **CAL** 171, **FAT** 5 g (1 g sat. fat), **CHOL** 5 mg, **SODIUM** 178 mg, **CARB** 27 g (5 g fiber, 12 g sugars), **PRO** 9 g

Overnight Peach-Raspberry French Toast

BAGEL THINS
TOAST FAST,
SO WATCH
CAREFULLY.

**Pumpkin- and
Fruit-Topped Bagels**

**Tropical Fruit
Breakfast Parfaits**

Tropical Fruit Breakfast Parfaits

23 g CARB

SERVES	8
HANDS ON	20 min.
TOTAL	40 min.

Nonstick cooking spray
- 4 cups regular rolled oats
- ⅓ cup shredded coconut
- ½ cup dry-roasted unsalted sunflower kernels
- ¼ cup honey
- 3 Tbsp. canola oil
- 2 Tbsp. packed brown sugar*
- 2½ cups cubed tropical fruits, such as mangoes, kiwifruits, papayas, bananas, and/or pineapple
- 2 cups coconut- or honey-flavor Greek yogurt
Toasted shredded coconut (optional)
Chopped macadamia nuts (optional)

1. For granola, preheat oven to 350°F. Lightly coat a 15×10-inch baking pan with cooking spray. In a medium bowl combine oats, the ⅓ cup coconut, and the sunflower kernels. In a small bowl combine honey, oil, and brown sugar. Drizzle honey mixture over oat mixture; stir until oats are coated. Spread evenly in prepared pan.

2. Bake 20 to 25 minutes or until lightly browned, stirring twice. Line a large baking sheet with foil or parchment paper. Spread granola onto prepared baking sheet; cool. Store in an airtight container at room temperature up to 1 week.

3. To make parfaits, place about 2 Tbsp. of the fruits in each of eight 6- to 8-oz. glasses. Add about 2 Tbsp. of the yogurt to each glass. Add about 1 Tbsp. of the granola to each glass. Repeat layers once more. Do not stir. If desired, top with toasted coconut and macadamia nuts. Serve immediately or cover and chill up to 4 hours.

Chia Pudding with Fruit

Tip You will have more granola than you need to make the parfaits. Use the extra granola to eat out of hand as a snack or to add crunch to salads.

PER SERVING *(1 parfait each)* **CAL** 155, **FAT** 5 g (2 g sat. fat), **CHOL** 8 mg, **SODIUM** 33 mg, **CARB** 23 g (2 g fiber, 14 g sugars), **PRO** 8 g

***Sugar Sub** Choose Splenda Brown Sugar Blend. Follow package directions to use 2 Tbsp. equivalent.
PER SERVING WITH SUB Same as above, except **CAL** 154, **CARB** 22 g

Peach Breakfast Parfaits Prepare granola as directed, except stir **1 tsp. ground cinnamon** into honey mixture. Assemble parfaits as directed, except substitute **chopped, peeled peaches** for the tropical fruits and use **peach- or honey-flavor Greek yogurt**. If desired, top with **sliced peaches** and purchased **glazed almonds or walnuts.**

PER SERVING *(1 parfait each)* **CAL** 120, **FAT** 2 g (0 g sat. fat), **CHOL** 0 MG, **SODIUM** 25 MG, **CARB** 19 g (2 g fiber, 13 g sugars), **PRO** 7 g

PER SERVING WITH SUB Same as above

Chia Pudding with Fruit

18 g CARB

SERVES	6
HANDS ON	20 min.
TOTAL	8 hr. 20 min.

- 1 14-oz. can unsweetened light coconut milk
- 1 cup plain fat-free Greek yogurt
- 2 Tbsp. pure maple syrup
- ½ tsp. vanilla
- ¼ cup chia seeds
- 2 cups chopped fresh fruit or berries, such as pineapple, strawberries, blueberries, raspberries, mango, and/or peach
- 6 tsp. unsweetened shredded coconut, toasted

1. In bowl stir together the first four ingredients (through vanilla). Stir in the chia seeds. Divide mixture among six bowls. Cover with foil; chill overnight.

2. To serve, spoon fruit over pudding in bowls. Sprinkle with coconut.

PER SERVING *(½ cup pudding + ⅓ cup fruit each)* **CAL** 161, **FAT** 8 g (4 g sat. fat), **CHOL** 0 mg, **SODIUM** 30 mg, **CARB** 18 g (4 g fiber, 12 g sugars), **PRO** 7 g

Strawberry-Pistachio Breakfast Quinoa

Ginger-Pear Overnight Oats

30 g
CARB

SERVES	2
HANDS ON	15 min.
TOTAL	8 hr. 15 min.

- 1 cup unsweetened vanilla almond milk
- ⅔ cup regular rolled oats
- 1 tsp. grated fresh ginger
- ¾ cup unpeeled ripe pear, cored and chopped
- 3 Tbsp. coarsely chopped walnuts, toasted

1. Divide the almond milk, oats, and fresh ginger between two single-serving containers with lids; stir. Top with the pear and walnuts. Cover and refrigerate overnight.

PER SERVING (1 cup each) **CAL** 228,
FAT 11 g (1 g sat. fat), **CHOL** 0 mg, **SODIUM** 91 mg,
CARB 30 g (6 g fiber, 7 g sugars), **PRO** 6 g

PINT-SIZE JARS WORK WELL, GIVING YOU AMPLE ROOM TO STIR TOPPINGS INTO OATS.

Strawberry-Pistachio Breakfast Quinoa

40 g
CARB

SERVES	4
TOTAL	20 min.

- 1 cup sliced fresh strawberries
- 1 tsp. sugar*
- 2 cups water
- 1 cup uncooked quinoa, rinsed and drained
- ¼ cup apple juice or apple cider
- 3 Tbsp. reduced-fat peanut butter spread
- ½ cup chopped fresh strawberries
- 4 tsp. chopped pistachio nuts

1. In a bowl combine sliced strawberries and sugar. Let stand 10 minutes, stirring occasionally. Meanwhile, rinse quinoa in a fine-mesh sieve; drain well. In a medium saucepan combine the water and quinoa. Bring to boiling; reduce heat to medium-low. Cook, covered, 10 to 15 minutes or until water is absorbed. Remove from heat. Stir in apple juice and peanut butter spread until combined. If necessary, stir in additional apple juice to make desired consistency. Stir in chopped strawberries. Divide quinoa mixture among four bowls. Top with sliced strawberries and pistachios.

PER SERVING (¾ cup each) **CAL** 270,
FAT 8 g (1 g sat. fat), **CHOL** 0 mg, **SODIUM** 91 mg,
CARB 40 g (5 g fiber, 7 g sugars), **PRO** 10 g

*****Sugar Sub** We do not recommend using a sugar sub for this recipe.

**Ginger-Pear
Overnight Oats**

**Berry-Banana
Smoothie Bowls**

Berry-Banana Smoothie Bowls

32 g
CARB

SERVES 4
TOTAL 15 min.

- 1½ cups pitted dark sweet cherries, frozen
- 1 cup unsweetened vanilla almond milk
- 1 6-oz. carton blueberry fat-free Greek yogurt
- ½ cup blueberries, frozen
- 1 medium banana, peeled, sliced, and frozen
- ½ cup ice cubes
- 1 cup fresh banana slices, blueberries, and/or pitted dark sweet cherries
- 1 Tbsp. sliced almonds, toasted
- 1 Tbsp. chopped crystallized ginger
- 1 Tbsp. chia seeds

1. In a blender combine the first six ingredients (through ice cubes). Cover and blend until smooth. Pour into bowls. Top with fresh banana slices, blueberries, and/or sweet cherries. In a bowl combine the remaining ingredients. Sprinkle over fruit.

PER SERVING (about ¾ cup each) **CAL** 172, **FAT** 3 g (0 g sat. fat), **CHOL** 1 mg, **SODIUM** 65 mg, **CARB** 32 g (5 g fiber, 19 g sugars), **PRO** 6 g

Cocoa PB Banana Smoothie

Cocoa PB Banana Smoothie

25 g
CARB

SERVES 2
TOTAL 10 min.

- 1 small banana, peeled, sliced, and frozen
- 1 5.3-oz. carton vanilla-flavor fat-free Greek yogurt
- ½ cup ice cubes
- ½ cup fat-free milk
- ½ cup fresh baby spinach
- 2 Tbsp. creamy peanut butter
- 1 Tbsp. unsweetened cocoa powder
  Fresh banana slices (optional)
  Honey (optional)

1. In a blender combine the first seven ingredients (through cocoa powder). Cover and blend until nearly smooth. Serve in tall glasses. If desired, top with fresh banana slices, a drizzle of honey, and/or a sprinkle of additional cocoa powder.

PER SERVING (1 cup each) **CAL** 218, **FAT** 9 g (2 g sat. fat), **CHOL** 3 mg, **SODIUM** 126 mg, **CARB** 25 g (3 g fiber, 17 g sugars), **PRO** 13 g

Nutty Chocolate
Granola Bars

Pumpkin Spice Breakfast Cookies

26 g CARB

SERVES 13
HANDS ON 20 min.
TOTAL 1 hr.

- 1½ cups rolled oats
- 1 cup almond meal
- ½ cup white whole wheat flour
- ⅓ cup toasted walnuts, chopped
- ¼ cup nonfat dry milk powder
- 1 tsp. pumpkin pie spice
- ¾ tsp. baking soda
- ¼ tsp. salt
- 1 egg, lightly beaten
- ¾ cup canned pumpkin
- ½ cup packed brown sugar*
- ¼ cup raisins, snipped
- ¼ cup almond butter
- 1 tsp. orange zest
- 1 tsp. vanilla
- ¼ cup pepitas or sliced almonds

1. Preheat oven to 350°F. Line a cookie sheet with parchment paper.
2. In a large bowl combine the first eight ingredients (through salt). In a medium bowl combine the next seven ingredients (through vanilla). Add egg mixture to flour mixture and stir until combined.
3. Using a ¼-cup measure, drop dough portions 2 inches apart onto prepared cookie sheet, making 13 mounds total. Sprinkle tops with pepitas, pressing into dough. Bake 13 to 15 minutes or until firm to the touch and lightly browned on top. Remove; cool on a wire rack.

To Store Place cookies in an airtight container at room temperature up to 3 days or freeze up to 3 months.

PER SERVING (1 cookie each) **CAL** 231, **FAT** 12 g (1 g sat. fat), **CHOL** 15 mg, **SODIUM** 156 mg, **CARB** 26 g (4 g fiber, 12 g sugars), **PRO** 8 g

*Sugar Sub We do not recommend using a sugar sub for this recipe.

Nutty Chocolate Granola Bars

24 g CARB

SERVES 12
HANDS ON 15 min.
TOTAL 35 min.

- 1 cup regular rolled oats
- ¼ cup slivered almonds, chopped
- ½ cup natural creamy peanut butter
- ⅓ cup honey
- ¼ cup refrigerated or frozen egg product, thawed, or 1 egg, lightly beaten
- 1 Tbsp. canola oil
- ½ cup oat bran
- ¼ cup almond meal
- ¼ cup chia seed powder or flaxseed meal
- ¼ tsp. salt
- ⅓ cup miniature semisweet chocolate pieces

1. Preheat oven to 325°F. In a shallow baking pan combine oats and almonds. Bake about 10 minutes or until lightly toasted, stirring twice; cool.

2. Meanwhile, in a large bowl combine the next four ingredients (through oil). Stir in oat mixture and the next four ingredients (through salt) until combined. Stir in chocolate pieces.
3. Line a baking sheet with parchment paper. On the prepared baking sheet shape oat mixture into a 6-inch square; cut square in half. Cut each half crosswise into 1-inch strips (12 bars total). Separate bars, leaving about 1 inch between bars.
4. Bake 10 to 12 minutes or until bars are set and edges are light brown. Remove; cool on a wire rack. If desired, wrap individual bars with plastic wrap.

To Store Place wrapped bars in an airtight container at room temperature up to 2 days or freeze up to 3 months.

PER SERVING (1 bar each) **CAL** 221, **FAT** 13 g (3 g sat. fat), **CHOL** 0 mg, **SODIUM** 105 mg, **CARB** 24 g (4 g fiber, 13 g sugars), **PRO** 7 g

Pumpkin Spice
Breakfast Cookies

MAKE & TAKE
LUNCHES

Think outside the lunchbox with fresh veggie-packed noon meals. These soups, salads, and sandwiches really bring the nutrition, energy, and balance.

Roast Beef, Arugula, and Pickled Onion Wrap

White Chicken Chili

Roast Beef, Arugula, and Pickled Onion Wrap

32 g
CARB

SERVES 1
HANDS ON 15 min.
TOTAL 8 hr. 15 min.

- 2 Tbsp. cider vinegar
- 1 tsp. honey
   Dash salt
- ¼ cup very thinly sliced red onion
- 1 8-inch low-carb whole wheat flour tortilla
- 1 Tbsp. mango chutney
- 2 oz. thinly sliced reduced-sodium cooked roast beef
- 1 cup arugula

1. In a small bowl combine vinegar, honey, and salt. Stir in onion. Cover and chill overnight.

2. Spread tortilla with chutney and top with meat and arugula. Drain onion, discarding liquid. Spoon onion over arugula. Roll up tortilla around filling.

Tip To make four wraps, use ½ cup cider vinegar, 1 Tbsp. honey, ⅛ tsp. salt, 1 cup onion, 4 tortillas, ¼ cup chutney, 8 oz. roast beef, and 4 cups arugula.

To Tote Wrap sandwich with plastic wrap. Pack in an insulated bag with ice packs.

PER SERVING (1 sandwich) **CAL** 239, **FAT** 5 g (2 g sat. fat), **CHOL** 40 mg, **SODIUM** 572 mg, **CARB** 32 g (8 g fiber, 17 g sugars), **PRO** 21 g

White Chicken Chili

36 g
CARB

SERVES 6
HANDS ON 25 min.
SLOW COOK 6 hr. 20 min.

- 3 15- to 16-oz. cans no-salt-added Great Northern, pinto, or cannellini (white kidney) beans, rinsed and drained
- 1½ cups chopped red, green, and/or yellow sweet peppers
- 1 cup chopped onion
- 1 to 2 fresh jalapeño chile peppers, seeded and chopped (tip, p. 58)
- 2 tsp. ground cumin
- 2 cloves garlic, minced
- ¾ tsp. salt
- ½ tsp. dried oregano, crushed
- 3½ cups reduced-sodium chicken broth
- 2½ cups chopped cooked chicken
   Monterey Jack cheese, shredded, and/or tortilla chips, broken (optional)

1. In a 3½- or 4-qt. slow cooker stir together the first eight ingredients (through oregano). Add broth. Cover and cook on low 6 to 8 hours or on high 3 to 4 hours. Mash some of the beans, then stir in chicken. Cover and cook 20 minutes more. If desired, top each serving with cheese and/or tortilla chips.

To Tote Transfer cooled chili to individual covered containers; chill. To tote, pack chili in an insulated bag with ice packs. To serve, if container is not microwavable, transfer chili to a bowl. Microwave, partially covered, 1 to 2 minutes or until hot, stirring once or twice. Alternately, heat chili at home and use an insulated food jar to keep it hot. Preheat food jar with boiling water, let stand for a few minutes, then drain it. Fill food jar with hot chili; cover tightly until ready to serve. Do not put food jar in bag with ice packs.

PER SERVING (1⅔ cups each) **CAL** 309, **FAT** 6 g (1 g sat. fat), **CHOL** 52 mg, **SODIUM** 453 mg, **CARB** 36 g (13 g fiber, 4 g sugars), **PRO** 26 g

Chipotle Shrimp, Mango, and Pasta Salad

55 g
CARB

SERVES 2
TOTAL 30 min.

- 6 oz. fresh or frozen peeled and deveined medium shrimp
- 3 oz. whole grain bow tie pasta
- ½ cup buttermilk
- ⅓ cup light mayonnaise
- 1 Tbsp. snipped fresh cilantro
- ¼ tsp. onion powder
- ¼ tsp. dry mustard
- ¼ tsp. ground chipotle chile pepper

Chipotle Shrimp, Mango, and Pasta Salad

- 1 medium red sweet pepper, cut into bite-size strips (¾ cup)
- ¾ cup chopped fresh mango
- ¾ cup thinly sliced carrot
- ¼ cup thinly sliced green onions
  Lime wedges

1. Thaw shrimp, if frozen. Rinse shrimp; pat dry. Halve shrimp lengthwise. Cook pasta according to package directions, adding shrimp during the last 2 minutes of cooking. Drain pasta and shrimp; rinse with cold water and drain again. Transfer pasta and shrimp to a large bowl.
2. Meanwhile, in a bowl stir together the next six ingredients (through ground chipotle chile pepper).
3. Add the next four ingredients (through green onions) to pasta and shrimp. Toss to combine. Add dressing; toss gently to coat. Sprinkle with additional snipped cilantro and serve with lime wedges. Serve immediately or cover and chill up to 2 days.

To Tote Divide salad between individual covered containers. Pack a container in an insulated bag with ice packs.

PER SERVING *(2¼ cups each)* **CAL** 406, **FAT** 9 g (2 g sat. fat), **CHOL** 145 mg, **SODIUM** 386 mg, **CARB** 55 g (8 g fiber, 19 g sugars), **PRO** 29 g

---

Chicken and Artichoke Spinach Salads

34 g
CARB

SERVES 4
TOTAL 45 min.

- ¼ cup dried quinoa
- ½ cup water
- 2 Tbsp. olive oil
- 2 Tbsp. balsamic vinegar
- 2 tsp. snipped fresh oregano
- ¼ tsp. salt
- ⅛ tsp. black pepper
- 4 cups fresh baby spinach
- ⅓ cup torn fresh basil
- 1 14-oz. can quartered artichoke hearts, drained and coarsely chopped
- 8 oz. cooked chicken breast or turkey breast, chopped
- ¾ cup grape tomatoes, halved
- ¾ cup quartered, thinly sliced red onion
- 4 tsp. shredded Parmesan cheese
- 2½ cups grapes

1. Rinse quinoa in a fine-mesh sieve; drain well. In a small saucepan combine quinoa and water. Bring to boiling; reduce heat. Simmer, covered, 12 to 15 minutes or until quinoa is tender and most of the liquid is absorbed. Drain if necessary. Set aside to cool slightly.
2. In a small bowl whisk together the olive oil, vinegar, oregano, salt, and pepper. Divide among four small containers.
3. In four pint-size jars evenly layer spinach, basil, cooked quinoa, and the next four ingredients (through Parmesan cheese). Drizzle with dressing just before serving. Serve with grapes.

To Tote Pack a salad, dressing container, and grapes in an insulated bag with ice packs. When ready to serve, drizzle salad with dressing.

PER SERVING *(2 cups each)* **CAL** 314, **FAT** 10 g (2 g sat. fat), **CHOL** 49 mg, **SODIUM** 446 mg, **CARB** 34 g (5 g fiber, 18 g sugars), **PRO** 23 g

Chicken and Artichoke Spinach Salads

FOR EASY EATING AND TOSSING, EMPTY SALAD INTO A BOWL.

Turkey, Apple, and Havarti Sandwich

27 g CARB

SERVES 1
TOTAL 10 min.

- 1 Tbsp. white wine vinegar
- 2 tsp. olive oil
- ½ tsp. Dijon-style mustard
  Dash black pepper
- ¼ cup fresh baby spinach
- ⅓ cup thinly sliced apple
- 2 oz. roasted turkey breast, thinly sliced
- 1 ¾-oz. slice Havarti cheese
- 2 slices reduced-calorie whole wheat bread

1. In a small screw-top jar combine vinegar, oil, mustard, and pepper; cover and shake well. Divide between two small storage containers.
2. Layer spinach, apple, turkey, and cheese between bread slices. To serve, drizzle one container dressing over sandwich filling.

Tip To roast turkey, preheat oven to 400°F. In a 10-inch oven-going skillet heat **2 tsp. canola oil** over medium-high. Add **one 1-lb. turkey breast tenderloin;** cook 3 minutes on one side or until golden. Turn turkey; transfer skillet to oven. Roast 15 to 20 minutes or until turkey is done (165°F). Transfer to a cutting board; cover with foil and let rest 10 minutes before slicing.

To Tote Wrap sandwich in plastic wrap or place in a sandwich container. Pack one dressing container and the sandwich in an insulated bag with ice packs. (Reserve remaining dressing for another sandwich or a tossed green salad.) To serve, drizzle dressing over sandwich filling.

PER SERVING (1 sandwich) **CAL** 325, **FAT** 14 g (5 g sat. fat), **CHOL** 60 mg, **SODIUM** 460 mg, **CARB** 27 g (6 g fiber, 8 g sugars), **PRO** 27 g

Turkey, Apple, and Havarti Sandwich

Asian Chicken and Noodle Salad

38 g
CARB

SERVES 1
HANDS ON 20 min.
TOTAL 20 min.

- 3 Tbsp. powdered peanut butter
- 2 Tbsp. water
- 3 Tbsp. unsweetened light coconut milk
- 1 Tbsp. lime juice
- 2 tsp. reduced-sodium soy sauce
- ¼ tsp. sriracha sauce
- 1 oz. dried whole grain spaghetti, broken in half, cooked, and drained
- ½ cup snow pea pods, trimmed and halved crosswise
- ⅓ cup chopped cooked chicken breast
- ¼ cup bite-size pieces red sweet pepper
- 1 tsp. snipped fresh cilantro
- 1 Tbsp. sliced green onion
- 1 Tbsp. chopped unsalted peanuts

1. In a medium bowl stir together powdered peanut butter and the water. Stir in the next four ingredients (through sriracha sauce) until smooth. Add the next five ingredients (through cilantro); toss to coat. Transfer to a storage container; sprinkle with green onion. Place peanuts in a small storage container. Cover and chill overnight.
2. To tote, pack containers in an insulated bag with ice packs. To serve, sprinkle salad with peanuts.

Tip Substitute 2 Tbsp. whipped peanut butter for the powdered peanut butter and reduce the water to 1 Tbsp.

PER SERVING *(1¾ cups)* **CAL** 378, **FAT** 12 g (3 g sat. fat), **CHOL** 48 mg, **SODIUM** 588 mg, **CARB** 38 g (9 g fiber, 8 g sugars), **PRO** 34 g

Asian Chicken and Noodle Salad

Chili-Cilantro Turkey Sandwiches

berries in an insulated bag with ice packs. Place tomato slices on sandwich just before eating.

PER SERVING (*1 sandwich each*) **CAL** 272, **FAT** 10 g (3 g sat. fat), **CHOL** 32 mg, **SODIUM** 612 mg, **CARB** 34 g (8 g fiber, 12 g sugars), **PRO** 16 g

Turkey Soup in a Jar

29 g
CARB

| SERVES 1 |
| TOTAL 20 min. |

- 1 tsp. reduced-sodium chicken base
- 1 clove garlic, minced
- ½ tsp. lemon zest
  Pinch ground ginger
- 2 Tbsp. dried whole wheat couscous
- ⅔ cup shredded or chopped cooked turkey breast or chicken breast
- 2 Tbsp. sliced green onion
- ¼ cup thinly sliced red sweet pepper
- 3 fresh shiitake mushrooms, stemmed and thinly sliced
- ½ cup packed fresh baby spinach

1. In a microwavable pint-size jar with lid layer all ingredients in the order given. Place lid on jar. Store in the refrigerator up to 3 days.
2. Before heating, let stand at room temperature 10 minutes or run warm water over the jar for a minute or so to warm slightly. Fill the jar nearly full with water (about 1 cup) and microwave, uncovered, 2 minutes. Cover and let stand 5 minutes. Stir to combine. (Alternately, fill the jar with hot water from a desktop kettle or hot water dispenser. Cover and let stand 5 minutes. Stir to combine.)

PER SERVING (*2 cups*) **CAL** 254, **FAT** 3 g (1 g sat. fat), **CHOL** 60 mg, **SODIUM** 617 mg, **CARB** 29 g (6 g fiber, 4 g sugars), **PRO** 32 g

Chili-Cilantro Turkey Sandwiches

34 g
CARB

| SERVES 4 |
| TOTAL 25 min. |

- 3 Tbsp. light mayonnaise
- 2 Tbsp. snipped fresh cilantro
- 1 tsp. hot or mild chili powder
- 8 slices very thinly sliced whole wheat bread
- 4 oz. thinly sliced lower-sodium cooked turkey
- 4 slices reduced-fat cheddar cheese (3 oz. total)
- 1 medium fresh poblano pepper, stemmed, seeded, and thinly sliced crosswise
- 1 medium fresh tomato, sliced
- 4 cups mixed fresh berries

1. In a small bowl stir together mayonnaise, cilantro, and chili powder. Spread on one side of each slice of bread.
2. Layer the next four ingredients (through tomato slices) on four of the bread slices; top with remaining bread slices. Cut sandwiches in half. Serve sandwiches with berries.

Tip Chile peppers contain oils that can irritate your skin and eyes. Wear plastic or rubber gloves when working with them.

To Tote Wrap tomato slices separately in plastic wrap. Wrap sandwich in plastic wrap or place in a sandwich container. Pack a sandwich, tomato slice, and

TO TOTE: PACK JAR IN AN INSULATED BAG WITH ICE PACKS.

Turkey Soup in a Jar

**Pineapple-Shrimp
Salad on Crackers**

Pineapple-Shrimp Salad on Crackers

34 g CARB

SERVES 1
TOTAL 15 min.

- 2 oz. peeled cooked shrimp, tails removed and coarsely chopped (about ⅓ cup)
- ¼ cup coarsely chopped pineapple
- 2 Tbsp. bias-sliced green onion
- 2 Tbsp. light mayonnaise
- ½ tsp. lime zest
- ¼ tsp. sriracha sauce
- 6 shredded wheat crackers
- 1 medium apple, sliced

1. Stir together the first six ingredients (through sriracha sauce). Serve shrimp mixture with crackers and apples slices.

To Tote Place shrimp mixture and crackers in separate covered containers. Pack containers and apple in an insulated bag with ice packs. To serve, spoon shrimp mixture on crackers.

PER SERVING (6 salad-topped crackers + 1 apple) **CAL** 316, **FAT** 13 g (2 g sat. fat), **CHOL** 118 mg, **SODIUM** 450 mg, **CARB** 34 g (4 g fiber, 9 g sugars), **PRO** 18 g

Turkey Chopped Salad with Orange-Poppy Seed Dressing

Turkey Chopped Salad with Orange-Poppy Seed Dressing

36 g CARB

SERVES 4
TOTAL 40 min.

- 2 6-inch corn tortillas
- 1 tsp. olive oil
- 2 cups frozen whole kernel corn
- 6 cups chopped romaine lettuce
- 2 cups chopped cooked turkey breast
- 1 cup seeded and chopped tomatoes
- ½ cup chopped orange sweet pepper
- ⅓ cup slivered red onion

- 2 slices turkey bacon, cooked according to pkg. directions and broken
- 1 recipe Orange-Poppy Seed Dressing

1. Preheat oven to 350°F. Cut tortillas into ¼-inch strips. Spread strips in a single layer on a baking sheet. Bake 8 to 10 minutes or until crisp; cool completely.
2. Meanwhile, in a 10-inch skillet heat oil over medium. Add corn; cook 6 to 8 minutes or until lightly browned, stirring occasionally. Remove from heat; cool completely.
3. Divide lettuce among four bowls. Top with the next five ingredients (through bacon) and the roasted corn. Drizzle salads with dressing.

Orange-Poppy Seed Dressing In a small jar with lid combine ¼ cup orange juice; 1 Tbsp. each olive oil, lime juice, and honey; and 1 tsp. poppy seeds. Shake well.

To Tote Divide tortilla strips among four small resealable plastic bags. Assemble salads in four covered containers. Divide dressing among four small containers. Pack salad and dressing containers in an insulated bag with ice packs. To serve, shake dressing. Drizzle one dressing portion over one salad. Cover and shake to combine or toss with a fork to combine. Top each with one portion of tortilla strips.

PER SERVING (2 cups salad + 2 Tbsp. dressing + tortilla strips from ½ of a tortilla each) **CAL** 334, **FAT** 8 g (2 g sat. fat), **CHOL** 76 mg, **SODIUM** 188 mg, **CARB** 36 g (5 g fiber, 11 g sugars), **PRO** 32 g

61

Miso-
Marinated
Tofu and
Cabbage
Wraps

Mediterranean Sandwich

38 g
CARB

SERVES 1

TOTAL 15 min.

- ½ cup canned no-salt-added garbanzo beans (chickpeas), rinsed and drained
- 1 Tbsp. lemon juice
- ¼ tsp. ground cumin
- ⅛ tsp. black pepper
  Dash salt
- ½ whole wheat pita bread round
- 1 Tbsp. finely chopped red onion
- 2 Tbsp. chopped cucumber
- 1 Tbsp. crumbled reduced-fat feta cheese
- 2 slices roma tomato

1. In a bowl coarsely mash the first five ingredients (through salt). Gently open pita bread to make pocket. Stuff with bean mixture and the remaining ingredients.

To Tote Prepare as directed, except do not add tomato. Wrap sandwich in plastic wrap or place in a covered container. Place tomato in a separate container. Pack containers in an insulated bag with ice packs. To serve, place tomato on sandwich.

PER SERVING (1 sandwich) **CAL** 206, **FAT** 3 g (1 g sat. fat), **CHOL** 3 mg, **SODIUM** 461 mg, **CARB** 38 g (7 g fiber, 4 g sugars), **PRO** 10 g

Miso-Marinated Tofu and Cabbage Wraps

32 g
CARB

SERVES 6

HANDS ON 25 min.

TOTAL 2 hr. 25 min.

- 1 18-oz. pkg. firm tofu (fresh bean curd)
- ⅓ cup rice vinegar
- ¼ cup snipped fresh mint
- 2 Tbsp. honey
- 2 Tbsp. white miso paste
- ¼ tsp. crushed red pepper
- 6 8-inch low-carb, high-fiber tortillas
- 6 napa cabbage leaves
- 1 cup julienned or coarsely shredded carrots
- 1 cup very thinly sliced radishes
- ¾ cup thinly sliced cucumber
- 2 small shallots, thinly sliced
- 6 medium fresh kiwifruit, peeled and sliced

1. Drain tofu and pat dry with paper towels. Cut tofu into 1-inch cubes. Place tofu in a resealable plastic bag set in a shallow dish. In a bowl whisk together the next five ingredients (through crushed red pepper). Pour over tofu. Seal bag; turn to coat. Marinate in the refrigerator at least 2 hours or up to 8 hours, turning bag occasionally.

2. Drain tofu, discarding marinade. Place a cabbage leaf on each tortilla. Layer drained tofu and the next four ingredients (through shallots) on cabbage leaves. Roll up tortillas; cut in half crosswise. Serve immediately or wrap in plastic wrap and chill up to 8 hours before serving. Serve wraps with kiwifruit.

To Tote Place kiwifruit in a covered container. Pack wrapped sandwich and kiwifruit in an insulated bag with ice packs.

PER SERVING (1 wrap each) **CAL** 197, **FAT** 5 g (0 g sat. fat), **CHOL** 0 mg, **SODIUM** 240 mg, **CARB** 32 g (11 g fiber, 13 g sugars), **PRO** 14 g

FOR BEST TOTING, ASSEMBLE SANDWICH IN THE MORNING.

Mediterranean Sandwich

**Black-Eyed
Pea Salad**

Cauliflower Soup

Cauliflower Soup

15 g
CARB

SERVES 1
TOTAL 20 min.

- 2 cups cooked cauliflower florets
- ⅔ to ¾ cup low-sodium chicken broth
  Dash garlic powder
  Dash black pepper
- 1 oz. reduced-fat cream cheese (neufchatel)
- ⅓ cup plain fat-free Greek yogurt
- 2 slices lower-sodium, less-fat bacon, crisp-cooked and crumbled
- 1 tsp. snipped fresh parsley
- ¼ tsp. lemon zest

1. In a blender or food processor combine cauliflower, ⅔ cup of the broth, the garlic powder, and pepper. Cover and blend until smooth. If desired, cover and chill overnight.
2. Transfer cauliflower mixture to a small saucepan. Bring just to boiling over medium. Whisk in cream cheese and enough of the remaining broth to reach desired consistency; heat through. Top soup with remaining ingredients.

To Tote Let soup cool, then transfer to a covered container; chill. Place yogurt in another covered container and bacon, parsley, and lemon zest in a third covered container. To tote, pack containers in an insulated bag with ice packs. To serve, if container is not microwavable, transfer soup to a bowl. Microwave, partially covered, 1 to 2 minutes or until hot, stirring once or twice. Alternately, heat soup at home and use an insulated food jar to keep it hot. Preheat food jar with boiling water, let stand for a few minutes, then drain it. Fill food jar with hot soup; cover tightly. Do not put food jar in bag with ice packs. To serve, top soup with yogurt and bacon mixture.

PER SERVING (1⅓ cups) **CAL** 229,
FAT 10 g (5 g sat. fat), **CHOL** 28 mg, **SODIUM** 348 mg,
CARB 15 g (6 g fiber, 9 g sugars), **PRO** 21 g

Black-Eyed Pea Salad

31 g
CARB

SERVES 4
HANDS ON 20 min.
TOTAL 2 hr. 20 min.

- ½ cup chopped yellow sweet pepper
- ¼ cup chopped green sweet pepper
- ¼ cup chopped red sweet pepper
- ¼ cup chopped red onion
- 1 fresh serrano chile pepper, stemmed, seeded, and thinly sliced
- 1 clove garlic, minced
- 1 11-oz. pkg. steamed ready-to-eat black-eyed peas, rinsed and drained, or one 15-oz. can black-eyed peas, rinsed and drained
- ⅔ cup chopped roma tomatoes
- ¼ cup seasoned rice vinegar
- 1 Tbsp. olive oil
- ¼ tsp. salt
- ¼ tsp. black pepper

1. In a bowl layer the first six ingredients (through garlic). Top with black-eyed peas and tomatoes. In another bowl whisk together vinegar, oil, salt, and black pepper. Drizzle over salad. Cover and chill 2 to 24 hours. Before serving, toss salad with a fork to combine.

Tip Chile peppers contain oils that can irritate your skin and eyes. Wear plastic or rubber gloves when working with them.

To Tote Assemble salads in four covered containers; drizzle evenly with dressing. Pack a salad container in an insulated bag with ice packs. Before serving, shake salad container or toss salad with a fork to combine.

PER SERVING (about 1 cup each) **CAL** 203,
FAT 4 g (0 g sat. fat), **CHOL** 0 mg,
SODIUM 317 mg, **CARB** 31 g (6 g fiber,
5 g sugars), **PRO** 11 g

Barbecue Chopped
Pork Salad

½ tsp. lemon zest
1 cup mixed baby salad greens
¼ cup cherry or grape tomatoes, halved
1 hard-cooked egg, sliced
1 Tbsp. chopped toasted walnuts
1 recipe Lemon-Chive Aïoli

1. Place a steamer basket in a saucepan. Add water to just below bottom of the basket. Bring water to boiling. Add beans and carrots to steamer basket. Cover and reduce heat. Steam about 5 minutes or until crisp-tender. Carefully remove basket from pan and place in a sink. Rinse with cold water; drain well. Meanwhile, toss lentils with parsley and lemon zest.
2. In a bowl arrange lentil mixture and the next three ingredients (through egg). Sprinkle with walnuts. Top with Lemon-Chive Aïoli.

Lemon-Chive Aïoli In a bowl stir together **2 tsp.** each **reduced-fat sour cream, light mayonnaise,** and **snipped fresh chives; 1 tsp. lemon juice;** and a **dash black pepper.**

Tip For cooked lentils, combine 2 cups reduced-sodium chicken broth and 1 cup rinsed and drained brown lentils. Bring to boiling; reduce heat. Simmer, covered, 25 to 30 minutes or until tender. Drain, if necessary. This yields about 2⅓ cups cooked lentils. Store leftovers, covered, in an airtight container in the refrigerator up to 3 days.

To Tote Assemble salad in a covered container. Place Lemon-Chive Aïoli in a separate small container. Pack containers in an insulated bag with ice packs. When ready to serve, top salad with aïoli.

PER SERVING (3 cups) CAL 380,
FAT 15 g (3 g sat. fat), CHOL 193 mg,
SODIUM 184 mg, CARB 42 g (15 g fiber,
9 g sugars), PRO 22 g

Barbecue Chopped Pork Salad

33 g
CARB

SERVES 1
TOTAL 20 min.

1 6-inch corn tortilla
  Nonstick cooking spray
2 cups chopped romaine lettuce
3 oz. chopped roasted lean boneless pork
¼ cup frozen roasted corn, thawed
¼ cup thinly sliced red onion
1 Tbsp. fat-free milk
1 Tbsp. light sour cream
1 Tbsp. barbecue sauce

1. Preheat oven to 450°F. Cut tortilla into strips. Spread on a baking sheet. Coat with cooking spray. Bake 5 to 7 minutes or until browned and crisp. Cool completely.
2. In a bowl combine the romaine, pork, corn, and red onion. In another bowl stir together milk, sour cream, and barbecue sauce. Spoon over romaine mixture; if desired, toss to coat. Top with tortilla strips.

To Tote Place romaine, pork, corn, and red onion in a covered container. In another covered container stir together milk, sour cream, and barbecue sauce. Place tortilla strips in a small resealable plastic bag. Pack all in an insulated bag with ice packs. To serve, add sour cream mixture to lettuce mixture and toss to coat. Top with tortilla strips.

PER SERVING (1 salad) CAL 322,
FAT 7 g (2 g sat. fat), CHOL 63 mg,
SODIUM 243 mg, CARB 33 g (5 g fiber,
14 g sugars), PRO 33 g

Lentil and Vegetable Bowl

42 g
CARB

SERVES 1
HANDS ON 10 min.
TOTAL 35 min.

2 oz. fresh green beans, trimmed
8 4×¼-inch carrot sticks
⅔ cup cooked brown lentils
1 Tbsp. snipped fresh parsley

Lentil and
Vegetable Bowl

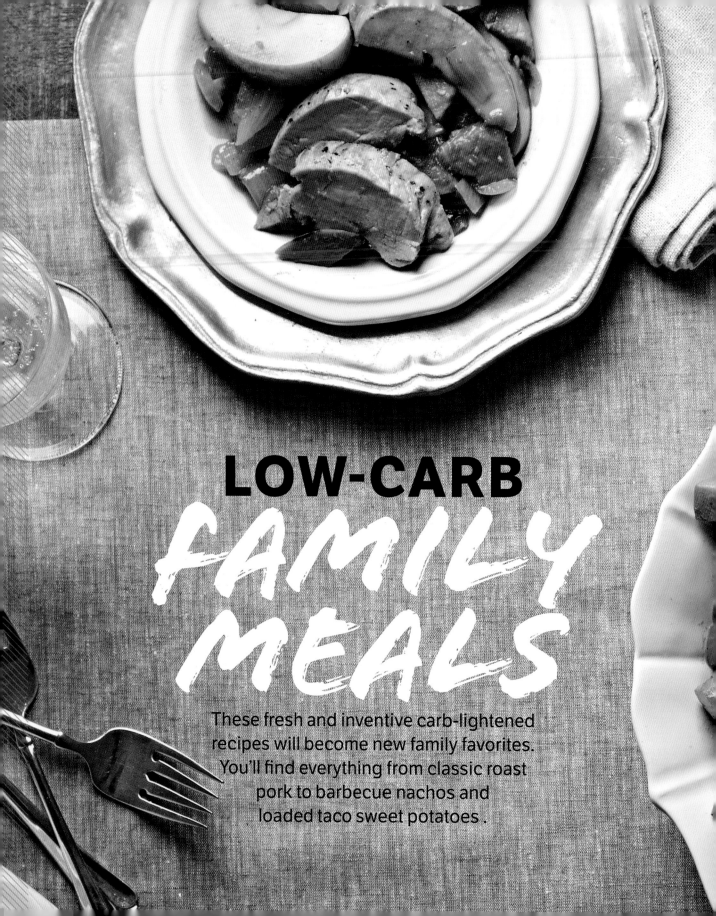

LOW-CARB
FAMILY MEALS

These fresh and inventive carb-lightened recipes will become new family favorites. You'll find everything from classic roast pork to barbecue nachos and loaded taco sweet potatoes.

Pork Tenderloin with Apple-Thyme Sweet Potatoes

44 g CARB

SERVES	4
HANDS ON	35 min.
TOTAL	1 hr.

- 1 1-lb. pork tenderloin, trimmed
- ½ tsp. kosher salt
- ¼ tsp. black pepper
- 1 Tbsp. canola oil
- 1 lb. sweet potatoes, peeled and cut into ½-inch pieces
- 2 cups chopped sweet onions
- 2 cloves garlic, minced
- ¼ cup apple cider
- ¼ cup cider vinegar
- 2 medium apples, such as Granny Smith or Honeycrisp, cored and cut into eighths
- 2 sprigs fresh thyme
- 2 bay leaves

1. Preheat oven to 350°F. Sprinkle meat with salt and pepper. In a 12-inch skillet heat oil over medium-high. Add tenderloin; cook 5 minutes or until browned on all sides. Transfer to a plate.

2. Add sweet potatoes to skillet. Cook over medium 2 minutes, stirring occasionally. Add onions and garlic; cook 3 to 5 minutes or until onions are tender, stirring occasionally. Stir in cider and vinegar. Return tenderloin and any juices to skillet. Add the remaining ingredients.

3. Transfer skillet to oven. Bake 20 to 25 minutes or until pork is done (145°F), turning and basting tenderloin occasionally. Remove and discard thyme and bay leaves.

4. Transfer tenderloin to a cutting board. Cover with foil and let stand 3 minutes. Cut meat into ¼-inch slices. Serve with potato mixture and, if desired, top with additional thyme.

PER SERVING (3½ oz. meat + 1¼ cups potato mixture each) **CAL** 342, **FAT** 6 g (1 g sat. fat), **CHOL** 73 mg, **SODIUM** 257 mg, **CARB** 44 g (7 g fiber, 18 g sugars), **PRO** 27 g

Chicken Thighs with
Caramelized Onion
and Bacon Dressing

Chicken Thighs with Caramelized Onion and Bacon Dressing

21 g CARB

SERVES	4
HANDS ON	40 min.
TOTAL	1 hr. 25 min.

- 3 slices lower-sodium, less-fat bacon
- 3 large onions, halved and sliced (3 cups)
- 2 cups cubed multigrain ciabatta rolls (½-inch cubes), dried
- ½ cup reduced-sodium chicken broth
- ¼ cup refrigerated or frozen egg product, thawed, or 1 egg, lightly beaten
- 2 Tbsp. snipped fresh parsley
- ¼ tsp. black pepper
- 4 medium skinless, boneless chicken thighs (about 12 oz.)
- 1 Tbsp. olive oil

1. Preheat oven to 400°F. Heat a 10-inch skillet over medium. Cook bacon in hot skillet about 10 minutes or until brown and crispy, turning once. Drain bacon on paper towels. Reserve 1 Tbsp. of the bacon drippings in skillet. Add onions. Reduce heat to medium-low. Cook, covered, 13 to 15 minutes or until onions are tender, stirring occasionally. Uncover; cook and stir over medium-high 3 to 5 minutes or until golden. Remove from heat.
2. Chop the bacon. In a medium bowl combine bacon, caramelized onions, and the next five ingredients (through pepper). Stir gently to combine. Spoon dressing mixture into four individual 12- to 14-oz. casserole dishes.
3. In the same skillet brown chicken thighs in hot oil over medium about 5 minutes, turning once. Place one thigh in each casserole. Bake, uncovered, 15 to 20 minutes or until chicken is done (170°F). Sprinkle with additional snipped parsley.

PER SERVING (1 casserole each) **CAL** 256, **FAT** 8 g (2 g sat. fat), **CHOL** 82 mg, **SODIUM** 337 mg, **CARB** 21 g (3 g fiber, 5 g sugars), **PRO** 23 g

Chicken Caesar Flatbreads

16 g CARB

SERVES 4
HANDS ON 15 min.
TOTAL 25 min.

- 2 rustic white or spicy Italian artisan pizza thin-crust flatbreads
- 3 Tbsp. light sour cream
- 3 Tbsp. light Caesar dressing
- 1 cup shredded cooked chicken breast
- 1 cup shredded part-skim mozzarella cheese (4 oz.)
- 2 cups chopped romaine lettuce
- ½ cup quartered cherry tomatoes
- ¼ cup finely shredded Parmesan cheese
- 2 slices lower-sodium, less-fat bacon, cooked and crumbled

1. Preheat oven to 450°F. Cut pizza crusts in half crosswise. Place crusts on a large baking sheet. Bake 4 minutes.

2. In a bowl stir together sour cream and dressing. Spread 3 Tbsp. of the mixture over flatbreads. Top with chicken and mozzarella. Bake 3 to 5 minutes more or until cheese is melted and crust is golden brown.

3. Meanwhile, in a bowl toss romaine with remaining 2 Tbsp. sour cream-dressing mixture. Top pizzas with romaine and sprinkle with tomatoes, Parmesan cheese, and bacon.

Tip Use flatbread with no more than 25 g carbohydrate and 250 mg sodium per flatbread, such as Flat Out.

PER SERVING (½ flatbread each) **CAL** 255, **FAT** 10 g (5 g sat. fat), **CHOL** 56 mg, **SODIUM** 534 mg, **CARB** 16 g (2 g fiber, 3 g sugars), **PRO** 25 g

Chicken Caesar Flatbreads

**Rosemary Chicken
with Vegetables**

Skillet Fajitas

38 g CARB

SERVES 4

TOTAL 40 min.

- 2 tsp. salt-free fiesta lime seasoning
- 1 tsp. garlic powder
- ⅛ tsp. salt
- ⅛ tsp. black pepper
- 1 lb. skinless, boneless chicken breast halves, cut into thin strips
- 2 tsp. canola oil
- 2 cups green, yellow, and/or red sweet pepper strips
- 1 large onion, thinly sliced
- 8 6-inch 100% whole wheat flour tortillas, heated according to pkg. directions
- ½ cup salsa
- ¼ cup snipped fresh cilantro
- ¼ cup plain fat-free Greek yogurt (optional)
- ¼ cup refrigerated avocado dip (guacamole) (optional)
- 1 lime, cut into 4 wedges

1. In a resealable plastic bag combine lime seasoning, garlic powder, salt, and black pepper. Add chicken strips, several at a time, shaking to coat.
2. In a 12-inch skillet heat 1 tsp. of the oil over medium. Add chicken; cook 3 to 4 minutes or until no longer pink, stirring frequently. Remove chicken.
3. In the same skillet heat remaining 1 tsp. oil over medium. Add sweet peppers and onion; cook 8 to 10 minutes or until tender and golden, stirring frequently. Stir in chicken; heat.
4. Serve chicken mixture in warm tortillas with the remaining ingredients.

PER SERVING (2 fajitas each) **CAL** 359, **FAT** 9 g (3 g sat. fat), **CHOL** 83 mg, **SODIUM** 588 mg, **CARB** 38 g (6 g fiber, 6 g sugars), **PRO** 33 g

Skillet Fajitas

Rosemary Chicken with Vegetables

45 g CARB

SERVES 4

TOTAL 30 min.

- 4 medium skinless, boneless chicken breast halves (1 to 1¼ lb. total)
- 1 tsp. lemon-pepper seasoning
- 1 Tbsp. olive oil
- 1 9-oz. pkg. refrigerated plain or spinach linguine
- 2 cloves garlic, minced
- 2 medium zucchini and/or yellow summer squash, halved lengthwise (if desired) and sliced ¼ inch thick (2½ cups)
- ⅔ cup apple juice
- 1 Tbsp. snipped fresh rosemary or 1 tsp. dried rosemary, crushed
- ¼ cup dry white wine or chicken broth
- 1 Tbsp. cornstarch
- 1 cup halved cherry or grape tomatoes

1. Sprinkle chicken with lemon-pepper seasoning. In a large 10-inch skillet heat hot oil over medium. Add chicken; cook 8 to 10 minutes or until chicken is done (165°F), turning once. Transfer chicken to a platter; cover and keep warm. Meanwhile, cook linguine according to package directions; drain. Return to pan; cover and keep warm.
2. Add garlic to skillet; cook and stir 15 seconds. Add zucchini, apple juice, and rosemary. Bring to boiling; reduce heat. Simmer, covered, 2 minutes.
3. In a bowl stir together wine and cornstarch; stir into skillet. Cook and stir until thickened and bubbly. Cook and stir 2 minutes more. Stir in tomatoes. Serve chicken with vegetable mixture and linguine. If desired, garnish with fresh rosemary sprigs.

PER SERVING (1 chicken breast half + ¾ cup vegetable mixture + 1 cup pasta each) **CAL** 398, **FAT** 8 g (2 g sat. fat), **CHOL** 110 mg, **SODIUM** 213 mg, **CARB** 45 g (3 g fiber, 8 g sugars), **PRO** 33 g

Peanut-Cilantro Chicken Pasta

Roasted Curried Chicken and Cauliflower

42 g CARB

SERVES 6
HANDS ON 20 min.
TOTAL 1 hr. 10 min.

¼ cup honey
¼ cup Dijon-style mustard
2 Tbsp. olive oil
1 Tbsp. curry powder
3 cloves garlic, minced
¼ tsp. crushed red pepper
6 6- to 8-oz. skinless, boneless chicken breast halves
2 cups cauliflower florets
1 large sweet potato (12 oz.), peeled and cut into 1-inch pieces
1 large red sweet pepper, cut into bite-size strips (1 cup)
2 cups hot cooked brown rice
Sliced green onions (optional)

Peanut-Cilantro Chicken Pasta

29 g CARB

SERVES 4
TOTAL 40 min.

3 cups packed fresh cilantro leaves and stems (3 oz.)
½ cup plain soymilk
2 Tbsp. rice vinegar
1 Tbsp. reduced-sodium soy sauce
2 cloves garlic, minced
½ tsp. salt
¼ tsp. crushed red pepper
½ cup dry-roasted salted peanuts
2 medium carrots, peeled
1 small zucchini, trimmed
3 oz. dried brown rice pad thai noodles
1 medium red sweet pepper, cut into thin strips
1 tsp. canola oil
12 oz. skinless, boneless chicken breast halves, cut into bite-size pieces
1 tsp. toasted sesame seeds
Lime wedges

1. In a food processor combine the first seven ingredients (through crushed red pepper); add ⅓ cup of the peanuts. Cover and process until nearly smooth.
2. Using a vegetable peeler, cut carrots and zucchini lengthwise into thin ribbons.
3. In a large saucepan cook noodles according to package directions, adding carrots and sweet pepper the last 1 minute of cooking; drain.
4. Meanwhile, in a 10-inch nonstick skillet heat oil over medium. Add chicken; cook and stir about 4 minutes or until no longer pink. Stir in cilantro mixture; heat. Stir in noodle mixture and zucchini.
5. Chop the remaining peanuts. Sprinkle pasta mixture with chopped peanuts and sesame seeds. Serve with lime wedges.

PER SERVING (1½ cups each) **CAL** 349, **FAT** 14 g (2 g sat. fat), **CHOL** 62 mg, **SODIUM** 587 mg, **CARB** 29 g (5 g fiber, 6 g sugars), **PRO** 28 g

1. Preheat oven to 375°F. In a bowl combine the first six ingredients (through crushed red pepper).
2. Arrange chicken in a 13×9-inch baking pan; brush with half of the mustard mixture. Add cauliflower, sweet potato, and sweet pepper; drizzle with remaining mustard mixture.
3. Roast, covered, 25 minutes. Uncover; roast about 25 minutes more or until chicken is done (165°F) and sweet potatoes are tender. Serve chicken and vegetables over rice and drizzle with cooking liquid. If desired, top with green onions and additional crushed red pepper.

Tip If you prefer, omit the honey and Dijon-style mustard and use ½ cup Dijon-style honey mustard.

PER SERVING (1 chicken breast half + ⅔ cup vegetables + ⅓ cup rice each) **CAL** 429, **FAT** 10 g (2 g sat. fat), **CHOL** 124 mg, **SODIUM** 353 mg, **CARB** 42 g (5 g fiber, 16 g sugars), **PRO** 42 g

Roasted Curried Chicken and Cauliflower

FOR EVEN COOKING, CUT CAULIFLOWER INTO SAME-SIZE FLORETS.

**Barbecued
Chicken Nachos**

Turkey-Pepper Popper Casserole

Barbecued Chicken Nachos

40 g
CARB

SERVES 4
HANDS ON 20 min.
TOTAL 35 min.

- 8 6-inch corn tortillas
   Nonstick cooking spray
- ¾ cup chopped poblano chile pepper (tip, *far right*) or red sweet pepper
- ½ cup chopped onion
- 2 tsp. canola oil
- 8 oz. shredded cooked chicken breast
- ½ cup no-salt-added pinto beans, rinsed and drained
- ⅓ cup bottled barbecue sauce
- ¾ cup shredded reduced-fat cheddar cheese (3 oz.)
- 1 recipe Crunchy Broccoli Slaw
- ¼ cup sliced green onions

1. Preheat oven to 375°F. Cut each tortilla into eight wedges. Arrange tortilla wedges in a single layer on a large baking sheet. Coat wedges with cooking spray. Bake 10 to 13 minutes or until wedges are crisp and golden brown on edges.
2. In a 10-inch skillet cook poblano pepper and onion in oil over medium 3 to 5 minutes or until tender. Stir in chicken, beans, and barbecue sauce; heat.
3. Arrange tortilla wedges on a platter. Top with chicken mixture, cheese, Crunchy Broccoli Slaw, and green onions.

Crunchy Broccoli Slaw In a bowl combine **2 Tbsp. plain fat-free Greek yogurt, 1 Tbsp. light mayonnaise, ½ tsp. lime juice,** and **⅛ tsp. chili powder.** Add **1½ cups packaged shredded broccoli slaw mix;** toss to coat.

PER SERVING *(16 chips + ½ cup chicken mixture + ⅓ cup slaw each)* **CAL** 381, **FAT** 12 g (4 g sat. fat), **CHOL** 65 mg, **SODIUM** 483 mg, **CARB** 40 g (6 g fiber, 12 g sugars), **PRO** 29 g

Turkey-Pepper Popper Casserole

34 g
CARB

SERVES 6
HANDS ON 30 min.
TOTAL 1 hr. 5 min.

   Nonstick cooking spray
- 6 oz. dried multigrain spaghetti, broken in half
- 2 tsp. olive oil
- 2 cups chopped red and/or green sweet peppers
- 1 cup thin bite-size slices fresh poblano chile pepper (seeded if desired)
- 1 to 2 fresh jalapeño peppers, halved, seeded (if desired), and thinly sliced
- 2 cloves garlic, minced
- 2 Tbsp. all-purpose flour
- ½ tsp. salt
- 1 cup evaporated low-fat milk
- ½ cup unsalted chicken broth
- 1 cup shredded reduced-fat cheddar cheese (4 oz.)
- 3 oz. reduced-fat cream cheese (neufchatel), cut up and softened
- 2 cups chopped cooked turkey breast (12 oz.)
- ⅓ cup whole wheat panko bread crumbs

1. Preheat oven to 375°F. Coat a 1½-qt. gratin dish or baking dish with cooking spray. Cook spaghetti according to package directions. Drain, reserving 1 cup of the cooking water.
2. Meanwhile, in a 12-inch nonstick skillet heat oil over medium-high. Add all peppers and the garlic; cook and stir 4 minutes. Sprinkle flour and salt over peppers; cook and stir 2 minutes. Add evaporated milk and broth; cook and stir about 5 minutes or until boiling and slightly thickened.
3. Remove skillet from heat. Add cheeses, stirring until melted. Add turkey and cooked spaghetti. Stir in enough of the reserved cooking water, ¼ cup at a time, to make desired consistency. Transfer to prepared baking dish. Sprinkle with panko; coat with cooking spray. Bake 25 to 30 minutes or until edges are bubbly and top is browned. Remove from oven. Let stand 5 minutes before serving.

Tip Chile peppers contain oils that can irritate your skin and eyes. Wear plastic or rubber gloves when working with them.

PER SERVING *(1 cup each)* **CAL** 358, **FAT** 12 g (5 g sat. fat), **CHOL** 70 mg, **SODIUM** 537 mg, **CARB** 34 g (4 g fiber, 8 g sugars), **PRO** 32 g

Chicken, Broccoli, and Farro Casserole

42 g CARB

SERVES 6
HANDS ON 35 min.
TOTAL 55 min.

- 1 Tbsp. olive oil
- ⅓ cup chopped onion
- 1 lb. skinless, boneless chicken breast halves, cut into bite-size pieces
- 3 cups sliced fresh cremini mushrooms (8 oz.)
- 3 Tbsp. all-purpose flour
- 1 12-oz. can evaporated fat-free milk
- 3 cups broccoli florets
- 1 cup cooked farro or brown rice
- 1 6-oz. carton plain fat-free Greek yogurt
- ⅓ cup light mayonnaise
- 2 Tbsp. fat-free milk
- ½ tsp. snipped fresh rosemary or ¼ tsp. dried rosemary, crushed
- ¼ tsp. salt
- ½ cup shredded reduced-fat Colby and Monterey Jack cheese (2 oz.)

Chicken, Broccoli, and Farro Casserole

1. Preheat oven to 350°F. In a 12-inch skillet heat oil over medium. Add onion; cook 5 minutes or until tender, stirring occasionally. Add chicken and mushrooms; cook and stir 5 minutes. Sprinkle with flour; cook and stir 2 minutes.

2. Stir in evaporated milk. Cook and stir until thickened and bubbly. Stir in broccoli; cook and stir 3 minutes more. Stir in the next six ingredients (through salt).

3. Transfer chicken mixture to a 2-qt. square or rectangular baking dish. Sprinkle with cheese. Bake 20 minutes or until bubbly and cheese is melted.

PER SERVING (1¼ cups each) CAL 405, FAT 11 g (3 g sat. fat), CHOL 67 mg, SODIUM 395 mg, CARB 42 g (5 g fiber, 12 g sugars), PRO 34 g

---

Baked Potato Chowder with Bacon-Cheddar Potato Skins

27 g CARB

SERVES 6
HANDS ON 20 min.
TOTAL 1 hr. 20 min.

- 3 medium (4 to 5 oz. each) Yukon gold potatoes
- 4 slices lower-sodium, less-fat bacon, chopped
- 1 cup chopped carrots
- ½ cup thinly sliced celery
- ½ cup chopped onion
- 3 cloves garlic, minced
- 2 14.5-oz. cans reduced-sodium chicken broth
- 2 cups ½-inch pieces peeled rutabaga or turnips (8 oz.)
- ½ cup shredded reduced-fat cheddar cheese (2 oz.)
- ⅓ cup light sour cream
- 3 Tbsp. snipped fresh chives
- 2 Tbsp. all-purpose flour
- 2½ cups fat-free milk
- 2 cups chopped cooked skinless, boneless chicken breast Black pepper (optional)

1. Preheat oven to 425°F. Line a shallow baking pan with foil. Scrub potatoes and prick with a fork; place potatoes on prepared pan. Bake 45 to 55 minutes or until tender; let cool.

2. Meanwhile, in a 4-qt. Dutch oven cook bacon over medium until browned and crisp, stirring occasionally. Using a slotted spoon, transfer bacon to paper towels. Discard all but 2 tsp. drippings in pot. Add carrots, celery, and onion. Cook over medium 5 minutes, stirring occasionally. Add garlic; cook and stir 1 minute more. Add broth and rutabaga. Bring to boiling; reduce heat. Simmer, uncovered, 10 to 12 minutes or until rutabaga is tender.

3. Cut cooled potatoes lengthwise in half. Using a spoon, scoop out the inside of each potato half and place in a large bowl, leaving ¼-inch-thick potato shells. Set potato flesh aside.

4. Increase oven temperature to 450°F. Place potato skins, skin sides down, in the same baking pan. Sprinkle tops of potato skins with the cheese and half of the cooked bacon. Bake 5 to 7 minutes or until cheese is melted and potato skins are heated through. Top with sour cream and sprinkle with half the chives.

5. Mash the reserved potato flesh. Stir in the flour. Gradually stir in milk until mixture is nearly smooth. Add potato mixture to soup. Cook, stirring occasionally, until thickened and bubbly. Add the chicken and remaining bacon. Cook and stir 5 minutes more or until heated.

6. Sprinkle with remaining chives and, if desired, pepper. Serve with potato skins.

PER SERVING (1½ cups soup + 1 potato skin each) CAL 279, FAT 7 g (3 g sat. fat), CHOL 56 mg, SODIUM 559 mg, CARB 27 g (3 g fiber, 10 g sugars), PRO 26 g

STUFF AND SERVE FIBER-LOADED SKINS ON THE SIDE.

Baked Potato Chowder with Bacon-Cheddar Potato Skins

Enchilada
Casserole

Enchilada Casserole

42 g
CARB

SERVES 6
HANDS ON 25 min.
TOTAL 1 hr. 5 min.

- 1 Tbsp. canola oil
- 1 Tbsp. all-purpose flour
- 1 8-oz. can no-salt-added tomato sauce
- ¾ cup reduced-sodium chicken broth
- 1 Tbsp. chili powder
- 1 tsp. dried oregano, crushed
- ½ tsp. ground cumin
- ⅛ tsp. ground cinnamon
- 1 15-oz. can no-salt-added black beans, rinsed and drained
- 1 15-oz. can no-salt-added pinto beans, rinsed and drained
- ¾ cup chopped green sweet pepper
- ½ cup chopped onion
- 1 4-oz. can diced green chile peppers, undrained
  Nonstick cooking spray
- 9 6-inch corn tortillas, cut into wedges
- 1¼ cups shredded reduced-fat cheddar cheese (5 oz.)
  Shredded lettuce, sliced pitted ripe olives, and/or chopped tomato (optional)

1. Preheat oven to 350°F. In a small saucepan heat oil over medium. Stir in flour until smooth. Stir in the next six ingredients (through cinnamon). Cook and stir until thickened and bubbly. Cook and stir 1 minute more.
2. In a bowl combine the next five ingredients (through chile peppers).
3. Coat a 2-qt. rectangular baking dish with cooking spray. Spread ⅓ cup of the tomato sauce mixture on the bottom of the prepared dish. Layer one-third of the tortillas on the sauce. Top with one-third of the bean mixture, one-third of the remaining sauce, and ½ cup of the cheese.

Repeat layers twice, starting with tortillas and setting aside the final ¼ cup cheese. Cover with foil.
4. Bake 35 minutes. Uncover. Sprinkle with the reserved ¼ cup cheese. Bake, uncovered, about 5 minutes more or until cheese is melted. Let stand 15 minutes before serving. If desired, top with lettuce, olives, and/or chopped tomato.

PER SERVING *(about 1 cup each)* **CAL** 305, **FAT** 9 g (3 g sat. fat), **CHOL** 17 mg, **SODIUM** 387 mg, **CARB** 42 g (11 g fiber, 5 g sugars), **PRO** 16 g

---

Harvest Chicken Lentil Chili

24 g
CARB

SERVES 8
HANDS ON 30 min.
TOTAL 1 hr. 30 min.

- 1 Tbsp. olive oil
- 2 cups coarsely chopped onions
- 1 cup coarsely chopped carrots
- 1 cup chopped celery
- 4 bone-in chicken thighs (about 2 lb. total), skinned
- 4 cups reduced-sodium chicken broth
- 1 cup water
- ¾ cup brown lentils, rinsed and drained
- 1 15-oz. can pumpkin
- 1 14.5-oz. can no-salt-added diced tomatoes, undrained
- 1 Tbsp. chili powder
- 1 tsp. ground cumin
- 1 tsp. dried oregano, crushed
- 1 to 2 Tbsp. Louisiana hot sauce
  Plain fat-free Greek yogurt, roasted pumpkin seeds (peptitas), and/or chili powder (optional)

1. In a 4-qt. Dutch oven with a tight-fitting lid heat oil over medium-high. Add onions, carrots, and celery. Cook 6 to

Harvest Chicken Lentil Chili

8 minutes or until onions are tender and carrots and celery are starting to soften, stirring occasionally. Add chicken, broth, and the water. Bring to boiling; reduce heat. Simmer, covered, about 20 minutes or until chicken is done (at least 175°F). Remove chicken from Dutch oven. When cool enough to handle, remove chicken from bones; discard bones. Chop chicken; chill until needed.
2. Meanwhile, stir lentils into broth mixture. Return to boiling; reduce heat. Simmer, covered, about 30 minutes or until lentils are tender.
3. Stir in cooked chicken and the next five ingredients (through oregano). Simmer, covered, about 10 minutes more or until heated. Stir in hot sauce.
4. If desired, top each serving with yogurt, pumpkin seeds, and/or additional chili powder.

PER SERVING *(1½ cups each)* **CAL** 223, **FAT** 5 g (1 g sat. fat), **CHOL** 64 mg, **SODIUM** 506 mg, **CARB** 24 g (10 g fiber, 7 g sugars), **PRO** 2 g

Enchilada Tostadas

Bacon-Wrapped Pork Tenderloin with Honey-Almond Green Beans

28 g CARB

SERVES 4
HANDS ON 20 min.
TOTAL 45 min.

- ¼ cup cherry preserves, large pieces snipped
- 1 tsp. red wine vinegar
- 10 slices lower-sodium, less-fat bacon
- 1 1-lb. pork tenderloin, trimmed
- 1 Tbsp. olive oil
- 8 oz. green beans, trimmed if desired
- ¼ cup reduced-sodium chicken broth
- 2 Tbsp. honey
- ¼ tsp. salt
- ¼ cup sliced almonds, toasted

1. Preheat oven to 425°F. Line a shallow roasting pan with foil. Place a rack in lined pan. In a bowl stir together cherry preserves and vinegar.
2. Lay bacon side by side on a work surface, overlapping slightly. Place tenderloin crosswise on bacon and wrap bacon around tenderloin. Place tenderloin, bacon ends down, on rack in the prepared pan. Roast 20 minutes. Brush top of wrapped tenderloin with preserves mixture. Roast 5 to 10 minutes more or until bacon is crisp and pork is done (145°F). Remove from oven; let stand 3 minutes.
3. Meanwhile, in a 10-inch skillet heat oil over medium-high. Add green beans; cook and stir 3 to 5 minutes or just until crisp-tender. Add broth, honey, and salt. Cook and stir about 3 minutes more or until liquid is nearly evaporated. Stir in almonds. Serve green beans with sliced tenderloin.

PER SERVING *(3 oz. cooked tenderloin + about ½ cup green beans each)* **CAL** 351, **FAT** 12 g *(3 g sat. fat)*, **CHOL** 82 mg, **SODIUM** 426 mg, **CARB** 28 g *(2 g fiber, 20 g sugars)*, **PRO** 31 g

Enchilada Tostadas

35 g CARB

SERVES 8
TOTAL 45 min.

- 1 recipe Enchilada Sauce
- 8 6-inch 100% whole wheat flour tortillas
  Nonstick cooking spray
- 1 lb. lean ground beef
- 1 15-oz. can reduced-sodium black beans, rinsed and drained
- 1 cup cooked brown rice
- ⅓ cup water
- 2 Tbsp. salt-free taco seasoning
- 2 cups shredded romaine lettuce
- 1 cup chopped roma tomatoes
- 1 cup plain fat-free Greek yogurt
- ½ cup thinly sliced radishes
- ½ cup snipped fresh cilantro

1. Prepare Enchilada Sauce. Meanwhile, preheat oven to 400°F. Coat both sides of tortillas with cooking spray and place on two large baking sheets. Bake 8 to 10 minutes or until crisp and golden, turning once and rotating pans halfway through baking.
2. Coat a 10-inch nonstick skillet with cooking spray; heat over medium-high. Add ground beef; cook until browned. Drain off any fat. Stir in beans, rice, the water, and taco seasoning. Cook until thick and heated through, stirring occasionally.
3. Spoon meat mixture onto tortillas. Drizzle with sauce and top with the remaining ingredients.

Enchilada Sauce In a small saucepan heat **2 tsp. canola oil** over medium. Stir in **2 tsp. all-purpose flour**; cook and stir 1 minute. Stir in **2 tsp. chili powder** and **1 tsp. dried oregano, crushed**; cook and stir 30 seconds more. Stir in **one 8-oz. can no-salt-added tomato sauce**, **¾ cup water**, and **½ tsp. salt**. Bring to boiling; reduce heat. Simmer, uncovered, 8 to 10 minutes or until slightly thick, stirring occasionally.

Tip If you like, use corn tortillas in place of the flour tortillas.

PER SERVING *(1 tostada each)* **CAL** 302, **FAT** 10 g *(3 g sat. fat)*, **CHOL** 37 mg, **SODIUM** 499 mg, **CARB** 35 g *(7 g fiber, 5 g sugars)*, **PRO** 22 g

Bacon-Wrapped Pork
Tenderloin with Honey-Almond
Green Beans

Pineapple Pork
Fried Rice

Pineapple Pork Fried Rice

41 g
CARB

SERVES 4
TOTAL 45 min.

- 1 egg
- 2 egg whites
- 2 tsp. canola oil
- 1 lb. pork tenderloin, trimmed and cut into bite-size pieces
- 1 Tbsp. canola oil
- 1 cup chopped fresh pineapple
- ½ cup thinly sliced carrot
- ½ cup thinly bias-sliced celery
- ½ cup sliced green onions
- 2 tsp. grated fresh ginger
- 2 cloves garlic, minced
- 2 cups cooked jasmine rice
- ½ cup frozen peas, thawed
- 3 Tbsp. reduced-sodium soy sauce
- 1 Tbsp. snipped fresh cilantro
  Finely chopped peanuts, lime wedges, and/or sriracha sauce (optional)

1. In a bowl whisk together egg and egg whites. In a 12-inch skillet or wok heat the 2 tsp. oil over medium-high. Add pork; cook and stir 3 to 5 minutes or until pork is no longer pink. Remove pork from skillet.
2. Add the 1 Tbsp. oil to the skillet. Add the next five ingredients (through ginger); cook and stir 3 to 4 minutes or until vegetables are tender. Add garlic; cook and stir 30 seconds more. Add egg mixture; let stand 5 to 10 seconds or until egg sets on bottom but remains runny on top. Add rice. Turn and toss mixture continuously 1 minute. Stir in cooked pork, the peas, soy sauce, and cilantro; heat. If desired, sprinkle with peanuts and serve with lime wedges and/or sriracha sauce.

Tip Instead of starting with a whole pineapple, pick up a container of cut-up pineapple from the produce section and finish chopping it at home.

PER SERVING *(1½ cups each)* **CAL** 386, **FAT** 11 g (2 g sat. fat), **CHOL** 144 mg, **SODIUM** 546 mg, **CARB** 41 g (4 g fiber, 8 g sugars), **PRO** 31 g

---

Hungarian-Style Pork Paprikash

44 g
CARB

SERVES 6
HANDS ON 15 min.
TOTAL 30 min.

- 2 Tbsp. all-purpose flour
- 1 Tbsp. paprika
- ¼ tsp. black pepper
- ¼ tsp. cayenne pepper
- 1 lb. pork tenderloin, trimmed and cut into 1-inch cubes
- 1 Tbsp. olive oil
- 2 medium carrots
- 2 14.5-oz. cans fire-roasted diced tomatoes, undrained
- 1 8-oz. can no-salt-added tomato sauce
- 1 medium yellow sweet pepper, cut into thin strips
- 8 oz. dried whole grain fettuccine
- ¼ cup light sour cream or plain fat-free Greek yogurt
  Snipped fresh parsley (optional)

1. In a resealable plastic bag combine the first four ingredients (through cayenne pepper). Add the pork; seal bag. Toss to coat pork. In a 10-inch skillet heat oil over medium-high. Add pork; cook about 5 minutes or until browned on all sides.

Hungarian-Style Pork Paprikash

2. Cut carrots in half crosswise. Cut each piece lengthwise into quarters, making a total of 16 carrot sticks. Add carrots and the next three ingredients (through sweet pepper) to skillet; stir to combine. Bring to boiling; reduce heat. Cover and simmer 10 minutes, stirring occasionally.
3. Meanwhile, cook pasta according to package directions; drain. Add pasta to pork mixture in skillet; toss to combine. Top with sour cream and, if desired, sprinkle with parsley.

PER SERVING *(1⅓ cups each)* **CAL** 315, **FAT** 6 g (1 g sat. fat), **CHOL** 52 mg, **SODIUM** 379 mg, **CARB** 44 g (8 g fiber, 9 g sugars), **PRO** 23 g

Pineapple-Bacon
Barbecue Burgers

Loaded Taco Sweet Potatoes

31 g
CARB

SERVES 4
HANDS ON 30 min.
TOTAL 1 hr. 20 min.

- 2 8- to 10-oz. sweet potatoes
- 8 oz. extra-lean ground beef
- 1 small onion, halved and sliced
- 1 small fresh poblano chile pepper, seeded and cut into bite-size strips
- ½ cup salsa
- 1 tsp. chili powder
- ¼ cup crumbled queso fresco or shredded reduced-fat cheddar cheese
- ¼ cup light sour cream
  Toppers: slivered red onion or sliced green onions, fresh cilantro, quartered grape tomatoes, sliced fresh jalapeno chiles, and/or chopped avocado

1. Preheat oven to 425°F. Scrub potatoes; pat dry. Pierce potatoes with a fork. Wrap potatoes individually in foil and place in a 15×10-inch baking pan. Bake 50 to 60 minutes or until tender.
2. Meanwhile, in a large nonstick skillet cook beef, onion, and poblano chile about 6 minutes or until beef is browned and vegetables are tender. Remove from heat; drain any fat. Add salsa and chili powder; toss to combine.
3. Cut baked sweet potatoes in half lengthwise. Scrape pulp with a fork to loosen. Top with beef mixture, cheese, and sour cream. Add desired toppers.

Tip Chile peppers contain oils that can irritate your skin and eyes. Wear plastic or rubber gloves when working with them.

PER SERVING (1 loaded sweet potato half each)
CAL 272, **FAT** 10 g (4 g sat. fat), **CHOL** 45 mg, **SODIUM** 417 mg, **CARB** 31 g (6 g fiber, 8 g sugars), **PRO** 17 g

Pineapple-Bacon Barbecue Burgers

35 g
CARB

SERVES 6
HANDS ON 15 min.
TOTAL 25 min.

- 1 egg, lightly beaten
- ⅓ cup canned crushed pineapple (juice pack), drained
- 6 slices lower-sodium, less-fat bacon, crisp-cooked and coarsely crumbled
- 1 lb. lean ground beef
- 6 Tbsp. barbecue sauce
- 6 Hawaiian sweet rolls, split and toasted
- 4 leaves red leaf lettuce
- 6 slices tomatoes
- ¼ cup very thinly sliced red onion

1. In a large bowl combine the first three ingredients (through bacon). Add ground beef; mix lightly to combine. (Do not overmix.) Form into six ¾-inch-thick patties.
2. Grease grill rack. Grill patties, covered, over medium-high 8 to 12 minutes or until done (160°F), turning once. Spread barbecue sauce over tops of burgers. Serve burgers in rolls with lettuce, tomatoes, and onion.

Tip The meat may appear a bit pink after grilling. Be sure to use an instant-read thermometer to measure the doneness.

PER SERVING (1 burger each) **CAL** 322, **FAT** 9 g (4 g sat. fat), **CHOL** 106 mg, **SODIUM** 432 mg, **CARB** 35 g (1 g fiber, 17 g sugars), **PRO** 24 g

**Loaded Taco
Sweet Potatoes**

USE A KNIFE
AND FORK TO
EAT THESE
POTATOES,
SKIN AND ALL.

WHOLE WHEAT PIZZA CRUSTS

STEP ONE: In a bowl stir together **¾ cup whole wheat flour**, **¼ cup all-purpose flour**, and **⅛ tsp. salt**. Gradually stir in **6 Tbsp. water** to make a soft dough, adding additional water, 1 tsp. at a time, if necessary. Shape dough into a ball. Sprinkle additional flour on a work surface. Knead dough on surface until smooth, elastic, and slightly sticky. Cover; let stand 10 minutes.

STEP TWO: Divide dough into six portions. Roll each into a smooth ball. Press balls to flatten; lightly coat with flour. Using a rolling pin, roll each ball into 6-inch circles. Grill circles on greased rack, covered, over medium 2 minutes or until firm, turning once. Makes 6 individual pizza crusts.

Southwestern
Steak Pizza

Southwestern Steak Pizza

29 g
CARB

SERVES 6
HANDS ON 20 min.
TOTAL 45 min.

- 8 oz. beef flank steak
- ¾ tsp. salt
- ½ tsp. black pepper
- 2 medium avocados, halved, seeded, and peeled
- 2 tsp. lime juice
- 1 tsp. salt-free fiesta lime seasoning blend
- ¼ tsp. ground cumin
- 1 recipe Whole Wheat Pizza Crusts *(opposite)*
- ¾ cup shredded reduced-fat Mexican cheese blend (3 oz.)
- ½ of a 15-oz. can (¾ cup) no-salt-added black beans, rinsed and drained
- 1 cup grape tomatoes, quartered
- 2 Tbsp. light sour cream (optional) Fresh cilantro leaves

1. Trim fat from steak. Sprinkle steak with ½ tsp. of the salt and ¼ tsp. of the pepper. Grill steak, covered, over medium heat 17 to 21 minutes for medium (160°F), turning once. Remove from grill; let stand 5 minutes. Thinly slice steak diagonally across the grain.
2. Meanwhile, in a bowl mash avocados. Stir in lime juice, fiesta lime seasoning, cumin, and the remaining ¼ tsp. each salt and pepper.
3. Spread avocado mixture on Whole Wheat Pizza Crusts; sprinkle with cheese. Top with steak slices, black beans, and tomatoes. Grill pizzas, covered, over low heat 2 to 3 minutes or until heated. Top with sour cream (if desired) and cilantro.

PER SERVING *(1 individual pizza each)*
CAL 291, **FAT** 12 g (3 g sat. fat), **CHOL** 32 mg, **SODIUM** 481 mg, **CARB** 29 g (7 g fiber, 1 g sugars), **PRO** 18 g

Hot Beef Sundaes

Hot Beef Sundaes

22 g
CARB

SERVES 4
HANDS ON 20 min.
TOTAL 1 hr. 25 min.

   Nonstick cooking spray
- 1 lb. beef stew meat, trimmed of fat
- 1 14.5-oz. can reduced-sodium beef broth
- 3 cloves garlic, minced
- ¼ tsp. black pepper
- 2 cups cubed, peeled russet potatoes
- 2 cups small cauliflower florets
- 1 Tbsp. olive oil
- ¼ tsp. salt
- ⅛ tsp. black pepper
- 2 to 4 Tbsp. fat-free milk
- ¼ cup cold water
- 2 Tbsp. all-purpose flour
- ¼ cup shredded reduced-fat cheddar cheese (1 oz.)
- ¼ cup chopped green onions
- 4 cherry tomatoes

1. Coat a medium saucepan with cooking spray. Brown the stew meat, half at a time, over medium-high. Return all beef to pan. Add broth, 2 cloves of the garlic, and the ¼ tsp. pepper. Bring to boiling; reduce heat. Simmer, covered, about 1 hour or until very tender. Using a slotted spoon, remove meat from pan. Shred beef using two forks.
2. Meanwhile, in another medium saucepan combine potatoes and the remaining 1 clove garlic. Add enough water to cover by 1 inch. Bring to boiling; reduce heat. Simmer, covered, 5 minutes. Add cauliflower; return to boiling. Reduce heat. Simmer, covered, about 10 minutes more or until vegetables are very tender. Drain well.
3. In a bowl combine potato-cauliflower mixture, oil, salt, and the ⅛ tsp. pepper. Mash mixture. Gradually stir in enough milk to make potato-cauliflower mixture light and fluffy.
4. If desired, strain beef cooking liquid through a fine-mesh seive. Measure 1 cup liquid; return to pan. In a bowl stir together cold water and flour until smooth. Stir into cooking liquid in pan. Cook and stir over medium until thickened and bubbly; cook and stir 1 minute more. Return shredded meat to pan; stir to combine.
5. To serve, scoop potato-cauliflower mash into bowls. Top with beef mixture, cheese, green onions, and tomatoes.

PER SERVING *(1 cup each)* **CAL** 298, **FAT** 10 g (4 g sat. fat), **CHOL** 78 mg, **SODIUM** 489 mg, **CARB** 22 g (2 g fiber, 3 g sugars), **PRO** 31 g

Stroganoff-Style Beef with Broccoli

Balsamic Onion and Steak Pasta

50 g CARB

SERVES 4	
HANDS ON 20 min.	
TOTAL 40 min.	

- 2 Tbsp. olive oil
- 1 lb. sweet onions, halved and sliced (about 3½ cups)
- 2 cloves garlic, thinly sliced
- 8 oz. boneless beef sirloin steak, cut into thin bite-size strips
- 2 Tbsp. balsamic vinegar
- ¼ tsp. salt
- ¼ tsp. black pepper
- 1½ cups dried cavatappi or other short tube pasta
- 1 15- to 19-oz. can cannellini beans, rinsed and drained
- 6 cups torn fresh spinach
- 1 oz. shaved Parmesan cheese

1. In a 12-inch skillet heat 1 Tbsp. of the oil over medium-low. Add onions and garlic. Cook, covered, 13 to 15 minutes or until tender, stirring occasionally. Uncover; cook and stir over medium-high 3 to 5 minutes more or until golden. Remove onions from skillet.

2. Add the remaining 1 Tbsp. oil to skillet. Add beef; cook and stir 2 to 3 minutes or until browned. Stir in onions, vinegar, salt, and pepper. Keep warm.

3. Cook pasta according to package directions, adding beans the last 2 minutes of cooking. Drain, reserving ½ cup of the cooking water. Return pasta and beans to pan. Add spinach; toss to combine and wilt spinach. Add beef mixture; toss to combine. Add enough of the reserved pasta water to reach desired consistency. Top with Parmesan and additional pepper.

PER SERVING (1½ cups each) **CAL** 426, **FAT** 12 g (3 g sat. fat), **CHOL** 39 mg, **SODIUM** 596 mg, **CARB** 50 g (9 g fiber, 7 g sugars), **PRO** 28 g

Stroganoff-Style Beef with Broccoli

38 g CARB

SERVES 5	
TOTAL 30 min.	

- ½ cup light sour cream
- 3 Tbsp. all-purpose flour
- ¼ tsp. dried dill weed
- 1 lb. boneless beef top round steak
- 2 Tbsp. vegetable oil
- 1 small onion, cut into ½-inch slices
- 2 cups sliced cremini or baby bella mushrooms
- 1 clove garlic, minced
- 3 cups dried extra-wide noodles
- 3 cups broccoli florets
- 1 14.5-oz. can beef broth
- 3 Tbsp. tomato paste
- 1 tsp. Worcestershire sauce
  Black pepper
  Snipped fresh dill weed (optional)

1. In a bowl stir together sour cream, 1 Tbsp. of the flour, and the dried dill weed.

2. Trim fat from meat. Cut meat into thin bite-size strips. In a 10-inch skillet heat 1 Tbsp. of the oil over medium-high. Cook meat, half at a time, in hot oil until slightly pink in center. Remove meat from skillet. Add the remaining 1 Tbsp. oil to skillet; add onion, mushrooms, and garlic. Cook 8 to 10 minutes or until onion is tender, stirring occasionally.

3. Meanwhile, cook noodles according to package directions, adding broccoli the last 3 minutes of cooking; drain. Return noodle mixture to pan; cover and keep warm.

4. Sprinkle the remaining 2 Tbsp. flour over onion mixture in skillet; stir to coat. Add broth, tomato paste, and Worcestershire sauce. Cook and stir until thickened and bubbly. Cook and stir 1 minute more. Return meat to skillet; heat. Remove from heat. Season to taste with pepper. Stir in sour cream mixture. Serve meat mixture over noodle mixture. Top with additional pepper and, if desired, snipped fresh dill weed.

Tip Partially freeze beef for easier slicing.

PER SERVING (1¾ cups each) **CAL** 391, **FAT** 13 g (4 g sat. fat), **CHOL** 85 mg, **SODIUM** 472 mg, **CARB** 38 g (4 g fiber, 4 g sugars), **PRO** 31 g

Balsamic Onion
and Steak Pasta

Red Beans and
Rice with Squash

Red Beans and Rice with Squash

40 g CARB

SERVES 5
HANDS ON 25 min.
TOTAL 40 min.

- 8 oz. andouille smoked chicken sausage, bias-cut into ½-inch slices
- 1 tsp. canola oil
- 1 15- to 16-oz. can red kidney beans, rinsed and drained
- 2 cups cubed butternut squash (8 oz.)
- 1 cup chopped green sweet pepper
- 1 cup reduced-sodium chicken broth
- ¾ cup chopped celery
- ¾ cup chopped onion
- ¾ cup water
- ¼ cup no-salt-added tomato paste
- 1 bay leaf
- 1 Tbsp. snipped fresh thyme or 1 tsp. dried thyme, crushed
- ⅛ tsp. ground allspice
- 1⅔ cups hot cooked brown rice

1. In a 10-inch nonstick skillet cook sausage in hot oil over medium until lightly browned, stirring occasionally. Add the next 11 ingredients (through allspice). Bring to boiling; reduce heat. Simmer, covered, 10 minutes. Uncover; simmer about 5 minutes more or until mixture is slightly thickened. Remove and discard bay leaf. Serve bean mixture over rice.

PER SERVING *(1 cup beans and squash + ⅓ cup brown rice each)* **CAL** 271, **FAT** 6 g (1 g sat. fat), **CHOL** 35 mg, **SODIUM** 583 mg, **CARB** 40 g (8 g fiber, 7 g sugars), **PRO** 16 g

BLTs with Creamy Tomato-Avocado Spread

BLTs with Creamy Tomato-Avocado Spread

20 g CARB

SERVES 4
TOTAL 30 min.

- 6 dried tomatoes (not oil-packed) Boiling water
- 12 slices lower-sodium, less-fat bacon, halved
- 1 small avocado, halved, seeded, and peeled
- ¼ cup reduced-fat semisoft cheese with garlic and fines herbes
- 8 very thin slices whole wheat bread, toasted
- 2 medium orange, red, and/or yellow tomatoes, thickly sliced
- 1 cup watercress or fresh spinach leaves

1. In a small bowl combine dried tomatoes and enough boiling water to cover. Let stand, covered, 5 minutes. Drain and chop tomatoes. Meanwhile, in a 10-inch skillet cook bacon over medium until browned. Drain on paper towels.
2. In a medium bowl mash avocado. Stir in chopped tomatoes and cheese. Spread half of the bread slices with avocado mixture. Top with bacon, sliced tomatoes, watercress, and remaining bread slices.

PER SERVING *(1 sandwich each)* **CAL** 230, **FAT** 11 g (4 g sat. fat), **CHOL** 18 mg, **SODIUM** 454 mg, **CARB** 20 g (5 g fiber, 5 g sugars), **PRO** 11 g

**Grilled Pork Chops with Warm
Sweet Potato-Kale Salad**

Grilled Pork Chops with Warm Sweet Potato-Kale Salad

35 g
CARB

SERVES 4

TOTAL 1 hr.

- 1 10- to 12-oz. sweet potato, peeled
- 4 strips reduced-fat, reduced-sodium bacon, coarsely chopped
- 1 medium red cooking apple, cored and coarsely chopped
- ¼ cup thinly sliced shallots
- 4 cups coarsely chopped, stemmed kale
- 2 Tbsp. cider vinegar
- 2 tsp. spicy brown mustard
   Fresh thyme (optional)
- 4 ¾- to 1-inch-thick bone-in pork chops (2 lb. total)
- 2 tsp. snipped fresh thyme
- ¼ tsp. salt
- ¼ tsp. black pepper
- 1 recipe Maple-Ginger Cherry Sauce

1. Cut sweet potato lengthwise into quarters. Cut each quarter crosswise into ¼-inch-thick slices.

2. For salad, in a 12-inch nonstick skillet cook bacon over medium until crisp. Using a slotted spoon, transfer bacon to paper towels to drain. Remove and discard all but 2 Tbsp. drippings. Add the sweet potato slices to the skillet. Cook about 5 minutes, stirring occasionally, or until slices are lightly golden. Add the apple and shallots; cook 3 minutes. Stir

in the kale; 2 to 3 minutes or until potatoes and apple are tender, stirring occasionally.

3. In a bowl whisk together vinegar and mustard. Drizzle over kale mixture; toss to combine. Remove from the heat. Stir in reserved bacon. Keep warm.

4. Trim fat from pork chops. In a bowl combine 1 tsp. of the thyme, the salt, and pepper. Sprinkle evenly over both sides of pork chops, rubbing in with your fingers.

5. Grill pork chops, covered, over medium 8 to 10 minutes or until done (145°F), turning once. Cover chops with foil; let rest 3 minutes.

6. Serve pork chops with sweet potato salad and Maple-Ginger Cherry Sauce over pork chops. Top with remaining 1 tsp. thyme.

Maple-Ginger Cherry Sauce In a small saucepan combine ¾ cup frozen unsweetened pitted tart red cherries and 2 Tbsp. water; bring to boiling. Reduce heat; simmer, covered, about 5 minutes or until cherries start to break down. If needed, mash lightly with a fork. Stir together 1 Tbsp. water and 1 tsp. cornstarch; add 2 Tbsp. reduced-calorie maple-flavor pancake syrup and 2 tsp. finely chopped fresh ginger. Stir into cherry mixture; cook and stir 5 to 6 minutes more or until sauce is slightly thickened and bubbly. Remove from heat. Cool about 5 minutes before serving.

Tip If the sweet potatoes are long and slender instead of short and fat, cut them in half lengthwise instead of in quarters before slicing.

PER SERVING *(1 pork chop +1 cup salad + 4 tsp. cherry sauce each)* **CAL** 419, **FAT** 15 g (5 g sat. fat), **CHOL** 85 mg, **SODIUM** 421 mg, **CARB** 35 g (7 g fiber, 16 g sugars), **PRO** 36 g

Italian Meatball Rolls

36 g CARB

SERVES 4
TOTAL 30 min.

Nonstick cooking spray
2½ cups thinly sliced fresh cremini mushrooms
½ cup chopped onion
2 cloves garlic, minced
1 8-oz. can no-salt-added tomato sauce
2 Tbsp. balsamic vinegar
½ tsp. dried rosemary, crushed
½ tsp. dried oregano, crushed

8 oz. refrigerated Italian-style cooked turkey meatballs (8 meatballs), halved if desired
4 whole wheat hot dog buns, split
¼ cup finely shredded reduced-fat mozzarella cheese (1 oz.)
Snipped fresh oregano and sliced pepperoncini salad peppers (optional)

1. Preheat broiler. Coat a 10-inch nonstick skillet with cooking spray; heat over medium. Cook mushrooms, onion, and garlic in hot skillet 5 to 10 minutes or until tender, stirring occasionally. Stir in the next four ingredients (through dried oregano). Bring to boiling; reduce heat. Simmer, covered, 2 minutes. Stir in meatballs. Simmer, covered, about 5 minutes more or until meatballs are hot.

2. Meanwhile, open buns so they lie flat and place on a baking sheet. Broil 4 to 5 inches from heat about 1 minute or until lightly toasted. Divide meatball mixture among buns; sprinkle with cheese. Broil 1 to 2 minutes more or until cheese is melted. If desired, sprinkle with fresh oregano and pepperoncini peppers.

PER SERVING *(1 sandwich each)* **CAL** 320, **FAT** 11 g (3 g sat. fat), **CHOL** 65 mg, **SODIUM** 605 mg, **CARB** 36 g (4 g fiber, 9 g sugars), **PRO** 19 g

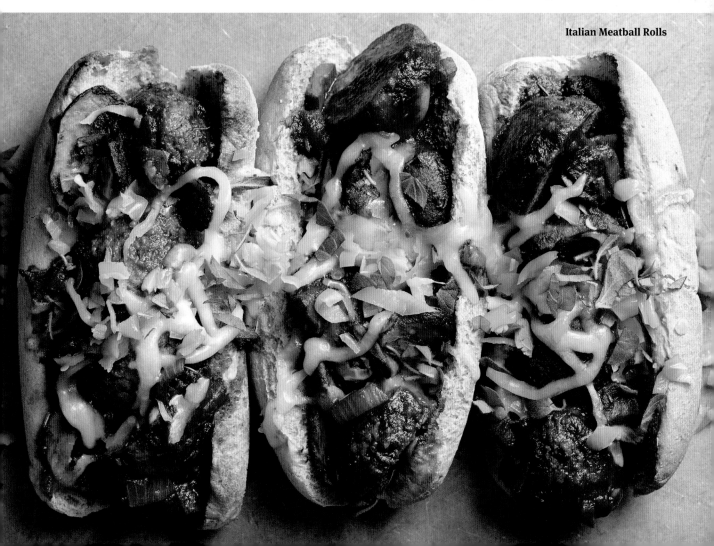

Italian Meatball Rolls

Shrimply Divine Pasta

Pork Tenderloin Sandwiches with Chimichurri Sauce

Pork Tenderloin Sandwiches with Chimichurri Sauce

30 g
CARB

SERVES 4
HANDS ON 25 min.
TOTAL 30 min.

- 1 lb. pork tenderloin, trimmed
- ¼ tsp. salt
- ¼ tsp. black pepper
- 2 tsp. olive oil
- 8 slices whole grain bread, toasted
- 4 leaves green leaf lettuce
- 1 recipe Chimichurri Sauce
- 8 slices tomato
- ¼ cup light mayonnaise (optional)

1. Cut tenderloin into four equal pieces. Using the flat side of a meat mallet, flatten tenderloin pieces between two pieces of plastic wrap to about ¼ inch thick. Sprinkle evenly with the salt and pepper.
2. In a 12-inch nonstick skillet heat olive oil over medium-high. Reduce heat to medium. Cook tenderloin pieces in hot oil 5 to 7 minutes or until just pink inside. Remove from heat.
3. Top four slices of toast with lettuce, tenderloin pieces, Chimichurri Sauce, and tomato slices. If desired, spread remaining toast slices with mayonnaise before adding to sandwiches. Serve immediately.

Chimichurri Sauce In a blender or food processor combine **1 cup packed fresh Italian parsley; 2 Tbsp.** each **snipped fresh oregano, finely chopped shallot, red wine vinegar,** and **lime juice; 1 Tbsp. olive oil; 3 cloves garlic, minced;** and **½ tsp. crushed red pepper.** Cover and blend until finely chopped, scraping sides as necessary.

PER SERVING *(1 sandwich each)* **CAL** 343, **FAT** 10 g (2 g sat. fat), **CHOL** 70 mg, **SODIUM** 506 mg, **CARB** 30 g (6 g fiber, 4 g sugars), **PRO** 32 g

Shrimply Divine Pasta

37 g
CARB

SERVES 4
TOTAL 20 min.

- 12 oz. fresh or frozen medium shrimp in shells
- 2 cups dried rotini or other small pasta
- 1 Tbsp. olive oil
- 3 cloves garlic, minced
- ½ cup bottled Italian salad dressing
- 1 tsp. Italian seasoning, crushed
- 1 5- to 6-oz. pkg. fresh baby spinach or 8 cups torn fresh spinach
  Finely shredded Parmesan cheese

1. Thaw shrimp, if frozen. Cook pasta according to package directions; drain. Return pasta to pan; cover and keep warm.
2. Meanwhile, peel and devein shrimp, leaving tails intact if desired. Rinse shrimp; pat dry with paper towels.
3. In a 10-inch skillet heat oil over medium-high. Add garlic; cook and stir 15 seconds. Add shrimp; cook and stir 2 to 3 minutes or until shrimp are opaque. Remove shrimp from skillet. Add salad dressing and Italian seasoning to skillet. Bring to simmering. Add spinach; cook and stir 1 to 2 minutes or just until wilted. Return shrimp to skillet.
4. Add cooked pasta to shrimp mixture; toss gently to combine. Serve with Parmesan cheese.

PER SERVING *(1 cup each)* **CAL** 340, **FAT** 11 g (2 g sat. fat), **CHOL** 120 mg, **SODIUM** 438 mg, **CARB** 37 g (2 g fiber, 4 g sugars), **PRO** 22 g

Tortilla Chip Flounder with Black Bean Salad

1 Tbsp. olive oil
2½ tsp. chili powder
1 tsp. reduced-sodium Old Bay seasoning or seafood seasoning
¼ tsp. salt
⅓ cup milk
⅓ cup all-purpose flour
⅓ cup fine dry bread crumbs
2 tsp. chili powder
1 tsp. paprika
¼ tsp. black pepper
2 Tbsp. butter, melted
Lemon wedges and/or fresh parsley (optional)

Tortilla Chip Flounder with Black Bean Salad

35 g CARB

SERVES 4
HANDS ON 30 min.
TOTAL 40 min.

4 3- to 4-oz. fresh or frozen flounder fillets or other white fish fillets
Nonstick cooking spray
4 oz. multigrain tortilla chips
⅛ to ¼ tsp. cayenne pepper
⅓ cup refrigerated or frozen egg product, thawed
1 15-oz. can no-salt-added black beans, rinsed and drained
½ cup halved cherry tomatoes
½ cup chopped green sweet pepper
¼ cup finely chopped red onion
2 Tbsp. snipped fresh oregano
2 Tbsp. snipped fresh Italian parsley
1 Tbsp. lemon juice
2 tsp. olive oil
¼ tsp. salt
¼ tsp. ground cumin
¼ cup crumbled queso fresco (1 oz.)

1. Thaw fish, if frozen. Preheat oven to 425°F. Line a baking sheet with foil; coat foil with cooking spray.
2. In a food processor combine tortilla chips and cayenne pepper. Cover and process until very finely crushed. Transfer to a shallow dish.
3. Rinse fish; pat dry. Pour egg into another shallow dish. Dip fish in egg, then in crushed tortilla chips, turning to coat and pressing to adhere. Place fish on the prepared baking sheet. Lightly coat top of fish with cooking spray. Bake 8 to 10 minutes or until fish flakes easily.
4. Meanwhile, for bean salad, in a bowl combine the next 10 ingredients (through cumin). Serve fish with salad. Sprinkle with queso fresco and, if desired, parsley.

PER SERVING (1 fish fillet + ⅔ cup bean salad each) CAL 361, FAT 11 g (2 g sat. fat), CHOL 46 mg, SODIUM 401 mg, CARB 35 g (8 g fiber, 3 g sugars), PRO 28 g

Spicy Oven-Baked Fish and Sweet Potato Fries

40 g CARB

SERVES 4
HANDS ON 20 min.
TOTAL 40 min.

1 lb. fresh or frozen white fish fillets, about ½ inch thick
Nonstick cooking spray
1 lb. sweet potatoes, cut into ¼- to ½-inch sticks

1. Thaw fish, if frozen. Rinse fish; pat dry. Cut fish into 3×2-inch pieces. Cover and chill until needed.
2. Preheat oven to 425°F. Line a large baking sheet with foil; lightly coat with cooking spray. Place potato sticks in a large bowl. Add the olive oil, ½ tsp. of the chili powder, the Old Bay seasoning, and ¼ tsp. of the salt; toss to coat. Arrange potatoes in a single layer on one half of the prepared baking sheet. Bake 10 minutes.
3. Meanwhile, place milk in a shallow dish. Place flour in another shallow dish. In a third shallow dish combine bread crumbs, the remaining 2 tsp. chili powder, the paprika, the remaining ¼ tsp. salt, and the pepper. Stir in melted butter until combined.
4. Dip fish pieces in milk; coat with flour. Dip again in the milk, then in the bread crumb mixture. Remove baking sheet from oven. Carefully turn potatoes over. Place fish on the other half of the hot baking sheet; return to oven. Bake 10 to 15 minutes more or until potatoes are golden brown and fish flakes easily. If desired, serve fish with lemon wedges and/or fresh parsley.

PER SERVING (2 pieces fish + 4 oz. fries each) CAL 384, FAT 13 g (5 g sat fat), CHOL 74 mg, SODIUM 640 mg, CARB 40 g (5 g fiber, 7 g sugars), PRO 28 g

Tortilla Chip Flounder with Black Bean Salad

Spicy Oven-Baked
Fish and Sweet
Potato Fries

POP THE
FLAVORS WITH
A SQUEEZE OF
LEMON.

Roasted Cauliflower
Mac and Cheese

Roasted Cauliflower Mac and Cheese

36 g CARB

SERVES 8
HANDS ON 40 min.
TOTAL 1 hr. 25 min.

- 6 cups small cauliflower florets
- 2 tsp. olive oil
- ¼ tsp. salt
- 2 cups dried elbow macaroni or cavatappi pasta
- 1 Tbsp. olive oil
- ¾ cup finely chopped onion
- 2 cloves garlic, minced
- 2½ cups fat-free milk
- 2 Tbsp. all-purpose flour
- ½ tsp. salt
- 2 oz. reduced-fat cream cheese (neufchatel), cut up
- 1½ cups shredded reduced-fat sharp cheddar cheese (6 oz.)
- 1 cup soft bread crumbs
- ¼ cup grated Parmesan cheese
- ½ tsp. snipped fresh thyme
- 1 tsp. olive oil

1. Preheat oven to 400°F. Line a 15×10-inch baking pan with parchment paper. Place cauliflower in prepared baking pan. Drizzle with 2 tsp. oil and sprinkle with ¼ tsp. salt; toss to coat. Roast about 20 minutes or until tender and browned. Remove from oven. Reduce oven temperature to 350°F.
2. Meanwhile, in a large saucepan cook macaroni according to package directions; drain. Rinse with cold water; drain again. Return macaroni to saucepan.
3. For cheese sauce, in a 10-inch nonstick skillet heat 1 Tbsp. oil over medium. Add onion; cook about 3 minutes or until tender, stirring occasionally. Add garlic; cook and stir 30 seconds. In a bowl whisk together the next three ingredients (through ½ tsp. salt) until smooth; gradually stir into onion mixture. Cook and stir until slightly thickened and bubbly. Reduce heat to low. Stir in cream cheese until melted. Remove from heat. Gradually add cheddar cheese, stirring just until melted.
4. Add cauliflower and cheese sauce to cooked macaroni; stir gently to combine. Transfer mixture to a 3-qt. rectangular baking dish. In a bowl combine the next three ingredients (through thyme). Drizzle with the 1 tsp. oil; toss to coat. Sprinkle crumb mixture over macaroni mixture. Bake, uncovered, 25 to 30 minutes or until heated and crumbs are light brown.

PER SERVING *(1 cup each)* **CAL** 295, **FAT** 11 g (5 g sat. fat), **CHOL** 24 mg, **SODIUM** 539 mg, **CARB** 36 g (3 g fiber, 7 g sugars), **PRO** 15 g

---

Mediterranean Lentil Skillet with Pita Chips

36 g CARB

SERVES 6
HANDS ON 30 min.
TOTAL 1 hr. 10 min.

- 1 Tbsp. olive oil
- ½ cup finely chopped onion
- ¼ cup finely chopped carrot
- ¼ cup finely chopped celery
- 1 tsp. dried thyme, crushed
- 2 cups low-sodium vegetable broth
- ¾ cup brown lentils
- ¼ cup dried currants or golden raisins
- 1 bay leaf
- 3 cups packed torn fresh kale
- ½ tsp. salt
- ½ tsp. black pepper
- 1 cup cherry or grape tomatoes, halved
- 1 Tbsp. red wine vinegar
- 1 Tbsp. lemon juice
- ¼ cup chopped walnuts, toasted
- 3 Tbsp. goat cheese
- 3 oz. unsalted pita chips

Mediterranean Lentil Skillet with Pita Chips

1. In a 10-inch skillet with a tight-fitting lid heat oil over medium. Add the next four ingredients (through thyme); cook and stir about 5 minutes or until vegetables are crisp-tender. Stir in the next four ingredients (through bay leaf). Bring to boiling; reduce heat. Simmer, covered, about 30 minutes or until lentils are tender. Remove and discard bay leaf.
2. Stir in the kale, salt, and pepper. Cook, uncovered, about 5 minutes more or until kale is slightly wilted and any remaining liquid is absorbed. Remove from heat.
3. Stir in tomatoes, vinegar, and lemon juice. Sprinkle with walnuts and goat cheese. Serve warm with pita chips.

PER SERVING *(⅔ cup each)* **CAL** 281, **FAT** 11 g (2 g sat. fat), **CHOL** 6 mg, **SODIUM** 434 mg, **CARB** 36 g (10 g fiber, 8 g sugars), **PRO** 12 g

VEGGIE-
PACKED

Boost your vegetable intake by loading your meal plan with a rainbow of colors. The benefit—more filling fiber, lots of antioxidants and good-for-you nutrients, and delicious variety.

Nectarine, Beet, and Goat Cheese Salad

Mexican Stuffed Acorn Squash

29 g
CARB

SERVES 6
HANDS ON 15 min.
TOTAL 1 hr. 15 min.

3 1¼-lb. acorn squash, halved and seeded
   Nonstick cooking spray
¾ tsp. salt
¼ tsp. black pepper
2 Tbsp. canola oil
12 oz. 93% lean ground turkey
¾ cup chopped green sweet pepper
½ cup chopped onion
1¼ cups cubed yellow summer squash
1 14.5-oz. can no-salt-added diced tomatoes, drained
1 tsp. salt-free fiesta lime seasoning
¼ tsp. crushed red pepper (optional)
6 Tbsp. crumbled queso fresco
3 Tbsp. snipped fresh cilantro

1. Preheat oven to 400°F. Pour ½ inch water into a large roasting pan; add acorn squash, cut sides down. Bake 30 minutes. Turn squash halves cut sides up; coat with cooking spray and sprinkle with ¼ tsp. of the salt and the black pepper. Bake 20 to 25 minutes more or until tender.
2. Meanwhile, in a 10-inch nonstick skillet heat 1 Tbsp. of the oil over medium. Add ground turkey; cook until browned. Remove turkey.
3. In skillet heat remaining 1 Tbsp. oil over medium. Add sweet pepper and onion; cook 5 to 7 minutes or until onion is tender, stirring occasionally. Add summer squash; cook and stir 3 minutes or just until squash is tender. Stir in turkey, remaining ½ tsp. salt, and the next three ingredients (through crushed red pepper); heat through.
4. Spoon turkey mixture into squash cavities. Bake 10 minutes. Top with queso fresco and cilantro.

PER SERVING (1 stuffed squash half each) **CAL** 262, **FAT** 11 g (3 g sat. fat), **CHOL** 47 mg, **SODIUM** 419 mg, **CARB** 29 g (5 g fiber, 4 g sugars), **PRO** 15 g

Mexican Stuffed Acorn Squash

Nectarine, Beet, and Goat Cheese Salad

22 g
CARB

SERVES 4
TOTAL 20 min.

4 cups fresh baby spinach
2 8-oz. pkg. refrigerated cooked whole baby beets, quartered
1 cup shredded cooked chicken (5 oz.)
2 fresh nectarines, pitted and cut into wedges
1 3.5-oz. container crumbled soft goat cheese (chèvre)
¼ cup balsamic vinaigrette salad dressing

1. Divide spinach among salad plates. Top with beets, chicken, nectarines, and goat cheese. Drizzle vinaigrette over salads. Season to taste with *salt* and *black pepper*.

Tip To make this salad vegan, substitute one 15-oz. can garbanzo beans (chickpeas), rinsed and drained, for the chicken and chopped toasted walnuts for the goat cheese.

PER SERVING (1 salad each) **CAL** 266, **FAT** 13 g (5 g sat. fat), **CHOL** 43 mg, **SODIUM** 519 mg, **CARB** 22 g (5 g fiber, 17 g sugars), **PRO** 18 g

Spaghetti Squash with Chicken and Mushroom Sauce

Succotash Salad with Buttermilk-Avocado Dressing

24 g
CARB

SERVES 4
HANDS ON 25 min.
TOTAL 45 min.

- 2 ears fresh sweet corn
- 1 cup fresh lima beans
- 1 large head butterhead (Boston or Bibb) lettuce, torn
- 2 cups sliced grilled or roasted chicken breast
- 6 slices lower-sodium, less-fat bacon, crisp-cooked and crumbled
- ½ cup finely chopped red onion
- ½ cup crumbled blue cheese or feta cheese (2 oz.)
- 1 recipe Buttermilk-Avocado Dressing

1. Cut corn kernels from cobs; discard cobs. In a small saucepan bring 1 cup lightly salted water to boiling. Add lima beans; simmer about 15 minutes or until tender. Remove with a slotted spoon. Add corn to water. Simmer about 3 minutes or until tender; drain.

2. Arrange lettuce on a large platter. Arrange the next four ingredients (through cheese) and the corn and lima beans in rows on lettuce. Serve with Buttermilk-Avocado Dressing.

Buttermilk-Avocado Dressing In a blender combine ¾ cup buttermilk; half of an avocado, seeded and peeled; 1 Tbsp. snipped fresh Italian parsley; ¼ tsp. each onion powder, dry mustard, salt, and black pepper; and 1 clove garlic, minced. Cover and blend until smooth.

PER SERVING (1¾ cups salad + about 3 Tbsp. dressing each) CAL 345, FAT 13 g (5 g sat. fat), CHOL 82 mg, SODIUM 609 mg, CARB 24 g (5 g fiber, 7 g sugars), PRO 33 g

Spaghetti Squash with Chicken and Mushroom Sauce

30 g
CARB

SERVES 4
HANDS ON 25 min.
TOTAL 45 min.

- 1 3-lb. spaghetti squash
- ½ cup water
- 1 Tbsp. olive oil
- 2 cups sliced fresh mushrooms
- ¼ cup chopped onion
- 2 cloves garlic, minced
- 2 links cooked desired-flavor chicken sausage, halved lengthwise and sliced
- 1 14.5-oz. can no-salt-added diced tomatoes, undrained
- 1 8-oz. can no-salt-added tomato sauce
- 1½ tsp. dried Italian seasoning, crushed
- ¼ tsp. salt
- ¼ tsp. black pepper
  Shaved or grated Parmesan cheese (optional)

1. Cut squash in half lengthwise; remove and discard seeds. Place one squash half, cut side down, in a 2-qt. rectangular microwave-safe baking dish; add ¼ cup of the water. Cover with vented plastic wrap. Microwave about 10 minutes or until tender. Remove squash half; keep warm. Repeat with the remaining squash half and the remaining ¼ cup water.

2. Meanwhile, for marinara sauce, in a medium saucepan heat oil over medium. Add mushrooms, onion, and garlic; cook about 7 minutes or until tender. Stir in the next six ingredients (through pepper). Bring to boiling; reduce heat. Simmer, uncovered, 15 to 20 minutes or until sauce reaches desired consistency, stirring frequently.

3. Use a fork to shred and separate the squash pulp into strands. Place squash pulp in a colander set in the sink; press pulp with a spatula to remove any excess moisture. Fluff drained squash with a fork. Spoon squash onto plates; top with sauce. If desired, sprinkle with Parmesan cheese.

PER SERVING (1 cup squash + ¾ cup sauce each) CAL 201, FAT 7 g (1 g sat. fat), CHOL 25 mg, SODIUM 509 mg, CARB 30 g (8 g fiber, 14 g sugars), PRO 11 g

SWAP
1 CUP FROZEN
CORN, THAWED,
FOR SWEET
CORN.

**Succotash Salad with
Buttermilk-Avocado Dressing**

Southwest Black Bean and Chicken Platter

Indian Cauliflower Fried Rice

Indian Cauliflower Fried Rice

20 g
CARB

SERVES 4
TOTAL 35 min.

- 1 medium head cauliflower (about 2 lb.), cored
- 2 Tbsp. canola oil
- 1 tsp. cumin seeds, crushed
- 1 clove garlic, minced
- 1 tsp. garam masala
- 1 tsp. grated fresh ginger
- ½ tsp. salt
- ½ tsp. ground turmeric
- ¼ to ½ tsp. cayenne pepper
- 12 oz. skinless, boneless chicken breasts, cut into bite-size strips
- 1 medium onion, cut into thin wedges
- 1 cup shredded carrots
- 1 cup fresh or frozen peas
- ½ cup crunchy falafel-flavor chickpeas or chopped peanuts Fresh cilantro

1. Break cauliflower into florets (about 8 cups). Place cauliflower in batches in a food processor. Cover and pulse each batch until crumbly and mixture resembles the texture of rice (about 6 cups).
2. In a wok or 12-inch skillet heat 1 Tbsp. of the oil over medium-high. Add cumin seeds; cook and stir 10 seconds. Add the next six ingredients (through cayenne); cook and stir 10 seconds. Add chicken. Cook and stir 3 to 4 minutes or until no longer pink (adding additional oil if necessary). Remove chicken from wok.
3. Add remaining 1 Tbsp. oil to wok. Add onion, carrots, and peas; cook and stir 2 minutes. Add cauliflower; cook and stir 4 minutes or until cauliflower is tender. Return chicken to wok; heat through. Top each serving with chickpeas and cilantro.

PER SERVING (1⅓ to 2 cups each) **CAL** 280,
FAT 11 g (1 g sat. fat), **CHOL** 62 mg,
SODIUM 649 mg, **CARB** 20 g (5 g fiber,
6 g sugars), **PRO** 26 g

Southwest Black Bean and Chicken Platter

22 g
CARB

SERVES 6
TOTAL 30 min.

- ¼ cup cider vinegar
- 3 Tbsp. olive oil or vegetable oil
- 3 Tbsp. snipped fresh cilantro
- 1 canned chipotle chile pepper in adobo sauce, drained and finely chopped
- 1 clove garlic, minced
- ½ tsp. salt
- 1 15-oz. can black beans, rinsed and drained
- ¾ cup cooked fresh or frozen whole kernel corn
- ½ cup chopped orange or yellow sweet pepper (optional)
- 3½ cups shredded cooked chicken
- 10 grape tomatoes, halved
- ¼ cup sliced green onions
- 10 cups coarsely shredded lettuce
- 1 avocado, halved, seeded, peeled, and sliced (optional)
- 1 lime, halved and cut into wedges

1. For dressing, in a screw-top jar combine the first six ingredients (through salt).
Cover and shake well. For relish, in a bowl combine black beans, corn, and, if desired, sweet pepper. Drizzle with 2 Tbsp. of the dressing; toss to coat. In another bowl toss together chicken and 1 Tbsp. of the dressing. In a third bowl combine tomatoes and green onions.
2. Line a large platter with shredded lettuce. Arrange tomato mixture, relish, chicken mixture, and, if desired, avocado slices in rows on top of lettuce. Drizzle with the remaining dressing. Serve with lime wedges.

Tip Chile peppers contain oils that can irritate your skin and eyes. Wear plastic or rubber gloves when working with them.

To Make Ahead Prepare salad as directed, except toss avocado slices with 1 Tbsp. lime juice to prevent browning and do not drizzle salad with dressing. Cover and chill salad and dressing separately up to 1 hour. Before serving, drizzle salad with the remaining dressing.

PER SERVING (about 2 cups each) **CAL** 319,
FAT 14 g (3 g sat. fat), **CHOL** 73 mg,
SODIUM 533 mg, **CARB** 22 g (6 g fiber,
5 g sugars), **PRO** 30 g

Chicken with Apple-Vegetable Slaw Stir-Fry

19 g
CARB

SERVES 4
TOTAL 40 min.

- ½ cup reduced-sodium chicken broth
- 2 Tbsp. cider vinegar
- 1 Tbsp. packed brown sugar
- 2 tsp. Dijon-style mustard
- 2 tsp. cornstarch
- 1 clove garlic, minced
- ½ tsp. crushed red pepper
- ½ tsp. salt
- 2 Tbsp. vegetable oil
- 12 oz. boneless, skinless chicken thighs, cut into bite-size pieces
- 2 cups quartered fresh cremini mushrooms
- ¼ cup sliced shallots
- 3 cups coarsley shredded green cabbage
- 8 oz. fresh asparagus spears, trimmed and cut into 2-inch pieces
- 1 medium tart apple, cored and thinly sliced
  Snipped fresh cilantro

1. For sauce, in a bowl stir together the first eight ingredients (through salt).
2. In a wok or 12-inch skillet heat 1 Tbsp. of the oil over medium-high. Add chicken; cook and stir 4 to 6 minutes or until chicken is no longer pink. Transfer to a bowl. Heat the remaining 1 Tbsp. oil in skillet. Add mushrooms and shallots; cook and stir 2 to 3 minutes. Add cabbage, asparagus, and apple; cook and stir 3 to 5 minutes more or until vegetables are crisp-tender.
3. Push vegetables to side of wok. Stir sauce; add to center of wok. Cook and stir until thickened and bubbly. Return chicken to wok. Cook and stir 1 minute more. Sprinkle with cilantro.

PER SERVING *(1½ cups each)* **CAL** 247, **FAT** 11 g (2 g sat. fat), **CHOL** 80 mg, **SODIUM** 514 mg, **CARB** 19 g (4 g fiber, 12 g sugars), **PRO** 20 g

Grilled Flank Steak Salad

31 g CARB

SERVES 4
HANDS ON 45 min.
TOTAL 1 hr. 15 min.

- 1 recipe Cilantro Dressing
- 1 lb. beef flank steak
- 4 small yellow and/or red sweet peppers, halved
- 2 ears fresh sweet corn
- 4 green onions, trimmed
  Nonstick cooking spray
- 4 cups torn romaine lettuce
- 8 cherry tomatoes, halved
- ½ of a small avocado, peeled and thinly sliced (optional)

1. Prepare Cilantro Dressing and divide it into two portions.

2. Score both sides of steak in a diamond pattern by making shallow diagonal cuts at 1-inch intervals. Place steak in a resealable plastic bag set in a shallow dish. Pour one portion of the Cilantro Dressing over steak. Seal bag; turn to coat steak. Marinate in the refrigerator 30 minutes.

3. Coat sweet peppers, corn, and green onions with cooking spray. Grill steak and corn, uncovered, over medium until steak is desired doneness and corn is tender, turning steak once and turning corn occasionally. For steak, allow 17 to 21 minutes for medium rare (145°F) to medium (160°F). For corn, allow 15 to 20 minutes. Add sweet pepper halves to the grill the last 8 minutes of grilling and green onions to the grill the last 4 minutes of grilling, turning frequently.

4. Thinly slice steak against the grain. Coarsely chop sweet peppers and green onions; cut corn from cob, leaving kernels in "sheets." Top romaine lettuce with steak, grilled vegetables, tomatoes, and, if desired, avocado slices. Drizzle with the reserved portion of the Cilantro Dressing.

Cilantro Dressing In a blender or food processor combine ⅓ cup lime juice; ¼ cup each **chopped shallots** and snipped fresh cilantro; 2 Tbsp. each **olive oil** and **water**; 4 tsp. honey; 2 cloves garlic, peeled and quartered; 1 tsp. chili powder; and ½ tsp. each **salt** and **ground cumin**. Cover and blend until combined.

PER SERVING (3 oz. cooked steak + 1 cup greens + ½ cup vegetables + 1½ Tbsp. dressing each) **CAL** 337, **FAT** 12 g (3 g sat. fat), **CHOL** 47 mg, **SODIUM** 375 mg, **CARB** 31 g (5 g fiber, 13 g sugars), **PRO** 29 g

Maple-Cider Pork with Roasted Beets and Cabbage

Eggplant, Fennel, and Siege Ziti

38 g CARB

SERVES 6
HANDS ON 25 min.
SLOW COOK 6 hr. (low) + 40 min. (high)

- 4 oz. bulk sweet Italian sausage
- 4 cups peeled and chopped eggplant
- 2 medium fennel bulbs, trimmed, cored, and thinly sliced
- 1 14.5-oz. can fire-roasted crushed tomatoes, undrained
- ½ cup water
- ¼ cup dry white wine
- 2 Tbsp. tomato paste
- 2 cloves garlic, minced
- 1 tsp. dried Italian seasoning, crushed
- 6 to 8 oz. dried cut ziti or penne pasta
- ½ cup snipped fresh basil
- 1 cup shredded part-skim mozzarella cheese (4 oz.)

1. In a 10-inch skillet cook sausage over medium-high until browned. Drain off fat.
2. In a 5- to 6-qt. slow cooker combine sausage and the next eight ingredients (through Italian seasoning). Cover; cook on low 6 to 7 hours or on high 3 to 3½ hours.
3. If using low, turn to high. Stir in pasta and basil. Cover and cook 30 minutes. Stir pasta mixture; sprinkle with cheese. Cover and cook 10 minutes more. Let stand, uncovered, 5 to 10 minutes. Sprinkle with additional basil.

Tip Cut 30 minutes of slow cooking by cooking pasta on the stove. Stir it into the eggplant mixture with basil. Sprinkle with cheese and continue as directed.

PER SERVING (1¼ cups each) **CAL** 255, **FAT** 5 g (3 g sat. fat), **CHOL** 18 mg, **SODIUM** 479 mg, **CARB** 38 g (6 g fiber, 7 g sugars), **PRO** 14 g

Caption (on photo): Eggplant, Fennel, and Sausage Ziti

Maple-Cider Pork with Roasted Beets and Cabbage

46 g CARB

SERVES 4
HANDS ON 25 min.
TOTAL 1 hr. 15 min.

- 6 cups coarsely shredded cabbage
- 1 lb. yellow or red beets, peeled and coarsely chopped
- 2 cups apple cider
- ½ tsp. salt
- ½ tsp. black pepper
- 2 cups coarsely chopped, peeled tart apples
- 1 Tbsp. olive oil
- 1 1-lb. natural pork tenderloin, trimmed
- 3 Tbsp. cider vinegar
- 3 Tbsp. pure maple syrup

1. Preheat oven to 400°F. In a roasting pan combine the cabbage, beets, apple cider, and ¼ tsp. each of the salt and pepper; toss to coat. Roast 20 minutes.

2. Meanwhile, sprinkle pork with the remaining ¼ tsp. each salt and pepper. In a 10-inch nonstick skillet cook pork in hot oil over medium-high 4 to 5 minutes or until browned on all sides.
3. Remove roasting pan from oven. Add apples; toss to combine. Place pork in pan and continue to roast 25 to 30 minutes or until done (145°F).
4. Transfer meat to a cutting board. Tent with foil and let rest 3 minutes. Using a slotted spoon, transfer cabbage mixture to a serving platter, reserving any remaining pan juices. Stir vinegar into roasting pan. Place pan over medium-high. Bring to boiling; reduce heat. Simmer 5 minutes. Stir in maple syrup. Slice pork and serve with cabbage mixture. Spoon sauce over top.

PER SERVING (3½ oz. pork + 1¼ cups cabbage mixture + ¼ cup sauce each) **CAL** 342, **FAT** 6 g (1 g sat. fat), **CHOL** 74 mg, **SODIUM** 444 mg, **CARB** 46 g (6 g fiber, 36 g sugars), **PRO** 26 g

Massaged Kale and Pork Salad

47 g
CARB

SERVES	4
HANDS ON	20 min.
TOTAL	25 min.

- 6 cups torn fresh kale, stems removed
- 1 recipe Honey-Grapefruit Vinaigrette
- 1 15-oz. can cannellini beans, rinsed and drained
- 1 grapefruit, peeled and sectioned
- 1 avocado, halved, seeded, peeled, and chopped
- ½ cup sliced radishes
- 1 1-lb. natural pork tenderloin, trimmed and cut crosswise into ¼-inch-thick slices
- ¼ tsp. salt
- ¼ tsp. black pepper
  Nonstick cooking spray

1. Place kale in a large bowl. Drizzle with Honey-Grapefruit Vinaigrette. Using clean hands, massage kale 3 to 4 minutes or until leaves are lightly wilted and glossy, making sure to massage all the kale evenly. Add the next four ingredients (through radishes); toss to combine.
2. Season pork with salt and pepper. Coat a 10-inch nonstick skillet with cooking spray. Heat over medium. Cook pork in hot skillet 3 to 4 minutes or until no longer pink, turning once. Serve over kale salad.

Honey-Grapefruit Vinaigrette In a screw-top jar combine **¼ cup grapefruit juice, 3 Tbsp. honey, 2 Tbsp. olive oil, 1 Tbsp. snipped fresh mint,** and **¼ tsp.** each **salt** and **black pepper.** Cover and shake well.

PER SERVING *(1½ cups each)* **CAL** 456, **FAT** 16 g (3 g sat. fat), **CHOL** 74 mg, **SODIUM** 624 mg, **CARB** 47 g (12 g fiber, 21 g sugars), **PRO** 35 g

IT IS NOT NECESSARY TO PEEL DELICATA SQUASH. THE SKIN IS TENDER AFTER COOKING AND IS A GOOD SOURCE OF FIBER.

Delicata Squash Salad with Pork Medallions

19 g CARB

SERVES 4
TOTAL 30 min.

- 12 oz. pork tenderloin, cut into ½-inch slices
- ¼ tsp. salt
- ½ tsp. black pepper
- 1 Tbsp. olive oil
- 3 slices lower-sodium, less-fat bacon
- 1 lb. delicata squash, halved, seeded, and cut into 1-inch pieces
- ¾ cup unsweetened apple juice
- ¼ cup water
- 2 shallots, thinly sliced
- 3 Tbsp. cider vinegar
- 1 tsp. snipped fresh thyme or ¼ tsp. dried thyme, crushed
- 6 cups fresh baby spinach

1. Sprinkle pork with salt and ¼ tsp. of the pepper. In a 10-inch nonstick skillet cook pork in hot oil over medium-high about 5 minutes or until browned but still slightly pink in center, turning once. Remove from skillet; keep warm.
2. In the same skillet cook bacon over medium until crisp. Drain bacon on paper towels; crumble bacon. Wipe out skillet. Add the next four ingredients (through shallots) to skillet. Bring to boiling; reduce heat. Cook, covered, 6 to 8 minutes or until squash is just tender.
3. Add vinegar, thyme, and the remaining ¼ tsp. pepper to skillet. Return pork and any accumulated juices to skillet; heat. Serve over spinach. Sprinkle with bacon.

PER SERVING *(1 cup pork and squash mixture + 1½ cups spinach each)* **CAL** 226, **FAT** 6 g (1 g sat. fat), **CHOL** 58 mg, **SODIUM** 315 mg, **CARB** 19 g (4 g fiber, 5 g sugars), **PRO** 22 g

Salmon-Stuffed
Zucchini

Almond-Coated Cod with Cabbage-Fennel Slaw

Salmon-Stuffed Zucchini

16 g
CARB

SERVES 4
HANDS ON 25 min.
TOTAL 35 min.

- 4 medium zucchini (about 8 oz. each)
- ⅓ cup finely chopped green onions
- ¼ cup roasted red sweet pepper, drained and chopped
- ¼ cup light mayonnaise
- 2 Tbsp. snipped fresh parsley
- 1 tsp. dried Italian seasoning, crushed
- 3 2.5-oz. pouches lemon-pepper or plain skinless, boneless pink salmon
- ½ cup panko bread crumbs
- ½ cup finely shredded Gruyère or Parmesan cheese (2 oz.) Lemon wedges

1. Preheat broiler. Trim ends of zucchini if desired; cut each zucchini in half lengthwise. Using a melon baller or a small spoon, scoop out and discard pulp, leaving ¼-inch-thick shells. Place zucchini shells, cut sides up, in a shallow baking pan. Broil 4 inches from the heat about 5 minutes or until edges of zucchini start to brown.
2. Meanwhile, in a bowl stir together the next five ingredients (through Italian seasoning). Add salmon and bread crumbs; stir gently to combine.
3. Spoon salmon mixture into broiled zucchini halves. Sprinkle with cheese. Broil about 3 minutes or until cheese is melted and golden. Serve with lemon wedges.

PER SERVING *(2 zucchini halves each)*
CAL 228, **FAT** 11 g (4 g sat. fat), **CHOL** 40 mg, **SODIUM** 558 mg, **CARB** 16 g (3 g fiber, 8 g sugars), **PRO** 19 g

Almond-Coated Cod with Cabbage-Fennel Slaw

22 g
CARB

SERVES 4
HANDS ON 20 min.
TOTAL 30 min.

- 4 4- to 5-oz. fresh or frozen skinless cod fillets
- 1 medium fennel bulb
- 1 medium orange
- 1 lemon
- 2 Tbsp. olive oil
- 1 Tbsp. honey
- 1 tsp. orange zest
- ¼ tsp. salt
- ¼ tsp. black pepper
- 4 cups shredded savoy or white cabbage
  Nonstick cooking spray
- 2 Tbsp. honey mustard
- ½ cup finely chopped sliced almonds

1. Thaw fish, if frozen. Preheat oven to 425°F. Snip 2 Tbsp. fennel fronds. Reserve additional fronds for garnish. Trim and discard fennel stalk and any damaged outer layer from bulb. Cut bulb in half lengthwise; remove and discard core. Thinly slice bulb.
2. Remove 1 tsp. zest from orange. Section the orange by cutting a thin slice from both ends using a paring knife. Place the flat end of the orange on a cutting board. Use the knife to cut away the peel and white pith from top to bottom. To remove sections, hold orange over a bowl to catch juices. Cut toward the center of the orange between one section and the membrane, then cut out along the membrane on the other side of the section to free each section. Set sections aside.
3. Remove 1 tsp. zest and squeeze 3 Tbsp. juice from lemon. Add lemon zest and juice and the next five ingredients (through pepper) to bowl with orange juice; whisk to combine. Add sliced fennel, the 2 Tbsp. snipped fennel fronds, and cabbage. Toss to combine. Gently stir in orange sections.
4. Preheat oven to 425°F. Line a large baking sheet with foil; coat foil with cooking spray. Measure thickness of fish. Arrange fish on prepared baking sheet. Brush tops of fish with mustard. Sprinkle almonds over fish, pressing onto fish to adhere. Lightly coat tops of fish with cooking spray. Bake 4 to 6 minutes per ½-inch thickness or until fish flakes easily. Serve with slaw. Top with additional reserved fennel fronds.

PER SERVING *(1 fish fillet + 1¼ cups slaw each)*
CAL 331, **FAT** 14 g (2 g sat. fat), **CHOL** 61 mg, **SODIUM** 318 mg, **CARB** 22 g (6 g fiber, 13 g sugars), **PRO** 30 g

115

Salmon in Parchment Paper

13 g
CARB

SERVES 4
HANDS ON 30 min.
TOTAL 55 min.

- 1 lb. fresh or frozen skinless salmon or halibut fillets, ¾ to 1 inch thick
- 4 cups fresh vegetables (such as sliced carrots; trimmed fresh green beans; sliced zucchini or yellow summer squash; sliced fresh mushrooms; and/or sliced red, yellow, and/or green sweet peppers)
- ½ cup sliced green onions
- 1 Tbsp. snipped fresh oregano or 1 tsp. dried oregano, crushed
- 2 tsp. orange zest
- ¼ tsp. salt
- ¼ tsp. black pepper
- 4 cloves garlic, halved
- 4 tsp. olive oil
- 1 medium orange, halved and thinly sliced
- 4 sprigs fresh oregano (optional)

1. Preheat oven to 350°F. Thaw fish, if frozen. Rinse fish; pat dry with paper towels. If necessary, cut into four serving-size pieces. Tear off four 14-inch squares of parchment paper. In a large bowl combine the next seven ingredients (through garlic); toss gently.

2. Divide vegetable mixture among the four pieces of parchment, placing vegetables on one side of each parchment square. Place one fish piece on top of each vegetable portion. Drizzle 1 tsp. of the oil over each fish piece. Top with orange slices. Fold parchment over fish and vegetables; fold in the open sides several times to secure, curving the edge into a circular pattern. Place parchment packets in a single layer in a 15×10-inch baking pan.

3. Bake 25 to 30 minutes or until fish flakes easily. Cut an "X" in the top of a parchment packet to check doneness; open carefully (steam will escape). If desired, garnish with fresh oregano sprigs.

Tip If using carrots and/or green beans, precook them. In a covered medium saucepan cook the carrots and/or green beans in a small amount of boiling water 2 minutes. Drain.

PER SERVING *(1 packet each)* **CAL** 262, **FAT** 12 g (2 g sat. fat), **CHOL** 62 mg, **SODIUM** 359 mg, **CARB** 13 g (4 g fiber, 8 g sugars), **PRO** 25 g

COOKING IN PARCHMENT

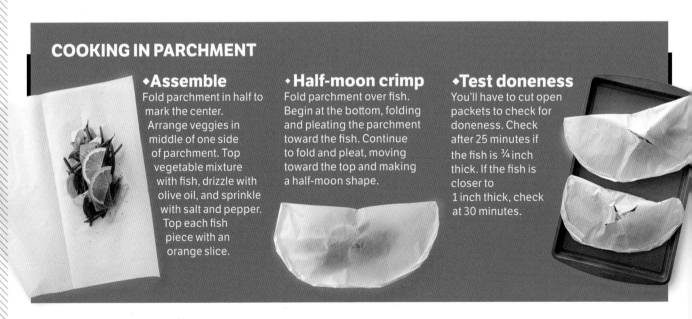

◆Assemble
Fold parchment in half to mark the center. Arrange veggies in middle of one side of parchment. Top vegetable mixture with fish, drizzle with olive oil, and sprinkle with salt and pepper. Top each fish piece with an orange slice.

◆Half-moon crimp
Fold parchment over fish. Begin at the bottom, folding and pleating the parchment toward the fish. Continue to fold and pleat, moving toward the top and making a half-moon shape.

◆Test doneness
You'll have to cut open packets to check for doneness. Check after 25 minutes if the fish is ¾ inch thick. If the fish is closer to 1 inch thick, check at 30 minutes.

Gingered
Vegetable-Tofu
Stir-Fry

ACE YOUR ASPARAGUS

Get the most out of your green spears with these must-know tips.

◆ Buying

Fresh asparagus should be firm with dark green or purple-tinged tips. If a bunch feels bendy, pass on it. Look for plump, straight spears without dry ends.

◆ Storing

Make asparagus last longer by wrapping the ends with a damp paper towel.

◆ Prepping

Break off the woody root ends of asparagus before cooking. It will naturally snap where the root ends and the fresh part begins.

◆ Cooking

Cook asparagus until crisp-tender—easily pierced with a fork but still has firmness. If it cooks too long, it will be mushy and bitter.

Vegetable and Tofu Soup

Vegetable and Tofu Soup

19 g
CARB

SERVES 4
HANDS ON 35 min.
TOTAL 2 hr. 35 min.

- 1 12-oz. pkg. extra-firm, tub-style tofu, drained and cut into ¾-inch cubes
- 2 Tbsp. olive oil
- 1 tsp. dried Italian seasoning, crushed
  Nonstick cooking spray
- 2 cups reduced-sodium chicken broth
- 1 14.5-oz. can no-salt-added diced tomatoes with basil, garlic, and oregano, undrained
- 3 cups sliced fresh button mushrooms
- ½ cup fresh or frozen peas, thawed
- ½ cup 1-inch pieces asparagus
- ½ cup chopped roasted red sweet pepper
- ⅓ cup oil-packed dried tomatoes, drained and finely chopped
- ¼ cup sliced green olives
  Shredded Parmesan cheese (optional)

1. Place tofu in a resealable plastic bag set in a shallow dish. Add oil and Italian seasoning. Seal bag; turn to coat tofu. Marinate in the refrigerator 2 to 4 hours.
2. Coat a 5- to 6-qt. Dutch oven with cooking spray; heat over medium-high. Cook undrained tofu in hot pan 5 to 8 minutes or until tofu is browned, turning once.
3. Add broth and canned tomatoes. Bring to boiling. Add the next three ingredients (through asparagus); reduce heat. Simmer, uncovered, 5 to 7 minutes or just until vegetables are tender. Stir in the next three ingredients (through olives); heat through. If desired, top servings with cheese.

PER SERVING *(1¾ cups each)* **CAL** 259,
FAT 15 g (2 g sat. fat), **CHOL** 0 mg, **SODIUM** 574 mg,
CARB 19 g (10 g fiber, 11 g sugars), **PRO** 16 g

Gingered Vegetable-Tofu Stir-Fry

37 g
CARB

SERVES 4
TOTAL 30 min.

- ¾ cup water
- ¼ cup dry sherry, dry white wine, or chicken broth
- 3 Tbsp. soy sauce
- 1 Tbsp. cornstarch
- ½ tsp. sugar
- 1 Tbsp. olive oil
- 2 tsp. grated fresh ginger
- 1 lb. asparagus, trimmed and cut into 1-inch pieces
- 1 small yellow summer squash, halved lengthwise and sliced
- ¼ cup sliced green onions
- 12 oz. extra-firm tofu, cut into ½-inch cubes and patted dry
- ½ cup chopped toasted almonds
- 2 cups hot cooked brown rice

1. For sauce, in a bowl stir together the first five ingredients (through sugar).
2. In a wok or 10-inch skillet heat oil over medium-high. Add ginger; cook and stir 15 seconds. Add the next three ingredients (through green onions); cook and stir 4 minutes or until asparagus is crisp-tender. Remove vegetables.
3. If necessary, add additional oil to wok. Add tofu; cook 2 to 3 minutes or until lightly browned, stirring gently. Remove tofu. Stir sauce; add to wok. Cook and stir until thickened and bubbly. Return cooked vegetables and tofu to wok. Cook and stir until heated Stir in almonds. Serve over rice.

PER SERVING *(1 cup tofu mixture + ½ cup rice each)* **CAL** 335, **FAT** 13 g (1 g sat. fat),
CHOL 0 mg, **SODIUM** 475 mg, **CARB** 38 g
(5 g fiber, 6 g sugars), **PRO** 14 g

Za'atar
Rice-
Stuffed
Peppers

Za'atar Rice-Stuffed Peppers

36 g
CARB

SERVES 8
HANDS ON 30 min.
TOTAL 1 hr.

- 1 Tbsp. olive oil
- ¾ cup chopped onion
- 1 Tbsp. za'atar spice mix
- 2 cloves garlic, minced
- ¼ tsp. crushed red pepper
- ⅛ tsp. salt
- ⅛ tsp. black pepper
- 1 15-oz. can garbanzo beans
  (chickpeas), rinsed and drained
- 1 15-oz. can tomato puree
- 3 cups cooked basmati rice
- 4 yellow, red, and/or green sweet
  peppers
- ½ cup water
- 1 5.3-oz. carton plain fat-free
  Greek yogurt
  Chopped cucumber and/or
  snipped fresh Italian parsley
  (optional)
  Lemon wedges (optional)

1. Preheat oven to 400°F. In a 10-inch skillet heat oil over medium heat. Add onion; cook 5 minutes or until tender, stirring occasionally. Add the next five ingredients (through black pepper); cook and stir 1 minute more. Stir in garbanzo beans and tomato puree; heat. Stir in rice.
2. Halve sweet peppers lengthwise; remove and discard seeds and membranes. Fill pepper halves with rice mixture. Place stuffed peppers in a 3-qt. rectangular baking dish. Pour the water into dish around stuffed peppers.
3. Bake, covered, about 30 minutes or until peppers are crisp-tender. Top with yogurt and, if desired, cucumber, parsley, and/or additional za'atar spice mix. If desired, serve with lemon wedges.

To Make Ahead Stuff peppers as directed in Step 2, but do not add water. Cover with foil; chill up to 24 hours. Add water and continue as directed in Step 3.

PER SERVING *(1 stuffed pepper half each)* **CAL** 192, **FAT** 3 g (0 g sat. fat), **CHOL** 0 mg, **SODIUM** 331 mg, **CARB** 36 g (4 g fiber, 6 g sugars), **PRO** 8 g

Triple Veggie Pasta

12 g
CARB

SERVES 4
TOTAL 30 min.

- 1 medium zucchini, trimmed
- 1 medium straight-neck yellow
  summer squash, trimmed
- 1 large carrot (1-inch diameter),
  peeled and trimmed
- 1 cup light Alfredo pasta sauce
- 1 Tbsp. basil pesto
- ⅛ to ¼ tsp. crushed red pepper
- 1 Tbsp. olive oil
- 1 cup sliced fresh cremini
  mushrooms
- 2 cups cooked chicken breast
  strips
- ½ cup halved grape or cherry
  tomatoes
- ½ cup frozen peas
  Small fresh basil leaves or
  snipped fresh basil

1. Using a spiral vegetable slicer fitted with the small blade, cut zucchini and yellow squash into long strands (about 7 cups lightly packed strands). Keeping carrot separate, cut carrot into long strands (about 1 cup lightly packed strands). If desired, cut through strands with kitchen scissors to make them shorter and easier to serve.
2. In a bowl combine Alfredo sauce, pesto, and crushed red pepper.
3. In a 12-inch skillet heat oil over medium. Add mushrooms; cook and stir 4 minutes. Add carrot; cook and stir 1 minute. Add squash mixture; cook and toss with tongs 2 minutes. Stir in Alfredo mixture, chicken, tomatoes, and peas; heat. Sprinkle with basil.

PER SERVING *(1½ cups each)* **CAL** 269, **FAT** 13 g (5 g sat. fat), **CHOL** 86 mg, **SODIUM** 456 mg, **CARB** 12 g (3 g fiber, 6 g sugars), **PRO** 26 g

IF YOU DON'T HAVE A SPIRAL SLICER, VERY THINLY BIAS-SLICE SQUASH AND CARROT.

Triple Veggie Pasta

Portobello-Blue Cheese Pitas with Chili Aïoli

Portobello-Blue Cheese Pitas with Chili Aïoli

42 g CARB | **SERVES** 4
HANDS ON 15 min.
TOTAL 20 min.

- ¼ cup light mayonnaise
- ½ tsp. chili powder
- 1 clove garlic, minced
- 1 Tbsp. olive oil
- 1½ tsp. white wine vinegar
- 3 cups mixed baby greens or arugula
- 4 large portobello mushrooms
- 2 tsp. olive oil
- ¼ tsp. salt
- ¼ tsp. black pepper
- 4 6-inch Greek pita flatbread rounds, warmed
- ¼ cup crumbled blue cheese

1. In a bowl stir together mayonnaise, chili powder, and garlic. In another bowl whisk together the 1 Tbsp. olive oil and the vinegar. Add greens; toss to coat.

2. Remove and discard stems from mushrooms. Slice mushroom caps into ½-inch-thick slices. In a 10-inch skillet heat the 2 tsp. olive oil over medium-high. Add mushrooms; sprinkle with salt and pepper. Cook about 5 minutes or until tender and golden on edges, stirring occasionally.

3. Spread mayonnaise mixture on pita bread rounds. Top with greens and mushrooms. Sprinkle evenly with cheese. Fold pita rounds over for sandwiches or eat open-face.

Tip If desired, use pita pockets instead of pita flatbread. Fill pita pocket with aïoli, greens, mushrooms, and blue cheese.

PER SERVING *(1 sandwich each)* **CAL** 320, **FAT** 13 g (3 g sat. fat), **CHOL** 9 mg, **SODIUM** 715 mg, **CARB** 42 g (4 g fiber, 5 g sugars), **PRO** 11 g

Pan-Roasted
Vegetable
Quinoa
with Eggs

Pan-Roasted Vegetable Quinoa with Eggs

39 g CARB | **SERVES** 4
HANDS ON 35 min.
TOTAL 40 min.

- 2 cups reduced-sodium vegetable broth or water
- 1 cup quinoa, rinsed and drained
- 2 cups sliced cremini mushrooms
- 1 large red onion, cut into thin wedges
- 1 cup sliced halved yellow summer squash
- 1 Tbsp. olive oil
- 2 cups torn fresh baby kale or spinach
- 1 cup grape tomatoes, halved
- 1 tsp. fresh thyme leaves
- ¼ tsp. salt
- ¼ tsp. black pepper
- 2 tsp. olive oil
- 4 eggs

1. In a medium saucepan bring broth to boiling. Stir in quinoa; reduce heat. Simmer, covered, about 15 minutes or until quinoa is tender. Drain if necessary.

2. Meanwhile, in a 10-inch skillet cook mushrooms, onion, and yellow squash in 1 Tbsp. hot oil over medium-high about 5 minutes or until tender, stirring frequently. Stir in the next five ingredients (through pepper). Reduce heat to medium. Cook about 3 minutes or until tomatoes soften. Stir into cooked quinoa.

3. Wipe out skillet. Heat the 2 tsp. oil in the same skillet over medium. Break eggs into skillet. Reduce heat to low. Cook eggs 3 to 4 minutes or until whites are completely set and yolks start to thicken. If desired, turn the eggs and cook 30 seconds more (for over-easy). Serve eggs over quinoa mixture. If desired, sprinkle eggs with additional pepper.

PER SERVING *(1¼ cups quinoa mixture + 1 egg each)* **CAL** 342, **FAT** 14 g (3 g sat. fat), **CHOL** 186 mg, **SODIUM** 515 mg, **CARB** 39 g (6 g fiber, 6 g sugars), **PRO** 18 g

BUILD A *HEALTHY* PLATE

One of the easiest ways to control portions doesn't even require using measuring cups or carb-counting books. Instead, plate healthful meals using the simple method described throughout this chapter.

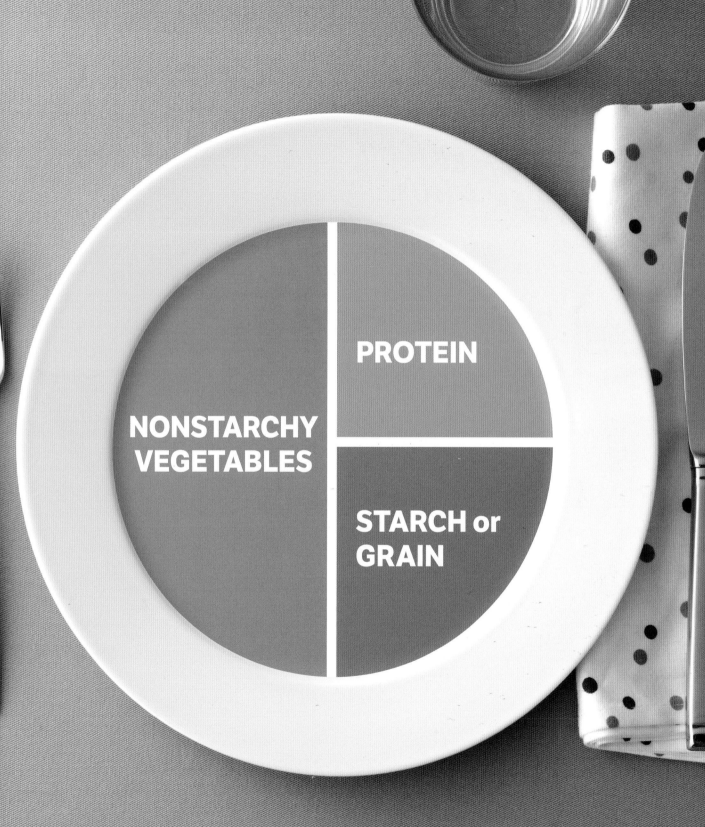

NONSTARCHY VEGETABLES

PROTEIN

STARCH or GRAIN

PLATE #1

ALL-AMERICAN STEAK DINNER

¼ PLATE
Starch, Grain, or Other Carb: potatoes, wine

½ PLATE
Nonstarchy Veggies: broccoli, carrots, mushrooms

¼ PLATE
Protein: beef

A flavorful red wine sauce gives basic pan-seared steak a lift in this satisfying take on meat and potatoes that has only 30 grams of carb per plate.

Wine-Glazed Steak

10 g CARB | **SERVES** 4
TOTAL 30 min.

- 1 lb. boneless beef top sirloin steak, cut ½ to ¾ inch thick
- 1 Tbsp. olive oil
- 2 cups sliced fresh mushrooms
- 4 cloves garlic, minced
- ¼ tsp. crushed red pepper
- ½ cup dry red wine or low-calorie cranberry juice
- ¼ cup balsamic vinegar
- 2 Tbsp. reduced-sodium soy sauce
- 2 tsp. honey

1. Trim fat from steak; cut steak into four equal portions. In a 10-inch skillet heat oil over medium-high. Add steaks. Reduce heat to medium; cook 10 to 13 minutes or until desired doneness (145°F for medium rare or 160°F for medium), turning steaks occasionally. If steaks brown too quickly, reduce heat to medium-low. Transfer steaks to plates; keep warm.

2. Add mushrooms to skillet; cook and stir 2 minutes. Spoon mushrooms over steaks. Add garlic and red pepper to skillet; cook and stir 30 seconds. Remove skillet from heat and carefully add wine or cranberry juice. Return to heat. Boil gently, uncovered, 3 to 5 minutes or until most of the liquid is evaporated. Add balsamic vinegar, soy sauce, and honey; return to simmering. Cook and stir about 2 minutes or until slightly thickened. Spoon sauce over steaks.

PER SERVING *(1 steak portion + about 2 Tbsp. mushroom mixture each)* **CAL** 229, **FAT** 7 g (2 g sat. fat), **CHOL** 57 mg, **SODIUM** 335 mg, **CARB** 10 g (1 g fiber, 7 g sugars), **PRO** 23 g

Steak Fries

14 g CARB | **SERVES** 4
HANDS ON 15 min.
TOTAL 45 min.

- 3 large red and/or yellow potatoes (about 12 oz. total)
- 2 tsp. olive oil
- ¼ tsp. dried rosemary, crushed
- ¼ tsp. dried thyme, crushed
- ¼ tsp. salt
- ⅛ to ¼ tsp. black pepper

1. Preheat oven to 450°F. Cut each potato into eight wedges. In a large bowl stir together the remaining ingredients. Add the potato wedges; toss to coat. Spread wedges in a single layer in a shallow roasting pan. Bake 30 to 35 minutes or until crisp, turning once.

PER SERVING *(6 wedges each)* **CAL** 80, **FAT** 2 g (0 g sat. fat), **CHOL** 0 mg, **SODIUM** 161 mg, **CARB** 14 g (2 g fiber, 1 g sugars), **PRO** 2 g

Steamed Broccoli and Carrots

7 g CARB | **SERVES** 4
TOTAL 10 min.

- 1 stalk broccoli
- 2 medium carrots

1. Wash and remove outer leaves and tough parts of broccoli stalk. Break into 3 cups florets. Peel and cut carrots into ½- to 1-inch pieces. Place steamer basket in a saucepan. Add water to just below bottom of basket. Bring water to boiling. Add vegetables to steamer basket. Cover pan; reduce heat. Steam vegetables 8 to 10 minutes or until crisp-tender.

PER SERVING *(1 cup each)* **CAL** 36, **FAT** 0 g, **CHOL** 0 mg, **SODIUM** 44 mg, **CARB** 7 g (3 g fiber, 3 g sugars), **PRO** 2 g

START WITH A 9-INCH PLATE

Portion control is easier when your plate is no more than 9 inches wide. If your dinnerware plates are larger than that, fill just inside the rim. A shallow rimmed bowl (like a pasta bowl) is also a good option as long as it measures 9 inches wide or less. Along with a right-size plate, use a 1-cup glass for milk, a ½-cup dish for fruit or dessert, and a 1-cup bowl for cereal or soup.

PLATE #2

ITALIAN-STYLE FEAST

½ PLATE
Nonstarchy Veggies: lettuce, spinach, mushrooms, dried tomatoes, red onion

¼ PLATE
Starch or Grain: pasta

¼ PLATE
Protein: turkey, cheese

Choose multigrain pasta over regular pasta whenever you can. The multigrain version contains more fiber and protein, making it a health-smart option.

Meatballs with Dried Tomato Sauce

25 g
CARB

SERVES 4

TOTAL 25 min.

Nonstick cooking spray
1 12-oz. pkg. (12) refrigerated or frozen cooked Italian-style turkey meatballs
1 clove garlic, minced
1 cup water
½ cup coarsely chopped dried tomatoes (not oil-packed)
1 Tbsp. balsamic vinegar
2 Tbsp. snipped fresh basil or 2 tsp. snipped fresh oregano
4 oz. dried multigrain spaghetti, cooked according to package directions
2 Tbsp. finely shredded Parmesan cheese

1. Coat an unheated 10-inch nonstick skillet with cooking spray. Heat over medium. Add meatballs; cook 5 to 10 minutes or until browned and heated, turning occasionally.
2. For sauce, lightly coat an unheated small saucepan with cooking spray; heat over medium. Add garlic to hot pan; cook and stir 10 seconds. Add water; bring to boiling. Remove from heat and add dried tomatoes. Cover and let stand 5 minutes. Transfer tomato mixture to a blender or food processor and add vinegar. Cover and blend until smooth. Stir in basil.
3. Add sauce to skillet with meatballs. Cook 1 minute or until sauce is heated, stirring to coat meatballs with sauce.
4. Serve meatballs and sauce over hot cooked spaghetti and sprinkle with Parmesan cheese.

PER SERVING *(3 meatballs + ½ cup spaghetti + ¼ cup sauce each)* **CAL** 310, **FAT** 13 g (4 g sat. fat), **CHOL** 93 mg, **SODIUM** 459 mg, **CARB** 25 g (3 g fiber, 4 g sugars), **PRO** 23 g

Leafy Green Salad

6 g
CARB

SERVES 4

TOTAL 10 min.

2 cups torn romaine lettuce
2 cups fresh baby spinach
½ cup thinly sliced red onion
½ cup thinly sliced fresh mushrooms
3 Tbsp. balsamic vinegar
1 Tbsp. olive oil

1. In a large bowl toss together the lettuce, spinach, red onion, and mushrooms. For dressing, in a screw-top jar combine balsamic vinegar and olive oil. Shake well. Drizzle dressing over salad and toss to coat.

PER SERVING *(1¼ cups each)* **CAL** 58, **FAT** 4 g (0 g sat. fat), **CHOL** 0 mg, **SODIUM** 17 mg, **CARB** 6 g (1 g fiber, 3 g sugars), **PRO** 1 g

DIVIDE YOUR PLATE

The plate method is a simple strategy to get your eating on track. If you mentally divide your plate into sections, it is easier to plan a balanced meal with the right mix of nutrients (including carbohydrate, protein, and fat) for better control of glucose and weight.

Divide your plate into the following categories.

½ NONSTARCHY VEGETABLES

Make nonstarchy vegetables the star of your meal. For variety, pick two nonstarchy vegetables per meal.

¼ STARCH OR GRAIN

This can be a serving of bread, pasta, rice, beans, or starchy vegetable. (Men may need two servings of starch.) Choose whole grains and beans to give meals a fiber boost.

¼ PROTEIN

Lean meat, fish, tofu, eggs, cheese, and nuts play a smaller than traditional role.

129

PLATE #3

MEDITERRANEAN TAPAS

¼ PLATE
Starch, Grain, or Other Carb: pita bread, hummus

½ PLATE
Nonstarchy Veggies: sweet peppers, cucumber

¼ PLATE
Protein: pork, hummus, yogurt

This appetizer-style plate of fresh and flavorful finger foods is a fun way to eat a well-balanced meal.

Greek Pork Tenderloin

4 g
CARB

SERVES 4
HANDS ON 20 min.
TOTAL 55 min.

- 1 lb. pork tenderloin
- 1 Tbsp. lemon zest
- ½ tsp. dried oregano, crushed
- ¼ tsp. salt
- ¼ tsp. dried rosemary, crushed
- ⅛ tsp. black pepper
- 2 tsp. olive oil
- 1 6-oz. carton plain low-fat yogurt
- 2 Tbsp. snipped fresh mint
- 1 clove garlic, minced

1. Preheat oven to 425°F. Trim fat from pork. In a bowl combine the next five ingredients (through pepper). Sprinkle over all sides of the pork and rub in with your fingers.
2. In a 10-inch oven-going skillet heat oil over medium-high. Add roast to hot skillet; cook about 4 minutes or until browned, turning to brown all sides. Transfer skillet to oven. Roast about 20 minutes or until done (145°F). Remove from oven and let stand, covered, 3 minutes.
3. Meanwhile, for sauce, in a bowl combine yogurt, mint, and garlic. Thinly slice pork and serve with yogurt mixture.

PER SERVING *(3½ oz. cooked pork + about 3 Tbsp. sauce each)* **CAL** 174, **FAT** 5 g (2 g sat. fat), **CHOL** 76 mg, **SODIUM** 236 mg, **CARB** 4 g (1 g fiber, 3 g sugars), **PRO** 26 g

Pita Bread Wedges

Preheat oven to 350°F. Wrap **2 whole wheat pita bread rounds** in foil. Bake about 10 minutes or until warm. To serve, cut each round into six wedges. Place three wedges on each plate. Makes 4 servings.

PER SERVING *(3 wedges each)* **CAL** 83, **FAT** 0 g, **CHOL** 0 mg, **SODIUM** 161 mg, **CARB** 17 g (1 g fiber, 0 g sugars), **PRO** 3 g

Crisp Vegetables

Cut **2 medium red sweet peppers** into strips to make 2 cups. Cut **1 large cucumber** into sticks to make 2 cups. Place ½ cup sweet pepper strips and ½ cup cucumber sticks on each plate. Makes 4 servings.

PER SERVING *(1 cup each)* **CAL** 27, **FAT** 0 g, **CHOL** 0 mg, **SODIUM** 3 mg, **CARB** 6 g (2 g fiber, 3 g sugars), **PRO** 1 g

Hummus

Using **one 7-oz. container roasted red pepper hummus**, spoon 3 Tbsp. hummus onto each plate. Makes 4 servings.

PER SERVING *(3 Tbsp. each)* **CAL** 92, **FAT** 6 g (0 g sat. fat), **CHOL** 0 mg, **SODIUM** 276 mg, **CARB** 9 q (1 g fiber, 1 g sugars), **PRO** 2 g

TAKE YOUR PICK

Create your own plate: Choose one item from each category, swapping for your favorite foods that fit into the sections.

LEAN PROTEIN

- Plain fish
- Skinless chicken breast
- Pork loin chop
- Low-fat cheese
- ¾ cup egg product, scrambled

STARCH OR GRAIN

- ½ cup corn
- ½ cup potatoes
- ½ cup green peas
- Half of a whole wheat English muffin
- 5 whole wheat crackers

NONSTARCHY VEGGIES

- Brussels sprouts
- Cauliflower
- Mixed salad greens
- Asparagus
- Carrot sticks and radishes

PLATE #4

BURGERS & SLAW

¼ PLATE
Starch or Grain:
whole wheat bun

½ PLATE
Nonstarchy
Veggies: broccoli
slaw mix, onion,
tomato, lettuce

¼ PLATE
Protein: lentils,
almonds, egg

Cooked lentils provide lean protein and meatlike
texture in these pan-fried burgers. Follow the
package directions when cooking the lentils.

Almond-Lentil Burgers

31 g
CARB

SERVES 4
HANDS ON 25 min.
TOTAL 50 min.

- 1 carrot
- ¼ of a medium red onion
- 5 tsp. olive oil
- ½ cup finely chopped celery
- 3 cloves garlic, minced
- 5 low-calorie whole wheat hamburger buns
- ⅓ cup sliced almonds, toasted
- 2 tsp. fresh oregano leaves
- 1 tsp. lemon zest
- ¼ tsp. salt
- ¼ tsp. black pepper
- ¾ cup cooked lentils
- 1 egg or ¼ cup refrigerated or frozen egg product, thawed
- 4 lettuce leaves
- 4 tomato slices
- 4 thin slices red onion

1. Using a large-hole grater, grate the carrot and the one-fourth onion. In an 8-inch skillet heat 2 tsp. of the oil over medium. Cook and stir grated vegetables, celery, and garlic in hot oil 4 to 5 minutes or until just crisp-tender. Remove from heat.

2. In a food processor process one of the hamburger buns to coarse crumbs. Measure out ½ cup; discard any remaining crumbs. Return the ½ cup crumbs to the food processor along with the next five ingredients (through pepper) and half of the lentils. Process until finely ground.

3. In a large bowl whisk egg. Add processed mixture, unprocessed lentils, and cooked carrot mixture; mix until combined. Let stand 20 minutes. Divide

mixture evenly into four portions and roll into balls; flatten with the palms of your hands into ¾-inch-thick patties.

4. Toast the remaining four buns. In a 10-inch nonstick skillet heat remaining 3 teaspoons oil over medium. Add burgers. Cook 6 to 8 minutes or until crisp and browned (160°F), turning once. Serve burgers on toasted buns with lettuce leaves, tomato slices, and onion slices.

PER SERVING (1 burger each) **CAL** 274, **FAT** 12 g (2 g sat. fat), **CHOL** 47 mg, **SODIUM** 372 mg, **CARB** 31 g (12 g fiber, 6 g sugars), **PRO** 12 g

Lemony Broccoli Slaw

12 g
CARB

SERVES 4
HANDS ON 15 min.
TOTAL 1 hr. 15 min.

- 1 small lemon
- 2 Tbsp. light mayonnaise
- 2 Tbsp. plain low-fat yogurt
- 1 Tbsp. honey
- 1 tsp. cider vinegar
- ¼ tsp. salt
- ¼ tsp. black pepper
- 4 cups packaged shredded broccoli (broccoli slaw mix)
- ¼ cup thinly sliced red onion
- 2 Tbsp. snipped fresh parsley
- 1 Tbsp. sliced almonds, toasted

1. Remove ¼ tsp. zest and squeeze 1 tsp. juice from lemon. In a large bowl combine zest, juice, and the next six ingredients (through pepper); mix well. Add the broccoli, red onion, and parsley. Stir until well combined. Cover and chill 1 to 4 hours. To serve, sprinkle slaw with almonds.

Tip To toast whole nuts or large pieces, spread them in a shallow baking pan lined with parchment paper. Bake in a 350°F oven 5 to 10 minutes or until golden, shaking pan once or twice.

PER SERVING (1 cup each) **CAL** 84, **FAT** 3 g (1 g sat. fat), **CHOL** 3 mg, **SODIUM** 225 mg, **CARB** 12 g (2 g fiber, 8 g sugars), **PRO** 3 g

USE THIS METHOD DINING OUT

Don't be afraid to ask the server for substitutions. If a grilled chicken dinner comes with corn, potatoes, and a roll, which are all starches, ask to swap two of them for steamed or sautéed nonstarchy vegetables, such as broccoli and asparagus.

PLATE #5

QUINOA BOWL

½ PLATE
Nonstarchy
Veggies: sweet
peppers, onion,
bok choy

¼ PLATE
Starch or Grain:
quinoa

¼ PLATE
Protein: tofu,
peanut butter,
quinoa

Quinoa is a cholesterol-free and low-fat
source of protein, making it a great substitute
for cooked rice in any stir-fried meal.

Spicy Peanut-Sauced Tofu Stir-Fry

26 g
CARB

SERVES 4
HANDS ON 10 min.
TOTAL 40 min.

- 1 12- to 14-oz. pkg. light extra-firm tofu, drained
- 1 Tbsp. olive oil
- ½ cup cold water
- 2 tsp. cornstarch
- ⅓ cup creamy peanut butter
- ¼ cup reduced-sodium soy sauce
- ¼ cup rice vinegar
- 2 Tbsp. honey
- 1 Tbsp. grated fresh ginger
- ¼ tsp. crushed red pepper
- 2 cloves garlic, minced
- 2 medium red sweet peppers, cut into strips
- 1 medium red onion, cut into thin wedges
- 4 cups sliced bok choy or small broccoli florets

1. Drain tofu and pat it dry. Cut into 1-inch cubes. In a 12-inch skillet heat 1 tsp. of the olive oil over medium. Add tofu cubes and cook on one side about 6 minutes or until browned and slightly crisp. Gently turn the tofu over and add another 1 tsp. of the oil. Continue cooking until all sides are browned and slightly crisp. Using a spatula, transfer tofu from pan to a bowl.

2. For peanut sauce, in a small saucepan stir the cold water into the cornstarch. Stir in the next six ingredients (through crushed red pepper). Cook and stir over medium until thickened and bubbly; cook and stir 1 minute more.

3. In the same skillet that was used for tofu heat the remaining 1 tsp. oil over medium-high. Add garlic, sweet peppers, and red onion; cook and stir 5 minutes. Add bok choy; cook and stir 2 minutes more. Add the browned tofu and peanut sauce; stir gently to coat and heat. If desired, sprinkle with additional crushed red pepper.

PER SERVING (1¼ cups stir-fry each)
CAL 292, FAT 15 g (3 g sat. fat), CHOL 0 mg, SODIUM 770 mg, CARB 26 g (4 g fiber, 18 g sugars), PRO 13 g

Quinoa

In a medium saucepan bring **1½ cups water** to boiling. Add **¾ cup rinsed and drained quinoa.** Reduce heat. Cover and simmer about 15 minutes or until done. Drain any excess water. Divide quinoa among plates. Makes 4 servings.

PER SERVING (½ cup each) CAL 117, FAT 2 g (0 g sat. fat), CHOL 0 mg, SODIUM 4 mg, CARB 20 g (2 g fiber, 0 g sugars), PRO 5 g

PORTION WITHOUT THE PLATE

If you don't have your 9-inch plate to help you measure, hold out your hand. This measuring tool is always with you. While not exact, these approximations are better than a guess.

1. Knuckles = ½ cup
2. Whole fist = 1 cup

3. Palm of hand = 3 ounces

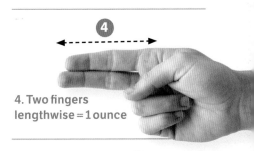

4. Two fingers lengthwise = 1 ounce

5. Tip of thumb = 1 teaspoon
6. Length of thumb = 1 tablespoon

PLATE #6
SURF & TURF KABOBS

½ PLATE
Nonstarchy Veggies: fennel, carrots, green onions, watercress

¼ PLATE
Starch or Grain: rice vermicelli, edamame

¼ PLATE
Protein: shrimp, chicken, edamame

Hot-off-the-grill kabobs and a cool Asian noodle salad make a pleasing summertime meal.

Miso-Marinated Shrimp and Chicken Skewers

3 g
CARB

SERVES 4
HANDS ON 25 min.
TOTAL 1 hr. 30 min.

- 12 oz. fresh or frozen large shrimp in shells
- 8 oz. skinless, boneless chicken breast halves
- 1 lime
- 2 Tbsp. rice vinegar
- 2 Tbsp. canola oil
- 2 Tbsp. miso (soybean paste)
- 1 tsp. grated fresh ginger
- 8 10-inch skewers

1. If using wooden skewers, soak in water 30 minutes. Thaw shrimp, if frozen. Peel and devein shrimp, leaving tails intact if desired. Rinse shrimp and pat dry. Place shrimp in a large resealable plastic bag set in a shallow bowl. Cut chicken breast halves lengthwise into ½-inch-thick strips. Place chicken strips in another large resealable plastic bag set in a shallow bowl.
2. For marinade, remove 1 tsp. zest and squeeze 2 Tbsp. juice from lime. In a bowl whisk together zest, juice, vinegar, oil, miso, and ginger. Pour half of the marinade over shrimp in bag. Pour remaining half of marinade over chicken in bag. Seal bags, turning to coat shrimp and chicken. Marinate in the refrigerator 1 to 2 hours, turning bags once or twice.
3. Drain and discard marinade from shrimp and chicken. Thread shrimp onto four skewers, leaving ¼ inch between shrimp pieces. Thread chicken strips, accordion-style, onto four skewers, leaving ¼-inch spaces.

4. Grill skewers, uncovered, over medium heat 6 to 10 minutes or until shrimp turn opaque and chicken is no longer pink, turning once. Remove skewers from the grill as they get done and keep warm.

PER SERVING (1 shrimp skewer + 1 chicken skewer each) **CAL** 166, **FAT** 7 g (1 g sat. fat), **CHOL** 108 mg, **SODIUM** 614 mg, **CARB** 3 g (0 g fiber, 1 g sugars), **PRO** 21 g

Edamame, Vermicelli, and Watercress Salad

23 g
CARB

SERVES 4
TOTAL 30 min.

- 2 oz. dried rice vermicelli or angel hair pasta
- 1 medium fennel bulb, trimmed, cored, and cut into thin strips
- 1 cup frozen shelled edamame, thawed
- 1 cup purchased coarsely shredded carrots
- 2 green onions, thinly sliced
- 3 Tbsp. rice vinegar
- 1 Tbsp. toasted sesame oil
- ¼ tsp. crushed red pepper
- ⅛ tsp. salt
- 4 cups fresh watercress, tough stems removed

1. Prepare rice vermicelli or pasta according to package directions; drain. Place the noodles in a large bowl. Add fennel, edamame, carrots, and green onions.
2. For dressing, in a screw-top jar combine vinegar, oil, crushed red pepper, and the salt. Cover and shake

well. Pour over edamame mixture; toss gently to coat. To serve, top watercress with edamame mixture.

PER SERVING (1 cup watercress + about 1 cup noodle mixture each) **CAL** 177, **FAT** 6 g (1 g sat. fat), **CHOL** 0 mg, **SODIUM** 160 mg, **CARB** 23 g (5 g fiber, 3 g sugars), **PRO** 7 g

ADDING TO YOUR MEAL

Good choices mean you have flexibility in eating.

ON THE SIDE

For at least one meal each day, and as your calorie allowance permits, enjoy a cup of low-fat milk or light yogurt and a small piece of fruit or ½ cup cut-up fruit. When you pick low-fat options, a meal with these side items and each of the three plate components typically totals fewer than 50 grams of carbohydrate and fewer than 500 calories.

PLATE #7

SEARED SALMON SUPPER

½ PLATE
Nonstarchy Veggies: asparagus, leek, sweet pepper, mushrooms, shallot

¼ PLATE
Starch, Grain, or Other Carb: potatoes, white wine

¼ PLATE
Protein: salmon

It's so easy—while the potatoes and asparagus are roasting in the oven, you can turn your attention to the salmon searing on the stove top.

Seared Salmon with Mushroom-Shallot Sauce

2 g CARB

SERVES 4
HANDS ON 20 min.
TOTAL 30 min.

- 4 4-oz. fresh or frozen skinless salmon fillets
- ¼ tsp. black pepper
- ⅛ tsp. salt
- 2 tsp. olive oil
- 1 cup sliced fresh cremini or button mushrooms
- 2 Tbsp. finely chopped shallot
- ⅓ cup dry white wine or reduced-sodium chicken broth
- 1 Tbsp. Dijon-style mustard
- 2 tsp. snipped fresh thyme or ½ tsp. dried thyme, crushed

1. Thaw fish, if frozen. Rinse fish and pat dry. Sprinkle with the pepper and salt. Measure thickness of fillets. In a 10-inch nonstick skillet cook salmon in hot oil over medium 4 to 6 minutes per ½-inch thickness or until salmon flakes easily, carefully turning once. Remove from skillet; cover and keep warm.
2. Add mushrooms and shallot to the same skillet. Cook 3 to 5 minutes over medium or until tender, stirring occasionally. Remove from heat and carefully add wine, mustard, and thyme. Cook and stir 1 to 2 minutes or until well combined and heated. To serve, top salmon with mushroom sauce.

PER SERVING *(1 salmon fillet + about 2 Tbsp. sauce each)* **CAL** 284, **FAT** 17 g (4 g sat. fat), **CHOL** 62 mg, **SODIUM** 232 mg, **CARB** 2 g (0 g fiber, 1 g sugars), **PRO** 24 g

Roasted Potatoes and Leeks

19 g CARB

SERVES 4
HANDS ON 15 min.
TOTAL 50 min.

- Nonstick cooking spray
- 12 oz. tiny new potatoes, scrubbed and quartered
- 1 Tbsp. olive oil
- ¼ tsp. salt
- ⅛ tsp. black pepper
- 1 medium red sweet pepper, cut into bite-size strips
- 1 medium leek, trimmed and cut into ¼-inch-thick slices (white part only)

1. Preheat oven to 425°F. Coat a 13×9-inch baking pan with cooking spray; add potatoes to pan. Drizzle with oil and sprinkle with salt and black pepper; toss to coat.
2. Roast, uncovered, 25 minutes, stirring once. Add sweet pepper and leek; toss to combine. Roast about 10 minutes more or until potatoes are tender and browned on the edges and pepper pieces are just tender.

PER SERVING *(¾ cup each)* **CAL** 112, **FAT** 4 g (1 g sat. fat), **CHOL** 0 mg, **SODIUM** 166 mg, **CARB** 19 g (2 g fiber, 3 g sugars), **PRO** 2 g

Quick Roasted Asparagus

2 g CARB

SERVES 4
HANDS ON 10 min.
TOTAL 20 min.

- 1 lb. fresh asparagus, trimmed
- 1 Tbsp. olive oil
- ⅛ tsp. salt
- ⅛ tsp. black pepper

1. Preheat oven to 425°F. Arrange asparagus in a shallow roasting pan. Drizzle with the oil and sprinkle with the salt and pepper. Toss to coat and arrange asparagus in an even layer. Roast, uncovered, 8 to 10 minutes or until crisp-tender, tossing once.

PER SERVING *(9 spears each)* **CAL** 42, **FAT** 3 g (0 g sat. fat), **CHOL** 0 mg, **SODIUM** 74 mg, **CARB** 2 g (1 g fiber, 1 g sugars), **PRO** 1 g

WATCH THE HEIGHT

Don't fall into the trap of piling food too high on your plate to make up for the plate's smaller size. Food should be no more than ½ inch high.

PLATE #8

ASIAN-STYLE NOODLE BOWL

½ PLATE
Nonstarchy Veggies: carrots, mushrooms, celery, pea pods, bok choy

¼ PLATE
Protein: pork

¼ PLATE
Starch or Grain: soba noodles

Five-Spice Pork and Soba Noodle Bowls

37 g
CARB

SERVES 4
HANDS ON 30 min.
TOTAL 45 min.

12 oz. pork tenderloin, cut into very thin bite-size strips
1½ tsp. five-spice powder
¼ tsp. ground ginger
     Nonstick cooking spray
2 cups thinly sliced carrots
2 cups thinly sliced, stemmed shiitake and/or button mushrooms
½ cup thinly sliced celery
1 Tbsp. canola oil
3 cups water
1 cup no-salt-added chicken broth
4 oz. dry soba (buckwheat noodles)
1 Tbsp. all-purpose flour
1 Tbsp. reduced-sodium soy sauce
3 cups thickly sliced, trimmed bok choy
2 cups snow peas, trimmed
½ cup thinly sliced green onions
¼ cup orange juice

1. In a medium bowl toss pork strips with five-spice powder and ginger. Coat an unheated 4- to 6-qt. nonstick Dutch oven with cooking spray. Heat over medium-high. Add pork strips. Cook 4 to 6 minutes or until pork is browned, stirring occasionally. Remove pork from pan.
2. In the same pan cook carrots, mushrooms, and celery in hot oil over medium 5 minutes, stirring occasionally. Add water and broth. Bring to boiling. Add soba; return to boiling and cook, uncovered, 3 to 4 minutes or until noodles are just tender.
3. Meanwhile, in a small bowl stir together flour and soy sauce until smooth. Add to noodle mixture along with bok choy, snow peas, green onions, and cooked pork. Cook and stir until just boiling; cook and stir 1 minute more. Remove from heat. Stir in orange juice.

PER SERVING (2 cups each) **CAL** 302, **FAT** 6 g (1 g sat. fat), **CHOL** 55 mg, **SODIUM** 541 mg, **CARB** 37 g (5 g fiber, 7 g sugars), **PRO** 27 g

PLATING COMBOS

You can use the plate method with mixed dishes such as casseroles, pizza, tacos, and sandwiches. Just break down the ingredients separately. A salad with grilled chicken and croutons could cover every category: greens, carrots, and tomatoes for the nonstarchy vegetables; chicken for the protein; and croutons for the starch or grain. Assemble casseroles in layers so you can see how much meat versus vegetables you are getting.

When in doubt, put a casserole with pasta, rice, or beans in the starch section.

An assortment of vitamin-packed vegetables pairs with pork and buckwheat noodles in this one-bowl meal that fits the healthful formula: half nonstarchy vegetables, a quarter protein, and a quarter grains.

PLATE #9

MAKE IT MOROCCAN

½ PLATE
Nonstarchy
Veggies:
Broccolini,
sweet pepper

¼ PLATE
Starch or Grain:
couscous,
garbanzo beans

¼ PLATE
Protein: chicken,
garbanzo beans

**Removing the skin from chicken thighs makes
them a healthful option. And there is plenty of
flavor once these Moroccan spice-coated thighs
are browned and baked to perfection.**

Moroccan Chicken Thighs

4 g
CARB

SERVES 4
HANDS ON 15 min.
TOTAL 55 min.

- 2 Tbsp. all-purpose flour
- 1 tsp. chili powder
- ½ tsp. ground cumin
- ½ tsp. ground ginger
- ¼ tsp. ground cinnamon
- 4 5-oz. bone-in chicken thighs, skinned
- 2 tsp. canola oil

1. Preheat oven to 375°F. In a large resealable plastic bag combine the first five ingredients (through cinnamon). Add chicken thighs to bag, one at a time, shaking to coat.
2. In a 12-inch oven-going skillet heat oil over medium-high. Add chicken thighs. Cook 5 to 6 minutes or until browned, turning once.
3. Transfer skillet to oven. Bake, uncovered, 35 to 40 minutes or until chicken is tender and done (170°F).

PER SERVING (1 chicken thigh each) **CAL** 138, **FAT** 6 g (1 g sat. fat), **CHOL** 81 mg, **SODIUM** 72 mg, **CARB** 4 g (0 g fiber, 0 g sugars), **PRO** 17 g

---

Steamed Broccolini

Trim **1 bunch broccolini** and measure 4 cups. Place steamer basket in a saucepan. Add **water** to just below the bottom of the basket. Bring water to boiling. Add Broccolini to steamer basket. Cover pan and reduce heat. Steam 6 to 8 minutes or until tender. Sprinkle lightly with a **dash salt.** Makes 4 servings.

PER SERVING (1 cup each) **CAL** 31, **FAT** 0 g, **CHOL** 0 mg, **SODIUM** 67 mg, **CARB** 6 g (2 g fiber, 2 g sugars), **PRO** 3 g

Moroccan-Style Couscous

38 g
CARB

SERVES 4
HANDS ON 15 min.
TOTAL 25 min.

- 2 tsp. canola oil
- ⅓ cup chopped onion
- ¼ cup chopped red sweet pepper
- 2 cloves garlic, minced
- 1 cup reduced-sodium chicken broth
- ½ tsp. chili powder
- ¼ tsp. salt
- ¼ tsp. ground cumin
- ¼ tsp. ground ginger
- ⅛ tsp. ground cinnamon
- ⅛ tsp. black pepper
- ⅔ cup couscous or whole wheat couscous
- ¼ cup no-added-salt canned garbanzo beans (chickpeas), rinsed and drained
- ¼ cup golden raisins
- 2 Tbsp. sliced green olives

1. In a small saucepan heat oil over medium. Add onion, sweet pepper, and garlic. Cook and stir about 5 minutes or until just softened.
2. Carefully add the next seven ingredients (through black pepper) to the saucepan; bring to boiling. Stir in couscous, garbanzo beans, raisins, and olives; remove from heat. Cover and let stand 5 minutes. Fluff couscous with a fork. Serve immediately.

PER SERVING (¾ cup each) **CAL** 206, **FAT** 3 g (0 g sat. fat), **CHOL** 0 mg, **SODIUM** 370 mg, **CARB** 38 g (3 g fiber, 7 g sugars), **PRO** 6 g

GO EASY ON THE EXTRAS

Choose low-fat versions of salad dressings, sauces, and spreads and skimp on the amounts.

PLATE #10

SUNDAY BRUNCH

½ PLATE

Nonstarchy
Veggies:
spinach,
mushrooms,
onion

¼ PLATE

Starch or Grain:
piecrust

¼ PLATE

Protein: chicken,
eggs, cheese

This plate showcases all the
components that make a
healthful meal. Add a sweet
bonus—a bowl of fresh berries.

Chicken-Spinach Quiche

15 g
CARB

SERVES 8
HANDS ON 30 min.
TOTAL 1 hr. 40 min.

- ½ of a 15-oz. pkg. rolled refrigerated unbaked piecrust (1 piecrust) Nonstick cooking spray
- 6 oz. skinless, boneless chicken breast, cut into ¾-inch chunks
- 2 cups shredded fresh spinach (about 2 oz.)
- 2 cups refrigerated or frozen egg product, thawed, or 8 eggs, lightly beaten
- ¾ cup shredded Gruyère or Swiss cheese (3 oz.)
- ½ cup fat-free milk
- ⅓ cup chopped roasted red sweet peppers
- 2 tsp. snipped fresh thyme or ¾ tsp. dried thyme, crushed
- ¼ tsp. salt
- ¼ tsp. black pepper

1. Preheat oven to 425°F. Let piecrust stand at room temperature according to package directions. Line a 9-inch pie plate with piecrust. Crimp edge as desired. Line unpricked piecrust with a double thickness of foil. Bake 8 minutes. Remove foil. Bake 4 to 5 minutes more or until piecrust is set and dry. Remove from oven. Reduce oven temperature to 350°F.
2. Coat an unheated 8-inch skillet with cooking spray. Heat skillet over medium. Add chicken to skillet; cook and stir 6 to 8 minutes or until chicken is no longer pink. Remove chicken from skillet. Return skillet to heat. Add spinach; cook over medium heat 1 to 2 minutes or until wilted, turning frequently.

3. In a large bowl whisk together chicken, spinach, and the remaining ingredients. Pour egg mixture into baked piecrust.
4. Bake 40 minutes. If necessary to prevent overbrowning, cover edge of quiche with foil. Bake 5 to 10 minutes more or until a knife inserted near center comes out clean. Let stand on a wire rack 10 minutes before serving. Cut into wedges.

Tip Cover leftover quiche with plastic wrap and refrigerate up to 24 hours. To reheat, preheat oven to 350°F. Remove plastic wrap from quiche. Cover loosely with foil. Bake about 40 minutes or until heated through (165°F).

PER SERVING (1 wedge each) **CAL** 209, **FAT** 10 g (5 g sat. fat), **CHOL** 28 mg, **SODIUM** 396 mg, **CARB** 15 g (1 g fiber, 1 g sugars), **PRO** 15 g

---

Baby Mixed Green Salad

5 g
CARB

SERVES 4
TOTAL 15 min.

- 5 cups baby mixed greens
- 1 cup sliced fresh mushrooms
- ½ cup thinly sliced red onion
- 1 Tbsp. white wine vinegar
- 1 Tbsp. lemon juice
- 1 Tbsp. olive oil
- 1 tsp. snipped fresh thyme
- 1 clove garlic, minced
- ¼ tsp. salt
- ¼ tsp. black pepper

1. In a medium bowl toss together the baby greens, mushrooms, and red onion.

2. For dressing, in a small bowl whisk together the remaining ingredients. Pour dressing over greens and toss to coat.

PER SERVING (1½ cups each) **CAL** 54, **FAT** 4 g (1 g sat. fat), **CHOL** 0 mg, **SODIUM** 156 mg, **CARB** 5 g (1 g fiber, 2 g sugars), **PRO** 2 g

MAKE FAIR TRADES

When you are calculating your servings of fruit, milk, and starch, trade one for another to keep your carbs in check. For example, if you want two pieces of bread for a sandwich, skip the milk or fruit for that meal. The fruit, milk, or starch serving can also be traded for a cup of broth-base soup or even ½ cup low-fat ice cream.

BETTER THAN
TAKEOUT

Bring fresh restaurant fare to your kitchen without the huge portions and high calories. Enjoy these lightened favorites and flavorful, contemporary dishes.

Spicy Chicken Tostadas with Charred Corn

Spicy Chicken Tostadas with Charred Corn

23 g
CARB

SERVES 4
TOTAL 30 min.

- 8 oz. shredded cooked chicken
- 1 tsp. salt-free Southwest chipotle seasoning
- ⅛ tsp. salt
- ¼ cup plain fat-free Greek yogurt
- 2 Tbsp. snipped fresh cilantro
- 1 tsp. lime juice
- 1 cup frozen fire-roasted corn or whole kernel corn, thawed
- 1 cup shredded coleslaw mix or finely shredded cabbage
- ½ small jalapeño pepper, seeded and finely chopped
- 1 medium avocado, halved, seeded, peeled, and mashed
- 4 tostada shells
- ½ cup halved and/or quartered cherry tomatoes
- ¼ cup crumbled cotija cheese or shredded reduced-fat Monterey Jack cheese
  Lime wedges

1. In a bowl combine chicken, chipotle seasoning, and salt; toss to coat.
2. For corn slaw, in a bowl stir together yogurt, cilantro, and the lime juice. Add corn, coleslaw mix, and jalapeño pepper; mix well.
3. Spread avocado on tostada shells. Top with chicken, the corn slaw, tomatoes, cheese, and additional cilantro leaves. Serve with lime wedges.

Tip Chile peppers contain oils that can irritate your skin and eyes. Wear plastic or rubber gloves when working with them.

PER SERVING (1 tostada each) **CAL** 272, **FAT** 15 g (4 g sat. fat), **CHOL** 59 mg, **SODIUM** 321 mg, **CARB** 23 g (5 g fiber, 4 g sugars), **PRO** 23 g

Chicken and Veggie Pinchos

Chicken and Veggie Pinchos

41 g
CARB

SERVES 4
TOTAL 45 min.

- 1 tsp. paprika
- ½ tsp. dried oregano, crushed
- ½ tsp. garlic powder
- ¼ tsp. onion powder
- ¼ tsp. salt
- ¼ tsp. black pepper
- ¼ tsp. ground annatto (optional)
- 1½ lb. skinless, boneless chicken thighs
- 1 medium green sweet pepper, seeded and cut into 1-inch pieces
- 1 medium red or yellow sweet pepper, seeded and cut into 1-inch pieces
- 1 medium sweet onion, halved crosswise and cut into 1-inch wedges
- 1 Tbsp. reduced-sugar ketchup
- 1 Tbsp. honey
- 1 tsp. lime juice
- ¼ tsp. ground ancho chile powder or chili powder
- 2 tsp. snipped fresh cilantro
- 2 cups hot cooked brown rice

1. If using wooden skewers, soak in enough water to cover at least 30 minutes. In a small bowl combine the first seven ingredients (through annatto if using). Cut chicken thighs into 1- to 1½-inch pieces. Place chicken in a medium bowl. Sprinkle with spice mixture; toss to coat.
2. Thread chicken, pepper pieces, and onion pieces on eight 10- to 12-inch skewers. For glaze, in a bowl stir together ketchup, honey, lime juice, and chile powder.
3. Grill skewers, covered, over medium heat 8 to 10 minutes or until chicken is no longer pink and vegetables are crisp-tender, turning once or twice and brushing both sides with glaze during the last 2 minutes of grilling. Serve chicken pinchos with rice. Sprinkle with cilantro.

PER SERVING (2 pinchos + ½ cup rice each) **CAL** 392, **FAT** 8 g (2 g sat. fat), **CHOL** 160 mg, **SODIUM** 332 mg, **CARB** 41 g (5 g fiber, 10 g sugars), **PRO** 38 g

Creamy Polenta with Chicken-Porcini Sauce

8 to 10 minutes or until chicken is done (165°), turning once. Transfer chicken to a plate; cover to keep warm.

3. Add fresh mushrooms and shallot to skillet. Cook over medium-high 5 to 7 minutes or until mushrooms start to brown, stirring occasionally. Carefully add wine; cook 3 to 4 minutes or until nearly evaporated. Add chopped mushrooms, ¼ cup of the reserved mushroom broth, and the half-and-half. Bring to boiling. Boil gently, uncovered, about 5 minutes or until slightly thickened, stirring frequently.

4. Serve chicken and porcini sauce with Creamy Polenta. Top with Parmesan cheese and parsley and/or rosemary.

Creamy Polenta In a medium saucepan bring **3 cups water** and **¼ tsp. salt** to boiling. Slowly add **¾ cup coarse-ground yellow cornmeal** to boiling water, whisking constantly. Cook and stir until mixture returns to boiling. Reduce heat to medium-low. Cook about 25 minutes or until mixture is very thick and tender, stirring frequently and adjusting heat as needed to maintain a slow boil. Add additional water as needed to maintain a soft, creamy texture. Stir in **⅓ cup finely shredded Parmesan cheese.**

PER SERVING (¾ cup polenta + 3 oz. cooked chicken + ½ cup sauce each) CAL 394, FAT 15 g (5 g sat. fat), CHOL 104 mg, SODIUM 619 mg, CARB 25 g (5 g fiber, 4 g sugars), PRO 38 g

Creamy Polenta with Chicken-Porcini Sauce

25 g
CARB

SERVES 4
TOTAL 55 min.

- ½ cup reduced-sodium chicken broth
- ⅓ cup dried porcini mushrooms
- ¼ tsp. garlic powder
- ⅛ tsp. salt
- ⅛ tsp. black pepper
- 1 lb. chicken breast tenderloins
- 1 Tbsp. canola oil
- 4 cups thinly sliced fresh cremini mushrooms
- 1 medium shallot, thinly sliced
- ¼ cup dry white wine or reduced-sodium chicken broth
- ½ cup half-and-half
- 1 recipe Creamy Polenta
- 1 oz. Parmesan cheese, shaved
  Fresh Italian parsley and/or snipped fresh rosemary

1. In a bowl microwave chicken broth just until boiling. Add dried mushrooms; cover and let stand 10 minutes. Drain mushrooms through a paper towel-lined sieve, reserving broth. Rinse and chop mushrooms; set aside.

2. Meanwhile in a small bowl combine garlic powder, salt, and pepper. Sprinkle over chicken. In a 10-inch skillet heat oil over medium-high. Add chicken. Cook

Mediterranean Chicken and Hummus Bowls

36 g
CARB

SERVES 4
HANDS ON 35 min.
TOTAL 2 hr. 35 min.

- 3 cups shredded red cabbage
- ¼ cup slivered red onion
- ¼ cup white wine vinegar
- 2 tsp. honey
- 2 8-oz. skinless, boneless chicken breast halves
- 1 Tbsp. snipped fresh oregano
- 1 tsp. lemon zest
- ⅛ tsp. salt
- 3 cups fresh baby spinach leaves
- 1 cup shredded carrots
- ¾ cup roasted red pepper hummus
- ¼ cup crumbled reduced-fat feta cheese (1 oz.)
- 2 Tbsp. sliced fresh basil
  Plain low-fat yogurt (optional)
- 2 whole wheat pita bread rounds, cut into wedges and, if desired, toasted

1. In a bowl combine cabbage and onion. Drizzle with vinegar and honey; toss to combine. Cover; chill at least 2 hours or up to 6 hours, stirring occasionally.

2. Fill a large saucepan halfway with lightly salted water. Bring to boiling; add chicken. Return to boiling; reduce heat. Simmer, covered, 15 to 17 minutes or until chicken is done (165°F).

3. Transfer chicken to a cutting board, reserving cooking water in the pan; cool chicken slightly. Coarsely shred chicken using two forks. In a bowl combine shredded chicken, 2 Tbsp. of the reserved cooking water, the oregano, lemon zest, and salt.

4. Arrange spinach, cabbage mixture, chicken, and carrots in separate piles in shallow bowls. Divide hummus among the bowls, spooning it into a mound in the center of each bowl. Sprinkle with feta cheese and basil. If desired, sprinkle chicken with additional lemon zest. Serve with yogurt, if desired, and pita wedges.

PER SERVING (1 bowl each) CAL 393, FAT 12 g (3 g sat. fat), CHOL 85 mg, SODIUM 619 mg, CARB 36 g (6 g fiber, 8 g sugars), PRO 35 g

Mediterranean Chicken and Hummus Bowls

TO EAT A BOWL, USE THE FORK TO TOSS EVERYTHING TOGETHER.

**Peanut-Ginger
Chicken Wraps**

Parmesan Chicken on Bruschetta-Style Vegetables

Peanut-Ginger Chicken Wraps

12 g CARB

SERVES 4
TOTAL 20 min.

- 2 cups chopped cooked chicken breast
- 2 cups shredded cabbage with carrot (coleslaw mix)
- 1 medium carrot, cut up
- 2 green onions, cut up
- 2 Tbsp. unsalted peanuts
- 1 tsp. minced fresh ginger
- ⅓ cup light Asian salad dressing
- ⅓ cup drained canned crushed pineapple
- 12 leaves butterhead (Boston or Bibb) or green leaf lettuce

1. In a food processor combine half of the first six ingredients (through ginger); cover and pulse several times until finely chopped. Transfer to a bowl. Repeat with remaining half of the same ingredients. Add dressing and pineapple to chicken mixture; stir to combine.

2. Spoon the chicken mixture onto lettuce leaves; roll up.

PER SERVING (3 wraps each) **CAL** 221, **FAT** 8 g (2 g sat. fat), **CHOL** 60 mg, **SODIUM** 267 mg, **CARB** 12 g (2 g fiber, 8 g sugars), **PRO** 24 g

Parmesan Chicken on Bruschetta-Style Vegetables

18 g CARB

SERVES 4
HANDS ON 20 min.
TOTAL 50 min.

- ½ cup panko bread crumbs
- 2 Tbsp. grated Parmesan cheese
- ½ tsp. dried Italian seasoning, crushed
- 1 egg white
- 4 5-oz. skinless, boneless chicken breast halves (1¼ lb. total) Nonstick cooking spray
- 1 Tbsp. olive oil
- ½ cup finely chopped onion
- 3 cups fresh spinach leaves
- 1½ cups sliced fresh mushrooms
- 2 to 3 cloves garlic, minced
- 3 cups peeled, seeded, chopped, and well-drained tomatoes
- 2 Tbsp. snipped fresh basil
- 1 Tbsp. balsamic vinegar
- ¼ tsp. salt
- ¼ tsp. black pepper Snipped fresh parsley (optional)

1. Preheat oven to 375°F. Place a rack in a shallow baking pan. In a shallow dish combine bread crumbs, cheese, and Italian seasoning. In another shallow dish beat egg white with a fork. Dip chicken in egg white, then in crumb mixture, turning to coat. Arrange chicken in the prepared baking pan. Lightly coat tops of chicken pieces with cooking spray. Bake about 30 minutes or until chicken is done (165°F) and coating is crisp. If desired, for better browning, turn the broiler on the last 2 to 3 minutes of cooking.

2. Meanwhile, in a 12-inch nonstick skillet heat oil over medium-high. Add onion; cook about 3 minutes or until tender, stirring occasionally. Add spinach, mushrooms, and garlic. Cook about 5 minutes or until spinach is wilted, mushrooms are tender, and liquid is evaporated, stirring occasionally. Remove from heat. Stir in the next five ingredients (through pepper).

3. Serve chicken with tomato mixture. If desired, sprinkle with snipped fresh parsley.

PER SERVING (1 chicken breast half + 1 cup tomato mixture each) **CAL** 296, **FAT** 8 g (2 g sat. fat), **CHOL** 93 mg, **SODIUM** 429 mg, **CARB** 18 g (4 g fiber, 7 g sugars), **PRO** 37 g

Coconut-Curry Chicken

3 Tbsp. light mayonnaise
1½ to 3 tsp. sriracha sauce
1 recipe Quick Pickled Veggies
4 light whole grain hamburger
buns, toasted
12 thin slices cucumber
¼ cup snipped fresh cilantro
Sliced fresh jalapeño chile
peppers (tip, *page 147*) (optional)

1. Place chicken in a resealable plastic bag set in a shallow dish. For marinade, in a bowl whisk together the next six ingredients (through crushed red pepper). Pour marinade over chicken. Seal bag; turn to coat chicken. Marinate in the refrigerator 2 to 4 hours, turning bag occasionally.
2. Drain chicken, discarding marinade. Grill chicken, covered, over medium heat 12 to 15 minutes or until done (165°F), turning once.
3. In a bowl combine mayonnaise and sriracha. Drain Quick Pickled Veggies.
4. Spread buns with mayonnaise mixture. Place cucumber slices on bottoms of buns. Top with chicken, Quick Pickled Veggies, cilantro, and, if desired, jalapeño peppers; add tops of buns.

Quick Pickled Veggies In a bowl combine ½ **cup** each **bite-size strips carrot** and **daikon** and 2 **Tbsp. thinly sliced onion.** In another bowl combine 2 **Tbsp. rice vinegar,** 1 **Tbsp. sugar,*** and ⅛ **tsp.** each **salt, crushed red pepper,** and **black pepper.** Microwave, covered, about 30 seconds or until sugar is dissolved. Pour over vegetables; toss to coat. Cover and chill 4 to 24 hours, stirring occasionally.

PER SERVING *(1 sandwich each)* **CAL** 335, **FAT** 11 g (2 g sat. fat), **CHOL** 93 mg, **SODIUM** 611 mg, **CARB** 23 g (7 g fiber, 8 g sugars), **PRO** 35 g

*Sugar Sub We do not recommend using a sugar sub for this recipe.

Coconut-Curry Chicken

38 g
CARB

SERVES 4
HANDS ON 25 min.
TOTAL 45 min.

Nonstick cooking spray
1 lb. skinless, boneless chicken thighs, cut into bite-size pieces
1 15-oz. can unsweetened light coconut milk
2 Tbsp. red curry paste
1 Tbsp. natural peanut butter
1 Tbsp. reduced-sodium soy sauce
2 cups fresh green beans (halved lengthwise if large)
1 medium red sweet pepper, cut into thin strips
2 medium carrots, cut into matchsticks
⅓ cup snipped fresh cilantro
¼ cup sliced green onions
2 cups hot cooked brown rice
Lime wedges

1. Coat a 12-inch nonstick skillet with cooking spray. Heat skillet over medium-high heat. Add chicken. Cook until no longer pink, stirring occasionally. Add the next four ingredients (through soy sauce); stir to combine. Add the next three ingredients (through carrots). Bring to boiling; reduce heat. Simmer, uncovered, 10 to 15 minutes or until vegetables are tender, stirring occasionally. Stir in cilantro and green onions. Serve over rice with lime wedges.

PER SERVING *(1 cup chicken mixture + ½ cup rice each)* **CAL** 393, **FAT** 14 g (7 g sat. fat), **CHOL** 106 mg, **SODIUM** 464 mg, **CARB** 38 g (6 g fiber, 8 g sugars), **PRO** 30 g

Chicken Banh Mi Sandwiches

23 g
CARB

SERVES 4
HANDS ON 25 min.
TOTAL 4 hr. 37 min.

4 5-oz. skinless, boneless chicken breast halves
1 Tbsp. rice vinegar
1 Tbsp. toasted sesame oil
2 tsp. reduced-sodium soy sauce
1 clove garlic, minced
½ tsp. ground ginger
½ tsp. crushed red pepper

Coconut-Curry Chicken

Chicken Banh Mi Sandwiches

NO DAIKON RADISH? USE REGULAR RED RADISHES.

Jerk Marinated Chicken
with Caribbean Rice

Jerk Marinated Chicken with Caribbean Rice

29 g CARB

| **SERVES** 4 |
| **HANDS ON** 25 min. |
| **TOTAL** 6 hr. 40 min. |

- 2 **8-oz. skinless, boneless chicken breast halves, halved horizontally**
- 2 **Tbsp. canola oil**
- 2 **Tbsp. red wine vinegar**
- 2 **Tbsp. orange juice**
- 2 **Tbsp. thinly sliced green onion**
- 1 **Tbsp. packed brown sugar**
- 1 **Tbsp. reduced-sodium soy sauce**
- 1 **Tbsp. seeded (if desired) and finely chopped fresh jalapeño chile pepper**
- 2 **tsp. Caribbean jerk seasoning**
- 3 **cloves garlic, minced**
- ⅛ **tsp. salt**
- 1 **recipe Caribbean Rice Lime wedges**

1. Place chicken in a resealable plastic bag set in a shallow dish. For marinade, in a bowl combine the next 10 ingredients (through salt). Pour marinade over chicken. Seal bag; turn to coat chicken. Marinate in the refrigerator 6 to 24 hours, turning bag occasionally.

2. Drain chicken, reserving marinade. Grill chicken, covered, over medium heat 4 to 5 minutes or until no longer pink, turning once.

3. Meanwhile, for glaze, in a small saucepan bring the reserved marinade to boiling; reduce heat. Simmer, uncovered, about 10 minutes or until reduced to ¼ cup. Slice chicken. Serve over Caribbean Rice with lime wedges and drizzle with glaze. If desired, sprinkle with additional jerk seasoning and/or snipped fresh cilantro.

Caribbean Rice Coat an 8-inch nonstick skillet with nonstick cooking spray; heat over medium-high. Add ½ **cup** each chopped fresh pineapple and chopped green sweet pepper; 1 Tbsp. seeded (if desired) and finely chopped fresh jalapeño chile pepper; ¼ tsp. each salt, garlic powder, and black pepper; and ⅛ tsp. ground cinnamon. Cook 5 minutes, stirring occasionally. Stir in one 8.8-oz. pouch cooked whole grain brown rice; ½ cup canned no-salt-added red kidney beans, rinsed and drained; and ¼ cup orange juice; heat. Stir in ¼ cup snipped fresh cilantro.

Tip Chile peppers contain oils that can irritate your skin and eyes. Wear plastic or rubber gloves when working with them.

PER SERVING *(3 oz. cooked chicken + ¾ cup rice + 1 Tbsp. glaze each)* **CAL** 286, **FAT** 6 g (1 g sat. fat), **CHOL** 83 mg, **SODIUM** 265 mg, **CARB** 29 g (5 g fiber, 5 g sugars), **PRO** 30 g

---

Orange-Ginger Chicken Stir-Fry

39 g CARB

| **SERVES** 6 |
| **TOTAL** 45 min. |

- 3 **Tbsp. olive oil**
- 1 **lb. carrots, cut into thin bite-size strips**
- 1 **medium red sweet pepper, cut into thin bite-size strips**
- 1 **lb. skinless, boneless chicken breast halves, cut into 1-inch pieces**
- 1 **cup frozen shelled edamame, thawed**
- 1 **Tbsp. grated fresh ginger**
- 3 **cloves garlic, minced**
- ½ **tsp. crushed red pepper (optional)**
- 1½ **cups reduced-sodium chicken broth**
- ¼ **cup frozen orange juice concentrate, thawed**

Orange-Ginger Chicken Stir-Fry

- 2 **Tbsp. reduced-sodium soy sauce**
- 2 **Tbsp. cornstarch**
- 2 **Tbsp. water**
- 3 **cups hot cooked quinoa**
- 1 **Tbsp. sesame seeds, toasted**

1. In a 10-inch skillet heat 1 Tbsp. of the oil over medium. Add carrots; cook and stir 5 minutes. Add sweet pepper; cook and stir about 3 minutes more or until carrots are tender. Transfer to a bowl. In the same skillet heat 1 Tbsp. of the oil over medium-high. Add chicken; cook and stir 4 to 5 minutes or until chicken is no longer pink. Transfer to the bowl with carrot mixture. Stir in edamame.

2. In the same skillet heat the remaining 1 Tbsp. oil over medium. Add ginger, garlic, and, if desired, the ½ tsp. crushed red pepper; cook and stir 30 seconds. Stir in broth, orange juice concentrate, and soy sauce. Bring to boiling.

3. Stir together cornstarch and the water; stir into broth mixture. Simmer 2 minutes. Add chicken mixture; cook and stir until heated. Serve chicken mixture over quinoa. Sprinkle with sesame seeds and, if desired, additional crushed red pepper.

PER SERVING *(⅔ cup chicken mixture + ½ cup quinoa each)* **CAL** 373, **FAT** 13 g (2 g sat. fat), **CHOL** 48 mg, **SODIUM** 481 mg, **CARB** 39 g (7 g fiber, 10 g sugars), **PRO** 26 g

Indian-Spiced Turkey Kabob Pitas

35 g CARB

SERVES	4
TOTAL	35 min.

- 1 tsp. whole cumin seeds
- 1 cup shredded cucumber
- ⅓ cup seeded and chopped roma tomato
- ¼ cup slivered red onion
- ¼ cup shredded radishes
- ¼ cup snipped fresh cilantro
- ¼ tsp. black pepper
- 1 lb. turkey breast, cut into 1-inch cubes
- 1 recipe Curry Blend
- ¼ cup plain fat-free Greek yogurt
- 4 2-oz. whole wheat pita bread rounds

Indian-Spiced Turkey Kabob Pitas

1. If using wooden skewers, soak in water 30 minutes. In a 6-inch dry skillet toast cumin seeds over medium heat about 1 minute or until fragrant. Transfer to a bowl. Add the next six ingredients (through pepper) to bowl; stir to combine.
2. In another bowl combine turkey and Curry Blend; stir to coat. Thread turkey cubes onto skewers. Grill kabobs, uncovered, over medium heat 8 to 12 minutes or until turkey is no longer pink, turning kabobs occasionally.
3. Remove turkey from skewers. Spread Greek yogurt on pita rounds. Using a slotted spoon, spoon cucumber mixture over yogurt. Top with grilled turkey.

Curry Blend In a bowl stir together **2 tsp. olive oil; 1 tsp. curry powder; ½ tsp.** each **ground cumin, ground turmeric,** and **ground coriander; ¼ tsp. ground ginger;** and **⅛ tsp.** each **salt** and **cayenne pepper.**

PER SERVING *(1 sandwich each)* **CAL** 322, **FAT** 5 g (1 g sat. fat), **CHOL** 70 mg, **SODIUM** 442 mg, **CARB** 35 g (5 g fiber, 2 g sugars), **PRO** 35 g

Eggplant-Turkey Pasta Bake

33 g CARB

SERVES	4
HANDS ON	25 min.
TOTAL	45 min.

- Nonstick cooking spray
- 4 oz. whole grain medium shells or penne pasta
- 1 cup light Alfredo pasta sauce
- 8 oz. lean ground turkey
- ½ of a 1-lb. eggplant, peeled if desired and cut into ½-inch cubes (4 cups)
- ½ cup + 1 Tbsp. chopped red onion
- 3 cloves garlic, minced
- 1½ cups chopped roma tomatoes
- 2 tsp. dried Italian seasoning
- 1 tsp. fennel seeds, crushed
- ½ cup shredded part-skim mozzarella cheese (2 oz.)
- 2 Tbsp. snipped fresh basil
- ⅛ tsp. black pepper

1. Preheat oven to 400°F. Coat four individual 10- to 12-oz. casseroles or ramekins with cooking spray. Cook pasta according to package directions. Drain, reserving ½ cup pasta cooking water; return pasta to pot. Stir in half of the Alfredo sauce and enough reserved cooking water to make creamy.
2. Meanwhile, in a 10-inch nonstick skillet cook turkey, eggplant, ½ cup of the onion, and garlic over medium-high until turkey is no longer pink, stirring occasionally. Stir in 1 cup of the chopped tomatoes, the Italian seasoning, and fennel seeds. Cover and cook 3 minutes. Stir in remaining Alfredo sauce.
3. Spoon half of the eggplant mixture into the prepared casseroles. Top with half of the pasta mixture. Repeat layers.
4. Bake casseroles, covered, 15 to 20 minutes or until heated through. Uncover; sprinkle with cheese. Bake 5 minutes more or until cheese is melted.
5. In a small bowl toss together the remaining ½ cup tomato, the basil, remaining 1 Tbsp. red onion, and the pepper. Sprinkle over baked pasta.

PER SERVING *(1 individual casserole each)* **CAL** 321, **FAT** 13 g (6 g sat. fat), **CHOL** 76 mg, **SODIUM** 467 mg, **CARB** 33 g (6 g fiber, 7 g sugars), **PRO** 20 g

Eggplant-Turkey Pasta Bake

Barbacoa Beef Tacos

Barbacoa Beef Tacos

34 g CARB

SERVES 8
HANDS ON 45 min.
TOTAL 3 hr.

- 1 cup reduced-sodium beef broth
- ½ of a 6-oz. can no-salt-added tomato paste
- ¼ cup cider vinegar
- 1 medium canned chipotle pepper in adobo sauce + 1 Tbsp. adobo sauce
- 4 cloves garlic, minced
- 2 tsp. ground cumin
- 1 tsp. dried oregano, crushed
- ¼ tsp. salt
  Nonstick cooking spray
- 1 2¼- to 2½-lb. boneless beef chuck arm roast, trimmed and cut into 2-inch chunks
- 1 large onion, halved and thinly sliced
- 1 medium red sweet pepper, chopped
- 1 recipe Quick Pickled Red Onions
- 16 6-inch corn tortillas, warmed
- 4 cups shredded lettuce
- ½ cup light sour cream
- 1 cup fresh salsa
- ½ cup snipped fresh cilantro

1. Preheat oven to 325°F. For sauce, in a blender combine the first eight ingredients (through salt). Cover; blend until smooth.

2. Coat a 3½- or 4-qt. Dutch oven with cooking spray; heat over medium. Cook meat, half at a time, until browned, stirring occasionally. Return all beef to Dutch oven. Add onion and red pepper. Pour sauce over beef and vegetables. Bring to boiling; cover and place in oven. Bake about 2½ hours or until beef is very tender.

3. Remove meat from pot, reserving cooking liquid. Shred meat using two forks; discard fat. Skim fat from cooking liquid. Place Dutch oven on burner over medium. Simmer about 5 minutes or until cooking liquid is reduced by half. Return meat to Dutch oven; toss to coat.

4. While beef is cooking, prepare Quick Pickled Red Onions. Drain onions before serving. To serve, top tortillas with beef and the remaining ingredients.

Quick Pickled Red Onions Place 1½ cups slivered red onion in a bowl. Add ½ cup lime juice and ¼ tsp. salt; toss to combine. Press down on onion with the back of a fork. Cover; chill at least 2 hours or up to 3 days. Drain before serving.

PER SERVING (2 tacos each) **CAL** 347, **FAT** 9 g (3 g sat. fat), **CHOL** 87 mg, **SODIUM** 432 mg, **CARB** 34 g (6 g fiber, 8 g sugars), **PRO** 33 g

Open-Face Meatball Sub with Caramelized Onions

Open-Face Meatball Sub with Caramelized Onions

29 g CARB

SERVES 4
HANDS ON 40 min.
TOTAL 1 hr.

  Nonstick cooking spray
- 1 large sweet onion, cut into thin wedges (about 1½ cups)
- 1 12-oz. jar roasted red sweet peppers, drained
- 2 tsp. balsamic vinegar
- 2 crusty kaiser, French, or hoagie rolls
- 1 recipe Sandwich Meatballs
- ½ cup shredded part-skim mozzarella cheese (2 oz.)

1. Coat a 10-inch nonstick skillet with cooking spray; heat skillet over medium-low. Add onion wedges. Cook, covered, 15 minutes, stirring occasionally. Uncover; increase heat to medium-high. Cook 5 to 10 minutes more or until onions are golden brown, stirring occasionally.

2. Transfer half of the onions to a blender. Add roasted peppers and vinegar. Cover; blend until smooth, scraping sides of blender as needed.

3. Preheat oven to 425°F. Line a baking sheet with foil; coat foil with cooking spray. Split rolls horizontally. Hollow out centers. Place roll halves on the prepared baking sheet. Bake about 6 minutes or until lightly toasted.

4. Spoon Sandwich Meatballs into roll halves. Top meatballs with blended sauce, the remaining caramelized onions, and the cheese. Bake 5 to 8 minutes or until heated and cheese is melted.

Sandwich Meatballs Preheat oven to 350°F. Line a baking pan with foil. In a bowl combine **1 egg, lightly beaten; ¼ cup whole wheat panko bread crumbs; 1 tsp. dried Italian seasoning; 2 cloves garlic, minced; and ¼ tsp. black pepper.** Add **12 oz. lean ground beef;** mix well. Shape mixture into 16 meatballs. Arrange meatballs in the prepared pan. Bake 20 to 25 minutes or until done (160°F). Drain meatballs on paper towels.

PER SERVING (1 sandwich each) **CAL** 346, **FAT** 13 g (5 g sat. fat), **CHOL** 109 mg, **SODIUM** 466 mg, **CARB** 29 g (3 g fiber, 6 g sugars), **PRO** 26 g

Bulgogi Beef and Vegetable Bowls

44 g CARB

SERVES 4
HANDS ON 35 min.
TOTAL 4 hr. 35 min.

- 1 lb. boneless beef sirloin steak, cut 1 inch thick
- ½ cup coarsely chopped onion
- ¼ cup honey
- ¼ cup water
- 2 Tbsp. reduced-sodium soy sauce
- 2 Tbsp. toasted sesame oil
- 1 Tbsp. finely chopped fresh ginger
- 4 cloves garlic, halved
  Nonstick cooking spray
- 1⅓ cups cooked brown rice
- 1 cup coarsely shredded carrots
- 1 cup finely shredded red cabbage
- ¾ cup cooked small broccoli florets
- ½ cup coarsely shredded cucumber
- ¼ cup snipped fresh cilantro or mint
- 1 to 2 tsp. sriracha sauce
- ½ cup kimchi (optional)

1. Trim fat from meat. Cut meat across the grain into very thin slices. Place meat in a resealable plastic bag set in a shallow dish. For marinade, in a blender or food processor combine onion, 2 Tbsp. each of the honey and water, the soy sauce, 1 Tbsp. of the sesame oil, the ginger, and garlic. Cover and blend until smooth. Pour marinade over meat. Seal bag; turn to coat meat. Marinate in the refrigerator 4 to 6 hours, turning bag occasionally.
2. Drain meat, discarding marinade. Coat a 10-inch nonstick skillet with cooking spray; heat over medium-high. Working in batches, add meat; cook and stir 40 to 60 seconds or just until slightly pink in center.
3. To assemble, divide meat and the next five ingredients (through cucumber) among shallow bowls, keeping ingredients in separate piles. In a small bowl combine the remaining 2 Tbsp. each

honey and water and the 1 Tbsp. sesame oil, the cilantro, and sriracha sauce. Top servings with honey mixture and, if desired, additional cilantro or mint. If desired, serve with kimchi.

Tip Partially freeze the meat for easier slicing.

Tip To cook rice, in a medium saucepan bring ⅔ cup water and ⅓ cup uncooked long grain brown rice to boiling; reduce heat. Simmer, covered, 35 to 45 minutes or until rice is tender and liquid is absorbed.

PER SERVING (1 bowl each) CAL 405, FAT 13 g (3 g sat. fat), CHOL 77 mg, SODIUM 434 mg, CARB 44 g (3 g fiber, 22 g sugars), PRO 30 g

SIMPLE SHREDDING

Different tools and techniques are used to shred various vegetables.

◆ Box shredder

A box shredder or flat shredder is a basic tool for manually shredding small amounts of straight vegetables like carrot, cucumber, zucchini, parsnip, and even potatoes.

◆ Chef's knife

Use a chef's knife to thinly slice (shred) vegetables like cabbage and Brussels sprouts. You can even cut straight veggies into short lengths, then into thin sticks if you don't have a shredder.

Bulgogi Beef
and Vegetable
Bowls

Korean Beef Lettuce Rolls

9g
CARB

| **SERVES** 4 |
| **TOTAL** 20 min. |

- 12 oz. extra-lean ground beef
- 3 Tbsp. reduced-sodium soy sauce
- 1 Tbsp. sriracha sauce
- 2 tsp. toasted sesame oil
- 1 12-oz. pkg. shredded broccoli slaw
- 8 butterhead (Boston or Bibb) lettuce leaves
- ½ cup red sweet pepper strips
  Chopped peanuts and/or sliced green onions (optional)
  Lime wedges

1. In a 12-inch skillet cook beef over medium-high until browned. Reduce heat to medium. Stir in soy sauce, sriracha sauce, and sesame oil. Stir in broccoli slaw. Cook and stir 2 to 3 minutes or until slaw mixture is just wilted.

2. Spoon beef mixture onto lettuce leaves. Top with sweet pepper and, if desired, peanuts and/or green onions and additional sriracha sauce. Roll leaves to enclose filling. Serve with lime wedges.

PER SERVING (2 lettuce cups each)
CAL 185, **FAT** 7 g (2 g sat. fat), **CHOL** 53 mg,
SODIUM 567 mg, **CARB** 9 g (3 g fiber, 5 g sugars),
PRO 21 g

*BUTTERHEAD LEAVES
HAVE THE FLEXIBILITY
TO WRAP AROUND
FLAVORFUL FILLING.*

Korean Beef
Lettuce
Rolls

Beef Gyros

19 g CARB

SERVES 8
HANDS ON 30 min.
TOTAL 1 hr. 15 min.

Nonstick cooking spray
- 1 cup chopped onion
- 2 Tbsp. water
- 1 lb. extra-lean ground beef
- 1 egg
- ¼ cup dry whole wheat bread crumbs
- 4 tsp. dried oregano, crushed
- 2 tsp. dried marjoram, crushed
- 3 cloves garlic, minced
- ½ tsp. kosher salt
- ½ tsp. black pepper
- 8 low-carb pita bread rounds
- 3 medium roma tomatoes, sliced
- ½ cup thinly sliced cucumber
- ¼ cup thinly sliced red onion
- ½ cup crumbled reduced-fat feta cheese (2 oz.)
- 1 recipe Tzatziki Sauce

1. Preheat oven to 325°F. Line a 9×5-inch loaf pan with parchment paper; coat paper with cooking spray.

2. In a food processor combine the 1 cup onion and the water; cover and process until smooth. Press pureed onion through a fine-mesh sieve to remove excess liquid; discard liquid. Return onion to food processor. Add the next eight ingredients (through pepper). Cover and process until mixture forms a paste.

3. Lightly press meat mixture into prepared loaf pan. Place loaf pan in a 13×9-inch baking pan. Pour enough boiling water into baking pan to reach halfway up sides of loaf pan. Bake 35 to 40 minutes or until done (160°F). Drain off fat. Cool 10 minutes. Remove loaf from pan; cut into slices about ¼ inch thick.

4. Fill pita rounds with meat, tomato, cucumber, and red onion slices; top with cheese. Serve gyros with Tzatziki Sauce.

Beef Gyros

Tip The meat may appear a bit pink after baking. Be sure to use an instant-read thermometer to measure the doneness.

Tzatziki Sauce In a small bowl stir together ½ of a 6-oz. carton plain fat-free Greek yogurt; ½ cup shredded, seeded cucumber; 1½ tsp. red wine vinegar; 1½ tsp. snipped fresh dill; 1 clove garlic, minced; and ¼ tsp. kosher salt. If desired, cover and chill up to 4 hours before serving.

Tip Don't have the time to make the tzatziki? You can purchase tzatziki in the deli section of your grocery store. Look for a version that uses fat-free Greek yogurt.

PER SERVING (1 sandwich + 1½ Tbsp. Tzatziki Sauce each) **CAL** 206, **FAT** 7 g (2 g sat. fat), **CHOL** 64 mg, **SODIUM** 610 mg, **CARB** 19 g (7 g fiber, 4 g sugars), **PRO** 24 g

Barley Tabbouleh
with Lebanese
Meatballs

Barley Tabbouleh with Lebanese Meatballs

30 g CARB

SERVES 6
HANDS ON 30 min.
TOTAL 1 hr. 50 min.

- 3½ cups unsalted chicken stock or water
- 1 cup hull-less barley or regular pearled barley
- 2 cups snipped fresh parsley
- 2 cups chopped unpeeled seedless cucumber
- 1 cup chopped tomatoes
- ½ cup finely chopped red onion
- 2 Tbsp. snipped fresh mint
- ¼ cup lemon juice
- 1½ Tbsp. olive oil
- 2 cloves garlic, minced
- ½ tsp. salt
- ¼ tsp. black pepper
- 1 recipe Lebanese Meatballs
- ¾ cup plain fat-free Greek yogurt (optional)

1. For tabbouleh, in a large saucepan combine broth and barley. Bring to boiling; reduce heat. Simmer, uncovered, about 1 hour or until desired tenderness; drain. Transfer barley to a bowl and let cool. Stir in the next five ingredients (through mint). In another bowl whisk together the next five ingredients (through pepper). Add to barley mixture; toss to coat. Set aside at room temperature.

2. In a 12-inch nonstick skillet cook Lebanese Meatballs over medium 15 to 18 minutes or until browned and done (160°F), turning occasionally. Serve with tabbouleh. If desired, top with yogurt and additional snipped fresh mint.

Lebanese Meatballs In a bowl combine **12 oz. lean ground beef; 2 Tbsp.** each **finely chopped onion** and **snipped fresh parsley; 1 Tbsp. snipped fresh mint; 1 clove garlic, minced; ½ tsp.** each **ground coriander** and **black pepper;** and ¼ **tsp.** each **ground cumin** and **salt;** mix well. Form mixture into 12 meatballs.

Tip Hull-less barley is a heartier form than pearled barley. It still has its bran and germ layers, so it is considered a true whole grain, making it richer in fiber and other nutrients.

Tip Lean meat may have some pink color even when it is cooked thoroughly (160°F).

PER SERVING (2 meatballs + 1 cup tabbouleh each) **CAL** 286, **FAT** 10 g (3 g sat. fat), **CHOL** 37 mg, **SODIUM** 406 mg, **CARB** 30 g (7 g fiber, 3 g sugars), **PRO** 19 g

Ginger-Plum Pork Sandwiches with Sesame Slaw

28 g CARB

SERVES 8
HANDS ON 30 min.
TOTAL 9 hr. 30 min.

- 1 2½- to 3-lb. boneless pork shoulder
- 2 tsp. ground coriander
- 1 tsp. ground ginger
- ½ tsp. salt
- ½ tsp. ground allspice
- ¼ tsp. black pepper
- 1 Tbsp. canola oil
- 1 medium onion, cut into thin wedges
- 8 dried pitted plums (prunes)
- ½ cup reduced-sodium chicken broth
- 8 whole wheat reduced-calorie hamburger buns, split and toasted
- 1 recipe Sesame Slaw

1. Cut roast into three equal portions. Trim all visible fat. In a bowl combine the next five ingredients (through pepper). Sprinkle over all roast portions, rubbing in with your fingers. In a 12-inch skillet heat oil over medium. Add roast portions and cook 8 to 10 minutes or until meat is browned, turning to brown all sides.

2. Place onion wedges, prunes, and broth in a 3½- or 4-qt. slow cooker. Top with browned roast portions. Cover and cook on low 9 to 10 hours or on high 4½ to 5 hours.

3. Transfer meat to a cutting board. Shred meat using two forks; discard any fat. Skim fat from cooking liquid. Measure 1 cup of the cooking liquid and discard any remaining cooking liquid. Transfer the 1 cup cooking liquid, the onion, and prunes to a blender. Cover; blend until smooth. Return to cooker with shredded pork; toss with tongs to combine.

4. Divide meat among buns. Top with some of the Sesame Slaw and pass any remaining slaw.

Sesame Slaw In a bowl toss together **4 cups shredded cabbage with carrot (coleslaw mix)** and **½ cup thinly sliced green onions.** In a screw-top jar combine **2 Tbsp.** each **vinegar** and **honey, 1 Tbsp.** each **sesame seeds** and **canola oil,** and **2 tsp. sesame oil.** Cover; shake well. Drizzle over cabbage mixture; toss to coat. Serve or cover and chill up to 4 hours.

PER SERVING (1 sandwich each) **CAL** 367, **FAT** 14 g (3 g sat. fat), **CHOL** 85 mg, **SODIUM** 443 mg, **CARB** 28 g (8 g fiber, 12 g sugars), **PRO** 32 g

Ginger-Plum Pork
Sandwiches with
Sesame Slaw

Cajun Shrimp and
Sausage Stir-Fry

Cajun Shrimp and Sausage Stir-Fry

35 g CARB

SERVES 4
TOTAL 30 min.

- 8 oz. fresh or frozen medium shrimp, peeled and deveined
- 2 Tbsp. canola oil
- 6 oz. cooked andouille sausage, sliced
- 3 cloves garlic, minced
- 1 tsp. salt-free Cajun seasoning
- ½ tsp. dried thyme leaves, crushed
- 8 oz. fresh okra, bias-sliced ½ inch thick, or frozen sliced okra, thawed
- ¾ cup coarsely chopped red sweet pepper
- 1 small onion, cut into ½-inch wedges
- ½ cup sliced celery
- 1 cup halved grape tomatoes
- 1 to 2 tsp. hot pepper sauce
- 2 cups hot cooked brown rice
  Lemon wedges (optional)
  Snipped fresh parsley (optional)

1. Thaw shrimp, if frozen. Rinse shrimp; pat dry.
2. In a wok or 12-inch skillet heat 1 Tbsp. oil over medium-high. Add shrimp and sausage; cook and stir 2 to 3 minutes or until shrimp turn opaque. Remove shrimp and sausage from wok.
3. Heat the remaining 1 Tbsp. oil over medium-high. Add garlic, Cajun seasoning, and thyme; cook and stir 30 seconds. Add okra; cook and stir 1 minute. Add sweet pepper, onion, and celery; cook and stir 2 to 3 minutes or until crisp-tender. Add tomatoes and hot pepper sauce; cook and stir 1 to 2 minutes or until tomatoes begin to soften. Return shrimp and sausage to wok along with any juices; heat. Serve over rice. If desired, serve with lemon wedges and top with parsley.

PER SERVING *(1⅓ cups shrimp mixture + ½ cup rice each)* **CAL** 359, **FAT** 15 g (3 g sat. fat), **CHOL** 79 mg, **SODIUM** 456 mg, **CARB** 35 g (5 g fiber, 4 g sugars), **PRO** 22 g

Coconut Shrimp with Mango Rice Pilaf

Coconut Shrimp with Mango Rice Pilaf

36 g CARB

SERVES 4
HANDS ON 25 min.
TOTAL 33 min.

- 1 lb. fresh or frozen extra-large shrimp in shells
  Nonstick cooking spray
- ¼ cup refrigerated or frozen egg product, thawed, or 2 egg whites, lightly beaten
- ¾ cup finely crushed reduced-fat or reduced-sodium shredded wheat crackers
- ⅓ cup shredded coconut
- ¼ tsp. ground ginger
- ¼ tsp. black pepper
- 1 8.8-oz. pkg. cooked brown rice
- ½ cup chopped fresh mango or chopped jarred mango, rinsed and drained
- ⅓ cup sliced green onions
- 2 Tbsp. snipped fresh cilantro

1. Thaw shrimp, if frozen. Preheat oven to 450°F. Lightly coat a large baking sheet with cooking spray. Peel and devein shrimp, leaving tails intact. Rinse shrimp; pat dry.
2. Place egg in a shallow dish. In another shallow dish combine crushed crackers, coconut, ginger, and pepper. Dip shrimp in egg, turning to coat. Dip in coconut mixture, pressing to coat, leaving tails uncoated. Arrange shrimp in a single layer on the prepared baking sheet.
3. Bake 8 to 10 minutes or until shrimp are opaque and coating is lightly browned. Meanwhile, heat rice according to package directions. Transfer to a serving bowl. Stir in mango and green onions. Serve rice with shrimp; sprinkle with cilantro.

PER SERVING *(4 or 5 shrimp + about ½ cup rice mixture each)* **CAL** 303, **FAT** 7 g (2 g sat. fat), **CHOL** 129 mg, **SODIUM** 249 mg, **CARB** 36 g (3 g fiber, 4 g sugars), **PRO** 23 g

Skewered Shrimp and Tomato Linguine

40 g CARB | **SERVES** 4
| **TOTAL** 40 min.

- 12 oz. fresh or frozen large shrimp, peeled and deveined
- 24 red and/or yellow cherry or grape tomatoes
- 1 Tbsp. olive oil
- 1 clove garlic, minced
- ¼ tsp. black pepper
- ⅛ tsp. salt
- 6 oz. dried whole grain linguine
- 1 Tbsp. butter
- 1 Tbsp. lemon juice
- 4 cups torn baby arugula
- 1 Tbsp. snipped fresh oregano
- ¼ cup finely shredded Parmesan cheese
  Freshly cracked black pepper
  Lemon wedges (optional)

Skewered Shrimp and Tomato Linguine

1. Thaw shrimp, if frozen. Rinse shrimp and pat dry. Thread shrimp and tomatoes onto four 10-inch metal skewers. In a bowl whisk together the next four ingredients (through salt). Brush over shrimp and tomatoes. Grill skewers, uncovered, over medium heat 5 to 8 minutes or until shrimp turn opaque, turning once

2. Meanwhile, prepare linguine according to package directions. Drain, reserving ⅓ cup of the cooking water. Return pasta to pot. Add butter and lemon juice; toss to combine. Add the reserved pasta cooking water, the grilled shrimp and tomatoes, the arugula, and oregano. Toss to combine. Sprinkle with Parmesan cheese and cracked black pepper. If desired, serve with lemon wedges.

PER SERVING *(1¼ cups each)* **CAL** 321, **FAT** 10 g (3 g sat. fat), **CHOL** 118 mg, **SODIUM** 603 mg, **CARB** 40 g (7 g fiber, 5 g sugars), **PRO** 20 g

Sweet Chili and Pistachio Mahi Mahi

28 g CARB | **SERVES** 4
| **HANDS ON** 25 min.
| **TOTAL** 40 min.

- 4 4- to 5-oz. fresh or frozen mahi mahi fillets
- 1 lime
- 5 tsp. honey, warmed
- 2 tsp. olive oil
- ¼ tsp. salt
- ¼ tsp. black pepper
- ½ cup salted dry-roasted pistachio nuts or whole almonds
- ¾ tsp. chili powder
- ¼ tsp. onion powder
- ¼ tsp. paprika
- 1⅓ cups cooked quinoa
- ½ cup chopped red sweet pepper
- ¼ cup chopped red onion
- ¼ cup snipped fresh cilantro

1. Thaw fish, if frozen. Preheat oven to 325°F. Line a baking sheet with parchment paper. For dressing, remove zest and squeeze juice from lime. In a small bowl combine zest, juice, 2 tsp. of the honey, the oil, salt, and black pepper.

2. In another bowl combine pistachio nuts, chili powder, onion powder, paprika, and 1 tsp. of the honey. Spread nuts on prepared baking sheet. Bake about 12 minutes or until toasted; cool. Place pistachios in a small food processor. Cover and process until finely crushed.

3. Increase oven temperature to 425°F. Reline baking sheet with parchment paper. Rinse fish; pat dry with paper towels. Place fish on the prepared baking sheet. Brush tops of fish with the remaining 2 tsp. honey. Sprinkle with crushed pistachios, pressing to adhere. Bake 10 to 15 minutes or until fish flakes easily.

4. Meanwhile, in a bowl combine the remaining ingredients. Stir in dressing. Serve fish with quinoa mixture. If desired, garnish with additional cilantro sprigs.

PER SERVING *(1 fish fillet + ½ cup quinoa mixture each)* **CAL** 322, **FAT** 12 g (2 g sat. fat), **CHOL** 83 mg, **SODIUM** 328 mg, **CARB** 28 g (4 g fiber, 10 g sugars), **PRO** 28 g

TRY COD OR SALMON IF YOU CAN'T FIND MAHI MAHI.

Sweet Chili and Pistachio Mahi Mahi

Udon Noodle Bowl

Udon Noodle Bowl

28 g CARB

SERVES 4
TOTAL 30 min.

- 2 tsp. sesame oil
- 1 cup quartered fresh mushrooms
- 1 cup shredded carrot
- 2 cloves garlic, minced
- 4 cups low-sodium vegetable broth
- 2 Tbsp. reduced-sodium soy sauce
- 2 tsp. rice vinegar
- 12 oz. extra-firm tofu, cut into 1-inch cubes
- 1 7.34-oz. pkg. refrigerated cooked udon noodles (any flavor), torn (discard seasoning packet)
- 1 medium zucchini, halved lengthwise and cut into ½-inch pieces
- 1 cup shredded red cabbage
- ¼ cup thinly bias-sliced green onion
- ¼ cup fresh cilantro leaves
- 2 Tbsp. chopped roasted, salted peanuts or cashews
  Lime wedges

1. In a large saucepan heat oil over medium. Add mushrooms, carrot, and garlic; cook and stir 3 minutes. Add broth, soy sauce, and vinegar. Bring to boiling; reduce heat. Simmer, uncovered, 5 minutes, stirring occasionally. Stir in tofu, noodles, and zucchini. Return to boiling; reduce heat. Simmer, uncovered, 3 minutes more, stirring occasionally.
2. Top noodle mixture with the next four ingredients (through peanuts). Serve with lime wedges.

PER SERVING (2 cups each) **CAL** 246, **FAT** 10 g (2 g sat. fat), **CHOL** 0 mg, **SODIUM** 493 mg, **CARB** 28 g (4 g fiber, 8 g sugars), **PRO** 14 g

Cauli-Rice and Smoky Black Bean Burger Stacks

36 g CARB

SERVES 4
HANDS ON 45 min.
TOTAL 1 hr. 15 min.

- 1 15-oz. can reduced-sodium black beans, rinsed and drained
- 1 egg, lightly beaten
- ½ cup finely chopped red sweet pepper
- ⅓ cup thinly sliced green onions
- ¼ cup yellow cornmeal
- 3 cloves garlic, minced
- 1 tsp. smoked paprika or regular paprika
  Nonstick cooking spray
- 3 cups cauliflower florets
- ¾ cup shredded Monterey Jack cheese (3 oz.)
- 1 egg, lightly beaten
- 2 cloves garlic, minced
- ½ cup refrigerated fresh salsa
- 1 avocado, halved, seeded, peeled, and chopped

1. In a large bowl combine half the beans and the egg. Mash beans until nearly smooth. Stir in remaining beans and the next five ingredients (through paprika). Using damp hands, shape mixture into four ¾-inch-thick patties. Cover and chill at least 30 minutes or up to 8 hours.
2. Preheat oven to 375°F. Coat four 6-oz. custard cups with cooking spray. Place cauliflower in a food processor. Cover and process until very finely chopped. Transfer cauliflower to a large microwave-safe bowl. Add 2 Tbsp. water; cover with vented plastic wrap. Microwave 3 minutes, stirring once. Cool slightly; squeeze cauliflower with a double thickness of paper towels to absorb some of the excess liquid.
3. For cauli-rice, in a bowl combine the cauliflower, cheese, egg, and garlic; mix well. Spoon cauliflower mixture into

Cauli-Rice and Smoky Black Bean Burger Stacks

prepared custard cups, pressing into cups with the back of a spoon. Bake 10 to 12 minutes or until done (160°F).
4. Coat a 10-inch nonstick skillet with cooking spray; heat over medium. Add bean patties. Cook 10 to 12 minutes or until done (160°F), turning once.
5. Place bean burgers on plates. Run a thin metal spatula or knife around edges of custard cups to loosen cauli-rice. Invert the cauli-rice on bean patties. Top with salsa and avocado.

PER SERVING (1 burger + ⅓ cup cauli-rice + 2 Tbsp. salsa + ¼ avocado each) **CAL** 344, **FAT** 15 g (6 g sat. fat), **CHOL** 112 mg, **SODIUM** 472 mg, **CARB** 36 g (9 g fiber, 5 g sugars), **PRO** 17 g

DINING OUT
with **DIABETES**

Most Americans eat out at least three times a week—that's more than 150 meals a year! This can have a big impact on your health, so eat right when you eat out.

DILEMMAS WITH DINING OUT
and *THE SOLUTIONS!*

Restaurant dining can be tough on your health. Learn how to navigate what's on the menu.

1.

DILEMMA: *Sodium counts skyrocket. From high-sodium ingredients and foods to generously salted sauces, sides, and entrées, the sodium in restaurant meals can quickly grow and top your daily quota.*

✓ **THE SOLUTION:**
When eating fast food, say no to cheese, bacon, cold cuts, and special sauce. Say yes to salads, but go easy on the dressing. Pile raw vegetables high on sandwiches. Ordering pizza? Choose thin crust, top it with veggies, and limit yourself to two slices. Eating at a sit-down restaurant? Steer clear of high-sodium ingredients, such as cheese and dips, and request that the chef go light on the sauce and salt. Remember, if you eat less food, you'll also consume less sodium.

2.

DILEMMA: *Fats and oils are in, on, and throughout foods. Restaurant foods are loaded with fats and oils so they taste good and stay moist.*

✓ **THE SOLUTION:** Rein in fat grams from start to finish. Send complimentary baskets of bread and butter or chips and salsa back to the kitchen. Request salad dressing on the side, then drizzle dressing on lightly or dip your greens or fork in it.

3.

DILEMMA: *Sipping and slurping racks up calories. Restaurants and fast-food joints serve big, bigger, and gigantic portions of sugar-sweetened beverages such as soda, lemonade, tea, specialty coffee drinks, smoothies, and alcoholic beverages.*

✓ **THE SOLUTION:** Keep the calories you spend on beverages to a bare minimum. Quench your thirst with water, club soda, unsweetened iced tea, coffee, diet soda, or diet lemonade. Low-fat milk and 100-percent fruit juice are healthful choices, but watch the portions and take into account the carbohydrate from these beverages. Skip the large calorie- and carb-dense coffees and teas and say no to smoothies. If drinking alcohol, keep it simple by choosing one light beer, a glass of wine, or a shot of liquor on the rocks mixed with a zero-calorie beverage.

4.

DILEMMA: *Protein portions dominate the plate. Menus, particularly those at American-style restaurants, focus on choices of beef, poultry, and seafood. Salads, vegetables, and grains often play second fiddle.*

✓ **THE SOLUTION:** Be creative and outsmart the menu by making your protein portion a side dish. Split and share a protein-focused main course or go vegetarian. Order nutritious salads and side dishes to fill your plate with raw or cooked vegetables, whole grains, and healthful starches.

5.

DILEMMA: *The portions are huge! When large portions are set in front of you, it's difficult to stop eating before you clean your plate.*

✓ **THE SOLUTION:** Don't eat it all. As soon as your plate arrives, cut the food in half and take the rest home to enjoy another day. Or request a split entrée to share with another person. You can even choose from soups, salads, and/or side dishes or request a half portion. At fast-food restaurants, choose regular, junior, or kids' meals.

TIME IT RIGHT

Eat on time to keep blood sugar in line. Try these tips to minimize lows from delayed eating.

◆ KEEP A SCHEDULE.
Eat meals about the same time every day to control blood glucose. Factor in the time needed for ordering and receiving your food.

◆ CALL AHEAD.
Many restaurants take reservations, offer faster seating if you call ahead, or have immediate seating in the bar.

◆ PACK A SNACK.
Keep a carb-containing snack on hand, such as raisins. If a meal takes longer than anticipated, you can keep your blood sugar from sliding.

ORDER *PLANNING*

Having a healthy restaurant routine can help you stay on track when dining out. Don't be shy to ask questions and make requests. A good restaurant wants you to come away satisfied.

1.
PRESELECT YOUR MEAL.
Visit a restaurant's website before you go so you can identify menu choices that are moderate in calories, fat, and sodium. If the nutrition information is listed, use it as a tool to identify good options.
If there is no nutrition information, make your best guess or use a calorie-counting app or website. Once you make your choice, stick to it.

2.
ORDER FIRST.
Once you are at the restaurant, try to be the first to order your meal so your dining companions don't influence your choices.

3.
BUILD IT YOUR WAY.
Ask to double the nonstarchy veggies and cut the amount of cheese, french fries, or other fatty ingredient/side in half. Request sauces on the side—or hold the sauce and ask for a lemon wedge instead.

4.
OPT FOR WHOLE, BASIC FOODS.
Choose lean grilled meat, such as skinless chicken breast or salmon, instead of a pasta entrée smothered in cream sauce. Similarly, pick steamed broccoli over broccoli casserole and a baked potato topped with salsa instead of french fries.

5.
GO FOR VEGGIES.
When in doubt about what's healthy, choose a leafy green salad (just watch the dressing and toppings) or a vegetarian burger—swapping out the beef could cut calories in half. If you do order a veggie (bean or quinoa) burger, be sure to take additional carbs into account.

6.
DON'T BE AFRAID TO ASK.
If you want fries but can't trust yourself to eat just a portion of what the restaurant serves, ask your server to bring you only a certain number of fries. Reward with a good tip if you get exactly what you want.

ABOUT *the* OPTIONS

Deciding what to eat can be stressful with diabetes. But some nutritional intel can help you control carbs and enjoy your meal.

Appetizers

Don't order an appetizer instead of an entrée. Many are fried, and most are sized to serve more than one. They can have as many (or more) carbs and calories as a main dish.

Soup

If you order soup, estimate 15–20 grams of carbohydrate per cup if it contains starchy vegetables, rice, barley, noodles, or beans, or if it's creamy, which often means milk, flour, or cornstarch has been added.

Bread and baked goods

Halve the carbs in a sandwich by eating it open-face. Watch out for muffins, which can have more calories and carbs than a cupcake.

Breaded meats

Grilled meats are mostly carb-free. Breaded items, like chicken-fried steak, are loaded with carbohydrate and fat.

Sauces and glazes

Gravies and sweet or savory sauces conceal carbohydrate grams from the ingredients used to make them, such as sugar, flour, and milk. Eat sauces sparingly.

Starchy sides

Restaurant portions of rice, beans, and french fries are often way too big, so eat half or less than what's served. Ask for brown rice if it is an option.

Beverages

Don't drink your calories. Besides obvious sources, such as soda, a lot of cocktails are full of sugar. And a fancy coffee drink or tall glass of orange juice, lemonade, or sweet tea could chew through your carbohydrate allowance for the meal.

UNDERSTAND THE MENU.

"Fried" and "gravy" are key watch-out words. Understanding the menu language can lead you to better choices.

RED FLAGS

- Bottomless
- Cheese/au gratin
- Cream/creamy
- Crispy/crusted
- Double or triple
- Hand-breaded/battered
- Loaded
- Prime
- Smothered
- Stuffed

LIGHTER LINGO

- Au jus
- Blackened
- Broiled
- Fresh
- Grilled
- Lighter
- Mini
- Petite
- Seasonal
- Steamed

Dark Chocolate and Peanut Popcorn

In a bowl combine **1 cup air-popped popcorn** and **1 Tbsp. roasted salted peanuts**. Drizzle with **¼ oz. dark chocolate, melted.**

SERVES 1. **CAL** 120, **CARB** 12 g (3 g fiber, 3 g sugars)

TOPPERS
POPCORN

Savory and sweet—these popcorn perk-ups are sure to satisfy. You'll keep your calories in check since they're all 131 calories or less.

Salted Caramel and Pretzel Popcorn

In a bowl combine **1 cup air-popped popcorn** and **½ oz. mini pretzel twists**. Top with **2 tsp. sugar-free caramel topping** and **a dash salt.** Toss to combine.

SERVES 1. **CAL** 116, **CARB** 27 g (1 g fiber, 0 g sugars)

Italian Popcorn

Place **1 cup air-popped popcorn** in a bowl; coat with nonstick butter-flavor cooking spray. Toss with **1 Tbsp. Parmesan** and **¼ Tbsp. Italian seasoning.**

SERVES 1. **CAL** 52, **CARB** 7 g (1 g fiber, 0 g sugars)

Sweet Chili Popcorn

In a bowl combine **1 cup air-popped popcorn,
2 tsp. honey,** and **1 tsp. chili powder.** Toss to combine.
SERVES 1. CAL 81, **CARB** 19 g (2 g fiber, 12 g sugars)

Tropical Popcorn

In a bowl combine **1 cup air-popped popcorn, 2 Tbsp.
snipped dried pineapple,** and **1 Tbsp. unsweetened
coconut flakes, toasted.** Toss to combine.
SERVES 1. CAL 126, **CARB** 24 g (2 g fiber, 14 g sugars)

Cranberry White Chocolate Popcorn

In a bowl combine **1 cup air-popped popcorn** and
1 Tbsp. chopped dried cranberries. Drizzle with
½ oz. white chocolate, melted. Toss to combine.
SERVES 1. CAL 131, **CARB** 21 g (2 g fiber, 14 g sugars)

BBQ Popcorn

In a bowl combine **1 cup air-popped popcorn** and
10 bite-size cheese crackers. Coat with **nonstick butter-flavor
cooking spray.** Toss with **¼ tsp. barbecue seasoning.**
SERVES 1. CAL 87, **CARB** 13 g (1 g fiber, 0 g sugars)

COTTAGE CHEESE

Brighten a bowl of cottage cheese with nutritious vegetables and fruits. The extras add bursts of flavor.

Veggieful Cottage Cheese

Top ⅓ cup low-fat (2%) cottage cheese with ¼ cup steamed small broccoli florets and 1 Tbsp. chopped roasted red peppers.
SERVES 1. CAL 73, **CARB** 6 g (1 g fiber, 4 g sugars)

Tropical Cottage Cheese

Top ⅓ cup low-fat (2%) cottage cheese with ¼ cup chopped pineapple, 2 Tbsp. chopped dried apricots, and 1 Tbsp. unsweetened flaked coconut, toasted.
SERVES 1. CAL 145, **CARB** 20 g (2 g fiber, 16 g sugars)

Radish-Chive Cottage Cheese

Top ⅓ cup low-fat (2%) cottage cheese with 2 medium radishes, thinly sliced; 1 tsp. snipped fresh chives; and, if desired, **cracked black pepper.**
SERVES 1. CAL 63, **CARB** 4 g (0 g fiber, 3 g sugars)

Blueberry-Honey Cottage Cheese

Top ⅓ cup low-fat (2%) cottage cheese with ¼ cup fresh blueberries, 1 Tbsp. finely chopped walnuts, and, if desired, 2 tsp. honey.

SERVES 1. CAL 130, **CARB** 10 g (1 g fiber, 7 g sugars)

Avo-Bacon Cottage Cheese

Top ⅓ cup low-fat (2%) cottage cheese with 3 thin slices avocado; 1 slice lower-sodium, less-fat bacon, crisp cooked and chopped; and ⅛ tsp. salt-free Southwest chipotle seasoning.

SERVES 1. CAL 112, **CARB** 5 g (1 g fiber, 3 g sugars)

Nutty-Peach Cottage Cheese

Top ⅓ cup low-fat (2%) cottage cheese with ¼ cup sliced fresh or frozen peaches, thawed, and 1 Tbsp. coarsely chopped toasted macadamia nuts.

SERVES 1. CAL 136, **CARB** 8 g (1 g fiber, 7 g sugars)

Caprese Cottage Cheese

Top ⅓ cup low-fat (2%) cottage cheese with ¼ cup cherry tomatoes, halved; 1 tsp. snipped fresh basil; and a pinch black pepper.

SERVES 1. CAL 70, **CARB** 5 g (1 g fiber, 4 g sugars)

TOPPERS
YOGURT

Sprinkle and drizzle healthful sundae toppings on a creamy bowl of plain yogurt. It's protein with pizzazz.

Purple Cow Yogurt

Top ½ cup plain fat-free Greek yogurt with ¼ cup blackberries, halved, and 1 Tbsp. low-sugar grape jelly, melted. **SERVES** 1. **CAL** 105, **CARB** 14 g (2 g fiber, 11 g sugars)

Chocolate-Strawberry Yogurt

Top ½ cup plain fat-free Greek yogurt with ¼ cup chopped fresh strawberries. Drizzle with 2 tsp. sugar-free chocolate-flavor syrup. **SERVES** 1. **CAL** 82, **CARB** 9 g (1 g fiber, 6 g sugars)

Caramel-Banana Yogurt

Top ½ cup plain fat-free Greek yogurt with ¼ of a medium banana, sliced; 2 tsp. sugar-free caramel-flavor ice cream topping; and 1 Tbsp. chopped peanuts. **SERVES** 1. **CAL** 175, **CARB** 21 g (2 g fiber, 9 g sugars)

Mango-Jalapeño Yogurt

Top **½ cup plain fat-free Greek yogurt** with **3 Tbsp. chopped fresh or jarred mango**; **½ to 1 tsp. finely chopped, seeded jalapeño chile pepper**; and **1 tsp. agave syrup**.

SERVES 1. **CAL** 105, **CARB** 15 g (1 g fiber, 13 g sugars)

Maple-Pecan Yogurt

Top **½ cup plain fat-free Greek yogurt** with **1 Tbsp. chopped toasted pecans**, **1 tsp. pure maple syrup**, and a **pinch coarse sea salt**.

SERVES 1. **CAL** 129, **CARB** 10 g (1 g fiber, 9 g sugars)

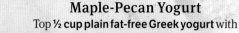

Honey-Pomegranate Yogurt

Top **½ cup plain fat-free Greek yogurt** with **2 Tbsp. pomegranate seeds** and **1 tsp. honey**.

SERVES 1. **CAL** 106, **CARB** 15 g (1 g fiber, 13 g sugars)

Raspberry-Pistachio Yogurt

Top **½ cup plain fat-free Greek yogurt** with **1 Tbsp. chopped salted dry-roasted pistachio nuts**. Drizzle with **1 Tbsp. raspberry spreadable fruit or low- or no-sugar raspberry jam, melted**.

SERVES 1. **CAL** 151, **CARB** 17 g (1 g fiber, 14 g sugars)

Strawberry Cream Apple Rings

Core and thinly slice **half of a medium apple** crosswise into rings. Stir together **1 oz. reduced-fat cream cheese (neufchatel), softened,** and **¼ tsp. vanilla.** Spread slices with cream cheese mixture and top with **¼ cup chopped fresh strawberries.**

SERVES 1. CAL 134, **CARB** 16 g (3 g fiber, 12 g sugars)

TOPPERS

APPLE RINGS

Swap apple slices for bread and crackers to carry tasty toppers. Smear or drizzle, then sprinkle with nutrient-loaded fruits, nuts, and more.

Core apples using a straight apple corer, not the kind that also cuts wedges. After removing the core, thinly slice apples crosswise. If you don't have a corer, slice apples, then cut a circle in the center of each slice with a small round cutter.

Mixed-Fruit Apple Rings

Core and thinly slice **half of a medium apple** crosswise into rings. Spread slices with **2 Tbsp. blueberry-flavor fat-free Greek yogurt** and top with **¼ cup fresh raspberries, halved.**

SERVES 1. CAL 100, **CARB** 22 g (4 g fiber, 15 g sugars)

Peanut Butter-Chocolate Apple Rings

Core and thinly slice **half of a medium apple** crosswise into rings. Drizzle slices with **2 tsp. peanut butter, melted,** and top with **1 tsp. miniature semisweet chocolate pieces.**

SERVES 1. CAL 134, **CARB** 18 g (3 g fiber, 13 g sugars)

Herbed Ricotta Apple Rings

Core and thinly slice **half of a medium apple** crosswise into rings. Spread slices with **2 Tbsp. part-skim ricotta cheese** and top with **½ oz. thinly sliced prosciutto or ham,** cut into thin strips, and **1 tsp. snipped fresh herbs (parsley, basil, thyme, and/or rosemary).**

SERVES 1. **CAL** 120, **CARB** 14 g (2 g fiber, 10 g sugars)

Cranberry-Cashew Apple Rings

Core and thinly slice **half of a medium apple** crosswise into rings. Spread slices with **2 tsp. cashew butter** and drizzle with **2 tsp. maple syrup.** Top with **1 Tbsp. finely chopped dried cranberries.**

SERVES 1. **CAL** 170, **CARB** 31 g (3 g fiber, 24 g sugars)

Blackberry-Mascarpone Apple Rings

Core and thinly slice **half of a medium apple** crosswise into rings. Stir together **1 Tbsp. each mascarpone cheese and plain fat-free Greek yogurt** and **¼ tsp. vanilla.** Spread slices with mixture; top with **¼ cup fresh blackberries** and **fresh mint** and/or **lemon zest.**

SERVES 1. **CAL** 156, **CARB** 27 g (4 g fiber, 21 g sugars)

Honey-Almond Apple Rings

Core and thinly slice **half of a medium apple** crosswise into rings. Drizzle slices with **2 tsp. honey** and top with **2 Tbsp. sliced almonds, toasted.**

SERVES 1. **CAL** 156, **CARB** 27 g (4 g fiber, 21 g sugars)

Vanilla Ice Cream
Sandwiches, *p. 187*

SWEET
TREATS

You can satisfy your sweet tooth and still lose weight
by working mindful, smartly portioned desserts
into your meal plan.

Classic Fudge Pops

Classic Fudge Pops

30 g
CARB

SERVES 9
HANDS ON 30 min.
TOTAL 4 hr. 25 min.

4 oz. bittersweet or semisweet chocolate, coarsely chopped
2¾ cups milk
1 tsp. vanilla
¾ cup sugar*
3 Tbsp. cornstarch
2 Tbsp. unsweetened Dutch-process cocoa powder
  Dash salt
  Frozen pop sticks
  Melted white chocolate and miniature semisweet chocolate pieces, and/or melted dark chocolate and finely crushed shortbread cookies (optional)

1. In a medium saucepan heat and stir chopped chocolate over low until melted. Gradually whisk in milk and vanilla. Meanwhile, in a bowl stir together the next four ingredients (through salt). Whisk sugar mixture into chocolate mixture. Cook and stir over medium until thickened and bubbly. Cook and stir 2 minutes more. Remove from heat; cool 45 minutes. Whisk until smooth.

2. Spoon mixture into nine 3-oz. frozen pop molds. Insert a frozen pop stick into each mold. Use a knife to stir the mixture in the molds to work out air bubbles; cover and freeze 3 to 4 hours or until firm. To serve, let stand 10 minutes before unmolding. If desired, dip pops in melted white chocolate and chocolate pieces, and/or dip in melted dark chocolate and crushed shortbread cookies.

Tip If you don't have frozen pop molds, use 3-oz. wax-lined paper cups. Spoon chocolate mixture into cups, stirring as directed; cover each with a piece of foil. Using a small sharp knife, make a slit in each piece of foil. Insert wooden pop sticks into slits. Freeze and serve as directed.

PER SERVING *(1 pop each)* **CAL** 179, **FAT** 6 g (4 g sat. fat), **CHOL** 6 mg, **SODIUM** 57 mg, **CARB** 30 g (1 g fiber, 25 g sugars), **PRO** 3 g

*Sugar Sub Choose Splenda Sugar Blend. Follow package directions for ¾ cup equivalent.
PER SERVING WITH SUB Same as above, except **CAL** 154, **CARB** 22 g (17 g sugars)

**Mint Cream-Filled
Chocolate Cupcakes**

Mint Cream-Filled Chocolate Cupcakes

28 g CARB

SERVES 24
HANDS ON 35 min.
TOTAL 1 hr. 25 min.

- 2 cups all-purpose flour
- ¾ cup unsweetened cocoa powder
- 1½ tsp. baking soda
- ½ tsp. salt
- 1⅓ cups sugar*
- ⅓ cup canola oil
- ¾ cup refrigerated or frozen egg product, thawed
- ½ tsp. vanilla
- ½ tsp. peppermint extract
- 1½ cups buttermilk
- 1 tsp. peppermint extract
  Green food coloring
- ½ of an 8-oz. container frozen light whipped dessert topping, thawed
- ½ cup semisweet chocolate pieces
- 1 tsp. shortening
- 24 miniature chocolate-covered mint cream candies, such as Junior Mints, or 12 layered chocolate mint candies, such as Andes, halved

1. Preheat oven to 350°F. Line twenty-four 2½-inch muffin cups with foil bake cups.
2. In a bowl combine the first four ingredients (through salt). In a large bowl combine sugar and oil; beat with a mixer on medium to high until combined. Beat in egg, vanilla, and the ½ tsp. peppermint extract. Alternately add the flour mixture and the buttermilk, beating on low after each addition until combined.
3. Spoon batter into prepared muffin cups, filling each cup about half full. Bake about 15 minutes or until tops of cupcakes spring back when lightly touched. Cool in muffin cups 5 minutes. Remove; cool on wire racks.
4. In a bowl fold 1 tsp. peppermint extract and about 12 drops green food coloring into the whipped topping. Transfer topping to a pastry bag fitted with a small round tip. Using a straw, poke a hole about halfway down in the center of each cooled cupcake. Insert tip of pastry bag into the hole in each cupcake and squeeze to fill with filling (stop when you see filling coming out of the hole).
5. In a bowl microwave chocolate pieces and shortening about 30 seconds or until melted and smooth, stirring every 10 seconds. Spoon or pipe chocolate in the center of each cupcake, covering the filled hole. Place a mint candy piece in the chocolate on each cupcake. Let stand about 30 minutes or until set.

PER SERVING (1 cupcake each) **CAL** 167, **FAT** 6 g (2 g sat. fat), **CHOL** 1 mg, **SODIUM** 160 mg, **CARB** 28 g (1 g fiber, 17 g sugars), **PRO** 3 g

*Sugar Sub Choose Splenda Sugar Blend. Follow package directions for 1⅓ cups equivalent.
PER SERVING WITH SUB Same as above, except **CAL** 150, **CARB** 22 g (11 g sugars)

Vanilla Ice Cream Sandwiches

Recipe pictured on p. 184.

26 g CARB

SERVES 24
HANDS ON 45 min.
TOTAL 1 hr.

- 4 oz. reduced-fat cream cheese, softened
- ½ cup butter, softened
- 1¾ cups sugar*
- 1 tsp. baking soda
- 1 tsp. cream of tartar
- ⅛ tsp. salt
- 3 egg yolks
- ½ tsp. vanilla bean paste or vanilla
- 1¼ cups all-purpose flour
- ½ cup white whole wheat flour
- 3 cups reduced-fat vanilla ice cream, softened

1. Preheat oven to 300°F. In a large bowl beat cream cheese and butter with a mixer on medium 30 seconds. Add the next four ingredients (through salt). Beat until combined, scraping bowl as needed. Beat in egg yolks and vanilla bean paste. Beat in both flours.
2. Shape dough into 1-inch balls. Place balls 2 inches apart on an ungreased cookie sheet lined with parchment paper.
3. Bake 14 to 16 minutes or until edges are set but not brown. Cool on cookie sheet 1 minute. Remove; cool on a wire rack.
4. Spread ice cream on bottoms of half of the cookies, using 2 tablespoons for each cookie. Top with remaining cookies, bottom sides down.

To Store Place sandwich cookies in a shallow baking pan and freeze at least 2 hours or until firm. Transfer to a freezer container and freeze up to 1 month.

PER SERVING (1 sandwich cookie each) **CAL** 167, **FAT** 6 g (4 g sat. fat), **CHOL** 39 mg, **SODIUM** 123 mg, **CARB** 26 g (0 g fiber, 18 g sugars), **PRO** 2 g

*Sugar Sub Choose Splenda Sugar Blend. Follow package directions for 1¾ cups equivalent.
PER SERVING WITH SUB Same as above, except **CAL** 145, **CARB** 18 g (11 g sugars)

Zucchini
Cupcakes with
Greek Yogurt
Frosting

Molasses Cookies

9 g
CARB

SERVES 48
HANDS ON 30 min.
TOTAL 1 hr. 40 min.

- ⅓ cup margarine, softened
- ⅔ cup packed dark brown sugar*
- 1 tsp. baking soda
- 1 tsp. ground ginger
- ½ tsp. ground cinnamon
- ¼ cup refrigerated or frozen
  egg product, thawed, or 1 egg
- ¼ cup mild molasses
- 1½ cups all-purpose flour
- ½ cup white whole wheat flour
  Nonstick cooking spray
- 2 Tbsp. granulated sugar*
- ½ tsp. ground cinnamon

1. In a bowl beat margarine with a mixer on medium to high 30 seconds. Add the next four ingredients (through cinnamon); beat until combined. Beat in egg and molasses. Beat in the flours. Cover and chill 1 hour.
2. Preheat oven to 350°F. Lightly coat a cookie sheet with cooking spray.
3. Shape dough into balls that are slightly less than 1 inch in diameter. In a small bowl combine the granulated sugar and ½ tsp. cinnamon. Roll balls in sugar-cinnamon mixture. Place balls 2 inches apart on the prepared cookie sheet. Using the bottom of a glass, flatten each ball to ½ inch thick. Bake about 7 minutes or until edges are set. Remove; cool on a wire rack.

PER SERVING (1 cookie each) **CAL** 48,
FAT 1 g (0 g sat. fat), **CHOL** 0 mg, **SODIUM** 45 mg,
CARB 9 g (0 g fiber, 5 g sugars), **PRO** 1 g

*Sugar Sub Choose Splenda Brown Sugar Blend for the brown sugar. Follow package directions for ⅔ cup equivalent. We do not recommend a sub for the granulated sugar. Baking time may need to decrease slightly.
PER SERVING WITH SUB Same as above, except **CAL** 44, **SODIUM** 44 mg, **CARB** 7 g (3 g sugars)

Zucchini Cupcakes with Greek Yogurt Frosting

24 g
CARB

SERVES 12
HANDS ON 20 min.
TOTAL 1 hr. 40 min.

- Nonstick cooking spray
- 1 cup whole wheat flour
- ¼ cup granulated sugar *
- ¼ cup packed brown sugar*
- 1 tsp. ground cinnamon
- ½ tsp. baking powder
- ½ tsp. salt
- ¼ tsp. baking soda
- 2 eggs
- ¼ cup fat-free milk
- 1 cup cooked quinoa
- 1 cup shredded zucchini
- ½ cup unsweetened applesauce
- ¼ cup canola oil
- 1 tsp. vanilla
- 1 recipe Greek Yogurt Frosting
- ½ to 1 tsp. lemon zest

1. Preheat oven to 350°F. Lightly coat twelve 2½-inch muffin cups with cooking spray. In a bowl stir together the next seven ingredients (through baking soda).
2. In another bowl beat together eggs and milk. Add the next five ingredients (through vanilla); stir until well mixed. Add quinoa mixture to flour mixture; stir gently to combine. Spoon batter into prepared muffin cups, filling each about three-fourths full.
3. Bake about 20 minutes or until a toothpick inserted in centers comes out clean. Cool in muffin cups 5 minutes. Remove cupcakes from pan; cool on wire rack. Frost cupcakes with Greek Yogurt Frosting; sprinkle with lemon zest.

Greek Yogurt Frosting In a bowl whisk together one **6-oz. carton plain fat-free Greek yogurt, 2 Tbsp. light agave nectar or 3 Tbsp. powdered sugar,*** and **1 tsp. vanilla** until combined.

Tip For 1 cup cooked quinoa, rinse and drain ⅓ **cup quinoa.** In a small saucepan combine quinoa and ⅔ **cup water.** Cook according to package directions. Cool. Measure out 1 cup. Use any remaining cooked quinoa in salads.

PER SERVING (1 cupcake each) **CAL** 167,
FAT 6 g (1 g sat. fat), **CHOL** 32 mg,
SODIUM 161 mg, **CARB** 24 g (2 g fiber,
13 g sugars), **PRO** 5 g

*Sugar Sub We do not recommend sugar subs for this recipe.

Molasses
Cookies

Crackled Sugar Cookies

LOW-TEMP
BAKING MAKES
A MELT-IN-
YOUR-MOUTH
SUGARY CRUST.

Crackled Sugar Cookies

12g
CARB

SERVES 48
HANDS ON 35 min.
TOTAL 50 min.

½ cup butter, softened
½ cup shortening
2 cups sugar*
1 tsp. baking soda
1 tsp. cream of tartar
⅛ tsp. salt
3 egg yolks
½ tsp. vanilla
1¾ cups all-purpose flour

1. Preheat oven to 300°F. In a bowl beat butter and shortening with a mixer on medium 30 seconds. Add the next four ingredients (through salt). Beat until combined, scraping bowl occasionally. Beat in egg yolks and vanilla. Beat in flour.
2. Shape dough into 1-inch balls. Place balls 2 inches apart on ungreased cookie sheets. Bake 12 to 14 minutes or until edges are set; do not let edges brown. Cool on cookie sheets 2 minutes. Remove; cool on wire racks.

To Store Layer cookies between sheets of waxed paper in an airtight container; cover. Store at room temperature up to 2 days or freeze up to 3 months.

PER SERVING (1 cookie each) **CAL** 88, **FAT** 4 g (2 g sat. fat), **CHOL** 17 mg, **SODIUM** 50 mg, **CARB** 12 g (0 g fiber, 8 g sugars), **PRO** 1 g

*Sugar Sub Use Splenda Sugar Blend. Follow package directions for 2 cups equivalent.
PER SERVING WITH SUB Same as above, except **CAL** 66, **CARB** 8 g (4 g sugars)

Sugar and Spice Popcorn Clusters

Sugar and Spice Popcorn Clusters

13g
CARB

SERVES 20
HANDS ON 20 min.
TOTAL 3 hr. 20 min.

1½ cups dark chocolate pieces
2 tsp. shortening
2 tsp. chili powder
1 tsp. ground cinnamon
¼ tsp. crushed red pepper
6 cups popped 94% fat-free microwave popcorn (most of 1 bag) or air-popped popcorn
½ oz. white baking chocolate, melted
Chili powder and/or crushed red pepper

1. In a large bowl combine dark chocolate pieces and shortening. Microwave, uncovered, 1½ to 2 minutes or until chocolate melts, stirring every 30 seconds.

2. In a small bowl combine the 2 tsp. chili powder, the cinnamon, and the ¼ tsp. crushed red pepper. Stir spice mixture into the melted chocolate mixture.
3. Slightly crush the popcorn; stir crushed popcorn into the spiced chocolate mixture. Stir until popcorn is evenly coated. Using two spoons, spoon popcorn mixture into 20 mounds onto waxed paper. Drizzle tops of the mounds with melted white baking chocolate; sprinkle with additional chili powder and/or crushed red pepper.
4. Let stand 3 to 4 hours or until completely set before serving.

Tip To crush popcorn, place popped popcorn in a resealable plastic bag; seal bag. Using a rolling pin, lightly pound and roll popcorn until slightly crushed.

PER SERVING (1 cluster each) **CAL** 99, **FAT** 6 g (4 g sat. fat), **CHOL** 0 mg, **SODIUM** 25 mg, **CARB** 13 g (2 g fiber, 10 g sugars), **PRO** 1 g

Peanut S'mores Cereal Bars

Peanut S'mores Cereal Bars

20 g
CARB

SERVES 16
HANDS ON 15 min.
TOTAL 1 hr.

Nonstick cooking spray
3½ cups high-fiber cluster-style cereal, such as Fiber One Honey Clusters
1 egg white, lightly beaten
2 Tbsp. butter, melted
¾ cup miniature semisweet chocolate pieces, melted
1 cup tiny marshmallows
½ cup unsalted peanuts, toasted and coarsely chopped

1. Preheat oven to 350°F. Coat a 9-inch square baking pan with cooking spray.
2. Place cereal in a resealable plastic bag; seal bag. Using a rolling pin, very finely crush cereal. In a bowl combine cereal, egg white, and melted butter. Lightly press cereal mixture evenly in the bottom of the prepared pan. Bake 10 to 12 minutes or until lightly browned.
3. Preheat broiler. Spread melted chocolate over crust. Top with marshmallows and peanuts. Broil 4 to 5 inches from heat 30 to 60 seconds or until lightly browned.
4. Place on wire rack and cool completely. Chill about 30 minutes or until firm. Cut into 16 bars.

To Store Place bars in a single layer in an airtight container. Store in the refrigerator up to 3 days.

PER SERVING (1 bar each) **CAL** 140, **FAT** 7 g (3 g sat. fat), **CHOL** 4 mg, **SODIUM** 80 mg, **CARB** 20 g (3 g fiber, 9 g sugars), **PRO** 3 g

Salted Caramel Blondies

Salted Caramel Blondies

22 g
CARB

SERVES 28
HANDS ON 25 min.
TOTAL 43 min.

Nonstick cooking spray
1¾ cups packed brown sugar*
⅓ cup butter
¼ cup canola oil
½ cup refrigerated or frozen egg product, thawed
2 tsp. vanilla
1 cup all-purpose flour
1 cup whole wheat flour
1 tsp. baking powder
½ tsp. salt
¼ tsp. baking soda
½ cup chopped pecans
½ oz. ridged potato chips (about ¼ cup), coarsely crushed
6 vanilla caramels, unwrapped
1 Tbsp. fat-free milk
¼ tsp. sea salt

1. Preheat oven to 350°F. Line a 13×9-inch baking pan with foil, extending over edges of pan; coat foil with cooking spray. In a medium saucepan combine brown sugar, butter, and oil; heat and stir over medium until smooth. Remove from heat; cool slightly. Stir in egg and vanilla.
2. In a bowl combine the flours, baking powder, the ½ tsp. salt, and the baking soda. Add the egg mixture to the flour mixture; stir to combine. Stir in pecans. Spread batter evenly in the prepared baking pan. Sprinkle with crushed potato chips.
3. Bake 18 to 20 minutes or until a toothpick inserted in center comes out clean. Cool in pan on a wire rack.
4. Meanwhile, in a 1-cup glass measure combine caramels and milk. Microwave on 50 percent power (medium) 1½ to 2 minutes or until smooth, stirring every 30 seconds. Drizzle mixture over cooled bars and quickly sprinkle with the sea salt. Using the edges of the foil, lift uncut bars out of the pan. Cut into 28 bars.

Tip Purchase a snack-size bag of potato chips and measure ¼ cup for this recipe.

PER SERVING (1 bar each) **CAL** 148, **FAT** 6 g (2 g sat. fat), **CHOL** 6 mg, **SODIUM** 128 mg, **CARB** 22 g (1 g fiber, 14 g sugars), **PRO** 2 g

*Sugar Sub We do not recommend using a sugar sub for this recipe.

Chocolate Chip Oatmeal Bars

Chocolate Chip Oatmeal Bars

20 g
CARB

SERVES 24	
HANDS ON 20 min.	
TOTAL 1 hr.	

- ¼ cup water
- 1½ tsp. ground chia seeds
- 1 cup regular rolled oats
- 1 cup white whole wheat flour
- ½ tsp. salt
- ½ tsp. baking powder
- ½ tsp. baking soda
- ¼ cup butter, softened
- ¾ cup packed brown sugar*
- ⅓ cup granulated sugar*

- ¼ cup refrigerated or frozen egg product, thawed, or 1 egg, lightly beaten
- 1 tsp. vanilla
- 1 cup semisweet chocolate pieces

1. Preheat oven to 350°F. Line a 13×9-inch baking pan with foil-lined parchment pan lining paper.
2. In a bowl combine the water and ground chia seeds; let stand 20 minutes.
3. Meanwhile, place ½ cup of the oats in a food processor. Cover and process until finely ground. Add the next four ingredients (through baking soda). Cover and process until combined.
4. In a large bowl beat butter and sugars with a mixer on medium until mixture starts to cling to the sides of the bowl. Beat in egg product, vanilla, and chia mixture until combined. Add the remaining ½ cup oats and the flour mixture, beating on low to medium until combined. Stir in chocolate pieces (dough will be stiff). Spread dough in the prepared pan.
5. Bake 18 to 20 minutes or until edges are golden. Cool in pan on a wire rack. Cut into 24 bars.

Tip If you have whole chia seeds, grind them using a spice grinder or a mortar and pestle.

PER SERVING (1 bar each) **CAL** 121, **FAT** 4 g (3 g sat. fat), **CHOL** 5 mg, **SODIUM** 108 mg, **CARB** 20 g (1 g fiber, 14 g sugars), **PRO** 2 g

*Sugar Sub Use Splenda Brown Sugar Blend for the brown sugar and Splenda Sugar Blend for the granulated sugar. Follow package directions for ¾ cup and ⅓ cup equivalents.
PER SERVING WITH SUB Same as above, except **CAL** 91, **SODIUM** 106 mg sodium, **CARB** 12 g (6 g sugars)

Deep Espresso Dark Cherry Chocolate Brownies

30 g
CARB

SERVES 12	
HANDS ON 15 min.	
TOTAL 45 min.	

- Nonstick cooking spray
- ½ cup unsweetened cocoa powder
- ⅓ cup all-purpose flour
- ⅓ cup white whole wheat flour
- 1½ tsp. baking powder
- 1 tsp. instant espresso coffee powder
- ⅛ tsp. salt
- 2 eggs, lightly beaten
- ¾ cup packed dark brown sugar*
- ½ cup granulated sugar*
- ⅓ cup canola oil
- 2 tsp. vanilla
- ½ cup frozen unsweetened pitted dark sweet cherries, thawed and chopped
- 1 Tbsp. powdered sugar*

1. Preheat oven to 350°F. Line an 8-inch square baking pan with foil, extending foil over edges of pan. Lightly coat foil with cooking spray.
2. In a bowl combine the next six ingredients (through salt). In another bowl whisk together the next five ingredients (through vanilla). Add the sugar mixture and cherries to flour mixture; stir until just combined. Spread evenly in the prepared pan.
3. Bake about 24 minutes or until slightly puffed. Cool in pan 5 minutes. Using the edges of the foil, lift uncut brownies out of pan; cool on a wire rack. Cut into 12 brownies. Dust with powdered sugar.

Tip The batter will continue to cook while cooling.

PER SERVING (1 brownie each) **CAL** 189, **FAT** 7 g (1 g sat. fat), **CHOL** 31 mg, **SODIUM** 103 mg, **CARB** 30 g (2 g fiber, 23 g sugars), **PRO** 3 g

*Sugar Sub We do not recommend using sugar subs for this recipe.

Deep Espresso Dark Cherry
Chocolate Brownies

5 DAYS
OF MEAL PLANS

Feel satisfied with fewer calories when you use this balanced meal plan to map out your weekday meals. Shoot for about 1,500 calories per day. It's OK if you are a little above or below that goal.

M	T	W	TH	F

These meal plans are ideal for people trying to lose weight. You might need more calories than this. Ask your health care team for a caloric goal that's right for you.

Breakfast
1 serving Black Bean-Corn Breakfast Burritos *(p. 33)* + ¾ cup fat-free milk

Midmorning snack
1 low-fat mozzarella cheese stick + ½ cup fresh raspberries

Lunch
1 serving Chicken and Artichoke Spinach Salads *(p. 54)*

Afternoon snack
1 serving Peanut Butter-Chocolate Apple Rings *(p. 182)*

Dinner
1 serving Bulgogi Beef and Vegetable Bowls *(p. 160)*

Dessert
1 serving Salted Caramel Blondies *(p. 193)*

TOTAL

CAL 1,437, **FAT** 54 g (16 g sat. fat), **CHOL** 287 mg, **SODIUM** 1,907 mg, **CARB** 163 g (20 g fiber, 85 g sugars), **PRO** 83 g

DAY 2

Breakfast
1 serving Blueberry Buckwheat Pancakes *(p. 38)* + ¾ cup vegetable juice

Midmorning snack
¼ cup whole almonds

Lunch
1 serving Barbecue Chopped Pork Salad *(p. 66)* + ½ cup carrots + 1 cup fat-free milk

Afternoon snack
1 serving Blueberry-Honey Cottage Cheese *(p. 179)*

Dinner
1 serving Turkey-Pepper Popper Casserole *(p. 77)* + 1 cup steamed broccoli

Dessert
¾ cup mixed fruit drizzled with 1 tsp. honey

TOTAL

CAL 1,500, **FAT** 52 g (12 g sat. fat), **CHOL** 155 mg, **SODIUM** 1,746 mg, **CARB** 170 g (27 g fiber, 77 g sugars), **PRO** 104 g

Breakfast
1 serving Berry-Banana Smoothie Bowls *(p. 49)* + 1 scrambled egg

Midmorning snack
3 graham cracker squares + 1 Tbsp. peanut butter

Lunch
1 serving Chili-Cilantro Turkey Sandwich *(p. 58)* + 1 serving Leafy Green Salad *(p. 129)*

Afternoon snack
¼ cup carrots + ¼ cup celery + ¼ cup hummus

Dinner
1 serving Tortilla Chip Flounder with Black Bean Salad *(p. 98)* + ⅓ cup cooked brown rice

Dessert
½ cup no-sugar-added vanilla ice cream + 2 Tbsp. sugar-free chocolate syrup

TOTAL

CAL 1,446, **FAT** 54 g (14 g sat. fat), **CHOL** 301 mg, **SODIUM** 1,632 mg, **CARB** 180 g (29 g fiber, 51 g sugars), **PRO** 71 g

DAY 4

Breakfast
1 serving Squash, Bacon, and Feta Breakfast Bake (*p. 34*) + 1 slice whole wheat toast + 1 Tbsp. light butter with canola oil

Midmorning snack
½ cup plain fat-free Greek yogurt drizzled with 2 tsp. honey

Lunch
1 serving Roast Beef, Arugula, and Pickled Onion Wrap (*p. 53*) + ½ cup fresh blackberries

Afternoon Snack
1 serving Cranberry-Cashew Apple Rings (*p. 183*)

Dinner
1 serving Bacon-Wrapped Pork Tenderloin with Honey-Almond Green Beans (*p. 82*) + 1 small whole wheat dinner roll

Dessert
1 serving Deep Espresso Dark Cherry Chocolate Brownies (*p. 194*)

TOTAL

CAL 1,507, FAT 49 g (13 g sat. fat), CHOL 362 mg, SODIUM 2,088 mg, CARB 187 g (26 g fiber, 113 g sugars), PRO 91 g

Breakfast
1 serving Strawberry-Pistachio Breakfast Quinoa *(p. 46)*

Midmorning snack
1 oz. reduced-fat cheddar cheese + 5 shredded wheat crackers

Lunch
1 serving Asian Chicken and Noodle Salad *(p. 57)*

Afternoon Snack
¼ cup whole pecans

Dinner
1 serving Chicken, Broccoli, and Farro Casserole *(p. 78)* + ½ cup steamed green beans

Dessert
2 cups air-popped popcorn drizzled with 1 tsp. light butter with canola oil

TOTAL
CAL 1,509, **FAT** 62 g (14 g sat. fat), **CHOL** 139 mg, **SODIUM** 1,429 mg, **CARB** 156 g (28 g fiber, 29 g sugars), **PRO** 97 g

MOVE *MORE*

Getting 150 minutes of moderate exercise each week is like free medicine for your body. Start with easy walks and stretches, then add strength training with basic at-home moves.

WHAT'S IN YOUR WAY?

STUCK ON YOUR PATH TO A HEALTHY WEIGHT?
Learn what a neuropsychologist says about the hidden barriers we all face and get advice from a motivational rock star to start breaking down roadblocks today.

Every morning, you tell yourself this is the day you're going to ditch the excuses. Snack less, move more, start the scale on a downward trend. But every night, you crawl into bed, pull up the covers, and ask yourself what went wrong.

It's like an invisible barrier is blocking the path to a healthier you.

Diane Robinson, Ph.D., says you're not imagining that roadblock. A neuropsychologist with the UF Health Cancer Center in Orlando, Robinson looks at the whole person, focusing on areas that boot camps and crash diets skip: biological, emotional, and social cues. She focuses on deeply rooted habits that sabotage health. If you've hit a roadblock, her findings may help you.

That blasted biology

Some of our attraction to certain foods can be traced back about 10,000 years, when humans hunted and gathered everything they ate. Back then, survival and reproduction depended on finding high-calorie foods that could get a person through a dry spell or a long winter.

Through natural selection, Robinson says, we can still easily pick out certain scents, including rich, sweet foods. But the challenge now is that agriculture— and convenience stores—make foods like that available nearly everywhere we look.

In short, the very skill that helped your ancestors survive could be what's challenging you most now.

Powerful emotions

Most of us believe we can handle our feelings. We're grown-ups, right?

Well, yes—but no. The coworker who shifted the blame, the mother you miss whenever you see pink peonies, the combative teen in place of that sweet toddler—it can all add up to an urge to bake a batch of Grandma's cookies.

The truth is once you understand the feelings in that plate of cookies, you can look for healthier ways to soothe yourself.

As a case in point, Robinson describes a veteran who had a long-standing ritual of slipping toffee candies in his pocket every morning, which was pushing his weight and glucose readings out of range.

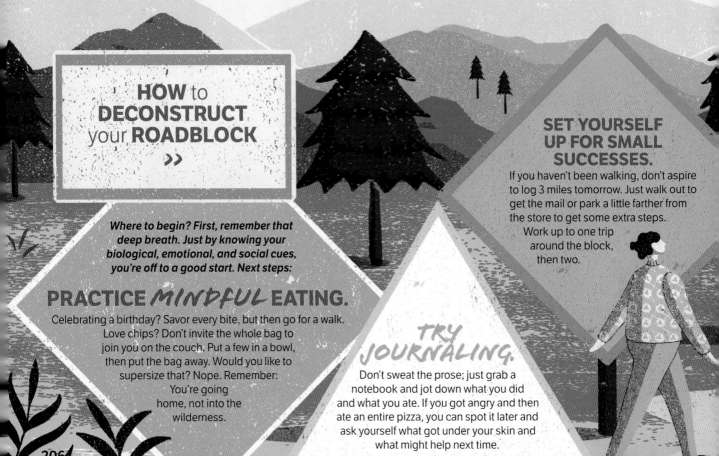

HOW to DECONSTRUCT your ROADBLOCK
»

Where to begin? First, remember that deep breath. Just by knowing your biological, emotional, and social cues, you're off to a good start. Next steps:

PRACTICE *MINDFUL* EATING.
Celebrating a birthday? Savor every bite, but then go for a walk. Love chips? Don't invite the whole bag to join you on the couch. Put a few in a bowl, then put the bag away. Would you like to supersize that? Nope. Remember: You're going home, not into the wilderness.

TRY JOURNALING.
Don't sweat the prose; just grab a notebook and jot down what you did and what you ate. If you got angry and then ate an entire pizza, you can spot it later and ask yourself what got under your skin and what might help next time.

SET YOURSELF UP FOR SMALL SUCCESSES.
If you haven't been walking, don't aspire to log 3 miles tomorrow. Just walk out to get the mail or park a little farther from the store to get some extra steps. Work up to one trip around the block, then two.

They talked about alternatives, and he decided to try sugar-free candies. "But that didn't really fly," Robinson says.

Next she asked why he wanted to improve his health. He began to talk about playing with his dog and grandkids and about the yardwork he used to enjoy.

They decided he would place pebbles in his pocket instead. "He still had his ritual. But now, it was pebbles representing the dog, the grandkids, and the garden," Robinson says.

"He started to respond to something much deeper when he would touch the pebbles. And that worked."

Social issues

Few of us second-guess cultural cues to eat. Who doesn't expect cake on their birthday? Then there's Thanksgiving, with its gravy and stuffing and "salads" with candy bars and whipped cream. Our daily choices aren't much better: lattes with syrup, burgers with fries.

Your family culture can stack your roadblock, too, especially if you snack together. If one person starts to change, that person can be given a hard time.

Still, Robinson says, "If you can make one small change—just a little thing—once a week, at the end of the year those 52 little changes can add up to a tremendous transformation."

Ready to start? Follow the path below.

OUTTHINK YOUR BARRIERS

Life coach Meshell Baker lends her advice for pushing past roadblocks:

◆ **Reframe negative thoughts.** Instead of thinking *I can't,* ask yourself: *How can I make this happen*?

◆ **Eyes on the prize.** "When you see people who have big results you want, ask yourself how you will incorporate a habit into your life to get the result you want."

◆ **Tempted? Wait 20 minutes.** Feelings often dissipate.

◆ **Have a 911.** Call a friend or reach for a podcast.

◆ **Tried everything? No, you haven't.** "You simply haven't found what works for you." Keep going. You'll find your way if you stay with it.

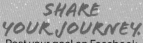

SHARE YOUR JOURNEY.
Post your goal on Facebook and follow up with photos. Support from friends makes success sweeter. You'll build confidence.

RECOGNIZE that **YOUR ROADBLOCK** is as **UNIQUE** as **YOU ARE.**

ADD
EXERCISE
to **YOUR DAY**

No time to exercise?
No problem! Sneak movement into your
everyday routines to help stay active, lose
weight, and manage your diabetes.

USE A STABILITY
BALL AS A CHAIR
TO IMPROVE CORE
STRENGTH.

YOUR CHECKLIST

Mix and match the following strategies help you burn calories, tone muscle, and feel more energized.

☑ **Walk when you can.**
There are easy ways to get a few more steps in your day. Park farther away in the parking lot so you have a longer walk inside. Be inefficient with your tasks—walk back and forth from the folding table to the dresser and put laundry away one piece at a time. Take the stairs instead of an elevator if you are only going one or two flights.

☑ **Stretch on the go.**
Stretch your lower back by turning your torso while sitting in a chair. Grab the side of the chair with both hands. Take a deep breath as you look over your shoulder. Twist as far as you can, then try it on the other side.

☑ **Exercise anywhere in the house.**
Do pushups in a standing position from a countertop. Stand a little more than arm length away and place your hands on the edge of the counter, shoulder width apart. Bend your elbows and lower your torso, then extend your arms by pushing up and away. Keep your body straight from head to heels. Do sets of 10 repetitions.

☑ **Have a walking meeting.**
Get more than your mouth moving. Walk and talk in person or on the phone. You'll burn more calories than if you stayed seated.

☑ **Increase your flexibility.**
When you pick something up from the floor, instead of hunching your back and bending from the waist, lengthen your spine and bend forward from the hips. With a straight back, lean forward as far as you can without rounding your back. Hold it for 10 seconds.

☑ **Tone while sitting at the computer.**
Sit on an exercise/stability ball when you are at your desk or using your laptop. While on the ball, your body constantly makes small adjustments to your posture and works your back, abdominal, glute, and leg muscles.

☑ **Don't waste commercial time.**
While watching television, get up and do a minute of jumping jacks or a minute of knee raises each time a commercial comes on. You can also lift small arm weights or do squats.

☑ **Set an alarm.**
Whether you're working or browsing websites at your desk, set an alarm on your computer or phone for every 50 minutes. When the alarm goes off, get up, stretch, and walk around for a few minutes.

☑ **Do all your own household chores.**
Clean the house, mow the lawn with a push mower, rake leaves, and wash your car by hand. Reaching, twisting, stretching, and lifting all burn calories. Instead of mopping your floor, get on your hands and knees to scrub if you can.

☑ **Park the cart.**
If you just need a handful of items at the supermarket, take two reusable bags and throw them over your shoulders. Put your items in the bags as you shop. While you wait to check out, hold the bags by your sides and do shoulder shrugs.

Exercise, even in small doses, is beneficial. The goal is to get moving for a total of 30 minutes over the course of the day.

YOUR FITNESS QUESTIONS ANSWERED

Being active with diabetes doesn't have to be a chore. We have you covered to make exercise safe and simplified.

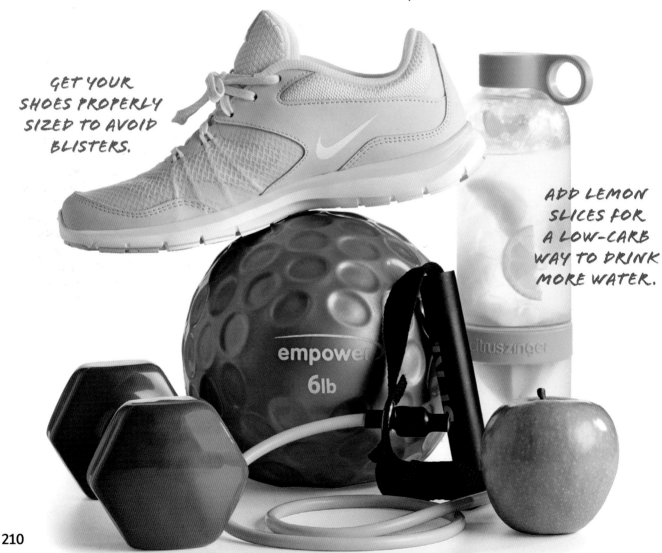

GET YOUR SHOES PROPERLY SIZED TO AVOID BLISTERS.

ADD LEMON SLICES FOR A LOW-CARB WAY TO DRINK MORE WATER.

empower 6lb

1.

Can exercise make glucose levels fall as well as rise?

A: Yes! If you have type 2 diabetes and don't take a glucose-lowering medication, then exercise will not cause glucose levels to fall too low. Exercise in most people with type 2 diabetes won't cause glucose levels to rise too high unless you've eaten a lot before exercising.

If you take insulin or another glucose-lowering medication that can cause hypoglycemia due to the way it works, then exercising without consuming carbs can cause hypoglycemia. Conversely, if people who take insulin vigorously exercise without taking enough rapid-acting insulin, their glucose levels can quickly rise.

2.

Are the guidelines for exercise different for people with type 1 and type 2 diabetes?

A: The general recommendations for both types of diabetes are similar, but key differences impact the approach. In type 1 diabetes and insulin-dependent type 2, a priority is to impart skills for people and their caregivers to manage glucose levels across the range of activities they do. However, both adults with type 1 and type 2 diabetes are encouraged to progress to and maintain a minimum of 150 minutes of moderate intensity (brisk pace) aerobic exercise with no more than 2 consecutive days without activity, and 2 to 3 days per week of resistance training (muscle-strengthening exercises) on nonconsecutive days. More activity may be needed to facilitate weight loss and for greater cardiovascular risk factor reductions (i.e., blood pressure cholesterol, etc.). Children and adolescents with diabetes (type 1 or 2) should aim for 60 minutes per day of moderate to vigorous aerobic activity with 3 or more days of muscle/bone-strengthening activities. (Diabetes Care, ADA Position Statement, 2016)

3.

Do you have to change your exercise routine every few months for it to be effective?

A: Yep! "Your body adapts to an exercise routine in about 12 weeks of doing it regularly," says Ryan Boisch, ACSM-CES, CDE, an exercise physiologist at Sanford Health in Fargo, North Dakota. If you usually walk and strength train with machines, try cycling and body weight exercises instead.

Does the time of day I exercise impact blood glucose control?

A: Gary Scheiner, M.S., CDE, an exercise physiologist and author of *Think Like a Pancreas*, promotes exercising after meals to lower the rise of glucose after eating. Walk a block or two after lunch or dinner, but don't buy the notion that there's a perfect time of day to exercise. "Do it daily. Treat exercise like medicine with this prescription: Take a reasonable dose daily for long-term health and happiness," he says.

ADD EXERCISE THROUGHOUT THE DAY TO MEET A GOAL FOR TOTAL MINUTES.

5.

Do I need an exercise stress test before I begin to exercise?

A: A stress test may be necessary if you've been inactive, are short of breath, are increasing exercise intensity or duration, or have or are at risk for heart problems. "Speak with your health care provider to know for sure," says Karen Kemmis, D.P.T., CDE, a physical therapist at the Joslin Diabetes Center in Boston.

6.

I am older and can't afford a gym. What types of exercise can I do on my own?

A: Research shows including adequate amounts of aerobic exercise and resistance training and reducing sedentary behavior are even more important as we age to keep muscles strong, increase flexibility, and optimize bone density. "Your home is your gym; your neighborhood is your track," says Richard Peng, M.S., ACSM-RCEP, CDE, an exercise physiologist for DaVita HealthCare Partners Medical Group in Los Angeles. No need for fancy gyms or equipment.

"Purchase rubber resistance bands. They're inexpensive and versatile," says Joy Keller, certified personal trainer in San Diego and executive editor of *IDEA Fitness Journal.* Or open your refrigerator or cabinets to find gallons of milk or cans of beans or soup. They double as tools for a successful resistance training program. Check out the countless free fitness videos on YouTube. "Do make sure the person offering the workout is certified," Keller says.

7.

How can I tell if exercise is helping me control my glucose levels over time?

A: The main way to tell is with the results of your A1C test. A1C provides the average of all the ups and downs of your glucose levels over the last two to three months. You'll be able to see the effects of regular exercise over a few weeks if you check your glucose at various times of the day—fasting and before and after meals.

8.

Can exercise alone help me lose weight?

A: Research shows that eating fewer calories than you need wins first place for weight loss or slowing weight gain. But regular exercise takes second place and offers a critical assist.

The National Weight Control Registry maintains that people who successfully keep weight off average 60–90 minutes of activity nearly every day. But exercise has other benefits: decreased insulin resistance, improved sleep, increased energy, prevention of chronic diseases like heart disease and some cancers, decreased joint pain, and a greater sense of well-being.

9.

Do I always need to eat or snack before I exercise or always bring food with me when I exercise?

A: "If your goal is weight loss and you don't take glucose-lowering medication that can cause hypoglycemia, it's generally unnecessary to eat or drink extra calories before you exercise," says Lisa Matthews, M.S., RD, a dietitian and certified fitness trainer at Williamson Medical Center in Franklin, Tennessee. If you need calories to raise glucose, portion out just what you need ahead of time.

If you take mealtime rapid-acting insulin shots, experiment with taking less insulin if you know you'll exercise within a few hours. If you use an insulin pump, try using the temporary basal feature to take less insulin during and several hours after you exercise. Taking an oral glucose-lowering medication? Tell your health care provider your glucose gets too low during exercise so he or she can make adjustments.

SNACKS & DRINKS NECESSARY OR NOT?

For Short-Duration Aerobic Activity *(under one hour)*

"It's not necessary for people who don't take insulin or another glucose-lowering medication that can cause hypoglycemia to carry snacks. Water or another no-calorie drink will suffice," Boisch says. For people who could become hypoglycemic when they exercise, Boisch suggests easy-to-carry glucose tablets or gel, dried fruit, Skittles candies, gummy bears, or packets of honey or sugar.

For Longer-Duration Aerobic Activity *(over one hour)*

"Rely on water as your main source of fluids. Some people may also need a small amount of carb-containing fluid such as Gatorade," Boisch says. "If you begin exercising at the low end of your target glucose range, or around 90 mg/dl, eat a snack like dried fruits and nuts, a piece of fruit, or crackers and peanut butter," Peng says.

Recommendations for longer-duration activity vary and must factor in the type of activity and intensity, individual needs, glucose-lowering medications and their timing, timing of exercise, and glucose levels at the start of and during exercise.

PAIR A PROTEIN AND A CARB FOR LONG-LASTING RESULTS.

WHY YOU NEED *to*

WALK

Fitness trends come and go, but this exercise never goes out of style. And for good reason.

Research on the incredible health benefits of walking just keeps coming.

Scientists at Cambridge University have reported that just 20 minutes of brisk walking each day can cut your risk of premature death by one-third.

A brisk half-hour daily walk can reduce your risk of myriad conditions, including cancer, heart disease, osteoporosis, dementia, and glaucoma.

New studies even found specific benefits for people with diabetes: A 15-minute walk after meals can help control your blood sugar.

For PWDs, walking should be a daily prescription, says exercise physiologist Carol Garber, Ph.D., director of the applied physiology program at Columbia University.

"It's essential that you exercise daily to keep your blood sugars under control," Garber says.

"Walking also helps maintain bone density—which is particularly important since diabetes has been linked to low bone mass."

Get ready.

Someone new to walking needs just one thing: the right shoes. They don't need to be expensive or super-fancy, but a reliable pair of good, sturdy, well-fitting walking shoes is essential.

The way those shoes fit is particularly important if you have diabetes because it's crucial to avoid blisters.

Your best bet, Garber says, is to visit an athletic shoe store and ask for guidance.

"Choose one that will let you try them on and walk around so that you don't get stuck with shoes that don't fit you well."

Though it's not necessary, adding a fitness tracker like a FitBit, Garmin, or Jawbone—or even a simple pedometer—to your walking arsenal might motivate you. "Each one has different advantages, and it's important to know that they may not all be perfectly accurate," Garber says. "But they can help push you to go farther or faster."

Take your first steps.

If you're just starting out, the recommendation to walk 30 minutes a day, five days a week, might seem overwhelming to you.

"It's better to start small than not to start at all," Garber says.

Try a short, 10-minute walk at first. Put it in your daily calendar as you would any other appointment, rather than saying you'll walk when you find the time—because you probably won't. If the weather is bad, hit the treadmill or the mall.

Many people find it easier to stick to a commitment to walk if they have a buddy. Ask a friend or officemate to join you a few times a week.

"Because walking is convenient, requires no special skill, and you're unlikely to get injured, it is the perfect exercise."

IF YOU CAN GET OUT OF A CHAIR AND MOVE, YOU CAN REAP THE HEALTH BENEFITS OF WALKING.

PROPER WALKING
FORM IS SIMPLE

A good stride helps prevent injury. Aim for comfortable, easy steps—don't overstride, which can cause pain or injury and doesn't really help you walk faster.

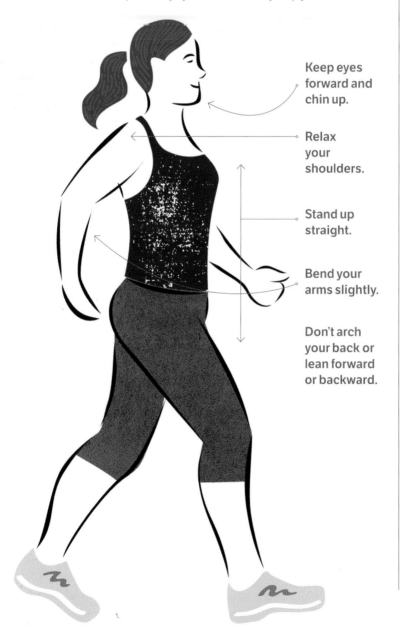

Keep eyes forward and chin up.

Relax your shoulders.

Stand up straight.

Bend your arms slightly.

Don't arch your back or lean forward or backward.

You can also find walking groups in your local area by using *meetup.com* (just search under Health & Wellness for a walking group near you).

Another way to find walking buddies is to ask around at the YMCA, medical center, or senior center.

Pump up your walk.

If you've been walking for exercise for a while and want to step it up, what's next?

There are lots of ways to boost your daily workout.

Increase your time first, then your speed, Garber says.

Every week or so, add 3 to 5 minutes to your walking time, until you're up to at least 30 minutes of walking at a stretch.

Once you're walking for those 30 minutes on a regular basis, try increasing your pace in small increments. As you begin to step up your pace, it becomes more important to get your muscles ready to move.

"Since diabetes puts you at risk for heart disease, it's a good idea to warm up for a solid 10 minutes before increasing your speed," Garber says.

Rather than warming up with so-called static stretches, such as the classic runner's stretch of grabbing a foot and pulling it up behind your body, start walking at a slow pace. Keep your pace controlled and gradually increase your speed over 10 minutes until you reach your exercise walking speed. To end your walk, reduce your pace to a cooldown speed over 5–10 minutes.

Then after your walk, when your muscles are warm and the blood is flowing, you can do static stretches like the runner's stretch or a hamstring stretch: Elevate your heel on a bench or rock—it doesn't have to be too high—and hold it for 20–30 seconds. Repeat twice with each leg.

If you've been walking on hills, calf stretches are a good idea, too. Stand on a step or curb and let your heels hang off the edge. Hold for 20–30 seconds, then repeat.

Push yourself a little.

After you've been walking awhile, you may find yourself ready to step it up again.

High-intensity interval training (HIIT) isn't just for runners and gym rats—you can adapt its benefits for a walking workout, too.

"Try walking as fast as you can for 2–4 minutes, then slow back down to your previous pace for a few minutes," Garber says.

Continue to switch paces throughout your session.

If you've been walking for 3–6 months and are feeling good, Garber suggests trying light jogging during intervals.

Add more fun stuff.

Playlists and podcasts can make those walking minutes fly by. Try the Ultimate Walking Playlist on Spotify—at 33 hours plus, you'll never run out of tunes. Or listen to fascinating podcasts such as *The Moth* or *Radiolab*.

To find the perfect music for your pace, create a playlist at *walk.jog.fm*. Just enter your minutes per mile, go through the list of songs that pop up, and add the ones you like.

When you're walking with confidence (even jogging a little), add strength training to your workout.

"Aerobic exercise is essential, but good muscular fitness and resistance exercises are also important for blood glucose control and muscle and joint health," Garber says.

Just don't add hand, wrist, or ankle weights to your walking workout, which can slow you down or change your form in a way that can stress your joints.

Instead, work in simple body-weight exercises you can do anywhere. These moves not only break up your routine, they allow you to get in a more comprehensive workout in about the same amount of time.

If you're doing a 30-minute session, for example, try taking a break after 10 minutes to do one exercise and again at 20 for another. Keep the strength moves simple, such as wall push-ups or lunges.

THIS IS HOW YOU ROLL

Most fitness crazes come and go. But here's one to embrace: foam rollers. Here are three things you should know about them—and four of the best moves.

3 TIPS FOR ROLLING

1 REAP THE BENEFITS.

Foam rollers target your fasciae, tissues that wrap around your muscles. When those tissues bind together from inactivity or repetitive motion, they can create painful knots, which limit movement and decrease flexibility. Get rolling to "break down adhesions between muscle fibers and increase blood flow," says Los Angeles fitness expert Ashley Borden.

2 KNOW WHEN TO ROLL.

Foam rollers are great for warming up or cooling down after a light workout, but they can be used any time. That might be while watching TV, after sitting at your desk for a while, or even after a long car ride. When you do it regularly, the discomfort of tenderizing those muscles will diminish.

3 FIND THE RIGHT FIT.

Rollers come in a variety of densities—soft to firm. As your muscles unwind, you can try a firmer model. Using foam rollers may cause discomfort and even a little pain, so start soft. A roller is too hard if you're losing your breath while using it.

IF YOU ARE NEW TO FOAM ROLLING, CHOOSE A SMOOTH ROLLER WITH LOW DENSITY. MOVE TO HARDER-TEXTURED ROLLERS AS YOU PROGRESS.

ROLL ON
4 MOVES TO TRY

Place the roller perpendicular to your body for these moves. Stay on soft tissue while rolling, avoiding bones and joints. If you reach an area that feels a little painful, hold for a few seconds to allow it to soften.

QUADRICEPS

FORM: Lie facedown on forearms with roller under thighs and legs extended behind you. Keeping head in line with spine, eyes down, and belly pulled in, crawl forward on forearms until roller is just above kneecaps. Reverse.
REPS: Do 3 sets of 10 each—one with toes pointed down, one with toes pointed in, and one with toes pointed out.

GLUTES

FORM: Sit on roller with knees bent, feet flat on floor, hands behind you. Cross left ankle over right knee. Tilt left knee down toward floor and slowly roll back and forth.
REPS: 10 times. Switch sides; repeat.

CALVES

FORM: Lie on back with roller under left calf and arms under head. Cross right ankle over left shin. Roll left leg side to side on top of roller 10 times. Slide roller up calf and repeat. Move up calf in small increments until full length of calf is rolled. Switch sides; repeat.

UPPER BACK

FORM: Lie on back with roller under shoulder blades and feet flat on floor. Interlock fingers behind head. Engage core and lift hips slightly off floor. Pushing into feet, slowly roll up and down from bottom of shoulder blades to top of shoulders.
REPS: Repeat 10 times.

6
SIMPLE STRETCHES

Ease your body's stiffness and improve stability with just a few daily moves.

1.
STANDING LATERAL REACH

This stretch helps lengthen the lateral back muscles, which can ease lower-back pain and improve posture.

STEP 1: Stand with your feet hip width apart, body weight evenly distributed. Reach both arms straight up with fingertips to the ceiling. With shoulders relaxed, attempt to bring your biceps toward your ears.

STEP 2: With the left hand, grasp the right wrist. Continue to reach upward as you lean the shoulders and rib cage to the left side, staying upright as if you are pressed between two sheets of glass. Keep the right biceps as close to your ear as possible.

STEP 3: Hold for 15–30 seconds and then return to the center, changing your wrist grip and repeating on the other side.

2.
STANDING
KNEE TO CHEST

This move helps with balance, strength, and stability while lengthening muscles in your lower back and hips. This stretch also can be done while seated or lying on your back.

STEP 1: Stand with your feet shoulder width apart. Bend your right knee and draw it up toward your chest by grasping just below the knee or behind the thigh with both hands to create a grip point. If you cannot maintain balance with both hands holding up your knee, put one hand on a chair or wall for support.

STEP 2: Pull the knee toward your body while maintaining a tall, erect posture. With each breath, try to bring your knee a little closer to the chest and torso.

STEP 3: Hold for 15–30 seconds, breathing and balancing, then release and switch sides.

IF YOU USE A CHAIR FOR BALANCE, MAKE SURE IT IS HIGH ENOUGH SO YOU AREN'T BENDING.

3.
LATERAL LUNGE

This stretch opens your hips and lengthens hamstrings in the legs.

STEP 1: Stand with feet wider than hip width apart, pointing your toes out slightly. Keep your weight evenly distributed.

STEP 2: Lean to the left, flexing your left knee while lengthening the right leg as you press into the hip. Stay upright as you lean to the side. You can place your hands on your thighs for help with balance. If you want to incorporate your back, extend your right arm up, fingertips reaching toward the ceiling.

STEP 3: Hold for 15–30 seconds, then release and switch sides.

4.
FIGURE 4

This stretch (often used in physical therapy) opens muscles deep in the hips and can alleviate lower-back pain, tightness, and discomfort, particularly after sitting for prolonged periods.

STEP 1: Lie on your back, placing the left foot on the floor with the knee bent toward the ceiling; draw your right knee up into your chest.
STEP 2: Cross the right leg over the left knee by resting your right ankle on the your thigh just above the knee.
STEP 3: Reaching through the legs, clasp your hands together on the left knee (under or on top), creating a grip point. Pull the knee toward the body, feeling the stretch in the right hip. Use your elbow to create more leverage to the stretch. Hold and repeat on the other leg.

5.
CHILD'S POSE

This common yoga stretch is ideal for relaxation and stretching your arms, sides, and lower back.

STEP 1: Begin on your hands and knees with hands placed slightly in front of the shoulders with fingers spread and knees directly under the hips. Relax your feet so your shoelaces are resting on the floor.
STEP 2: Push your hips back, allowing them to rest as close to the heels as possible as you lengthen your body and reach your arms out on the floor in front of you, as if someone were grasping your wrists and pulling your arms longer.
STEP 3: Tuck your chin and relax into the pose, holding the position for up to 60 seconds.

REGULAR STRETCHING CAN INCREASE YOUR BODY'S CIRCULATION, WHICH WILL GIVE YOU MORE ENERGY FOR THE DAY.

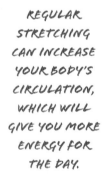

Cat

Cow

6.
CAT/COW STRETCH

These stretches move the spine through healthy ranges of flexion and extension, which lubricates the spine and allows for a connection between breath and movement.

STEP 1: Begin on your hands and knees with hands placed directly under the shoulders and knees directly under the hips. The spine should be neutral and your head relaxed.

CAT: For cat pose, round the back, dropping the head and tucking the tailbone. Exhale as you arch your back toward the ceiling.

COW: For cow pose, arch the back by dropping the belly, lifting the chin, and opening the chest and throat, taking full, deep breaths. Move between the two stretches 3–5 times.

ROLL YOUR WAY INTO *RELAXATION*

Fitness experts are starting to incorporate rollers into floor exercises. You lic on top of the roller and roll your body over it, focusing on one muscle group at a time.

Here is one stretch to try with a roller. See "This Is How You Roll," *p. 218*, for additional moves to try.

STEP 1: Sit on the floor. Place the roller behind you and lie back, resting your spine lengthwise on top of the roller. Your neck and head should be in contact with the roller.

STEP 2: Bend your knees and place your feet flat on the floor. If you struggle with balance on top of the roller, widen your feet for more stability. Allow the weight of your body and head to be fully supported by the roller.

STEP 3: Reach arms toward the ceiling, palms facing each other, directly above your shoulders. Like scissors, drop one arm behind your head toward the floor while the other arm simultaneously drops down by your side. Continue this scissor motion for 30–45 seconds.

THE 30-MINUTE WORKOUTS

225

30-MINUTE WORKOUT
EASY ON THE KNEES

Exercising isn't always easy. And if you have knee pain, you may talk yourself out of it altogether.

Knee pain is often caused by arthritis, a generic term for inflammation of one or more joints. About 22 percent of the population suffers from arthritis, and people with diabetes are nearly twice as likely to develop it. The most common form, osteoarthritis (OA), causes wear and tear of joint cartilage, creating bone spurs or cysts. When this happens, bones rub against each other, causing stiffness and joint pain that can feel worse after activity.

Here's good news: While joint damage is irreversible, exercise can help relieve stiffness without hurting joints, giving you better mobility.

Both aerobic and resistance exercises work—with some tweaks. Swimming and cycling are great for getting your heart pumping because they don't stress joints. The following resistance exercises reduce pain and disability by strengthening muscles that support the knees and improve range of motion (ROM).

Tweak exercises to accommodate knee mobility issues by determining your ROM (or how far you flex or extend a joint). When done regularly, they'll help make daily activities such as walking, getting out of chairs, and taking the stairs easier and less painful.

KEEP LEAD KNEE BEHIND YOUR TOES AND YOUR BACK STRAIGHT.

WARM-UP

To improve circulation and ROM before starting this workout, march in place at a comfortable pace for 1–5 minutes. Start by raising heels off ground and progress to a high march. Increase ROM and speed as it becomes easier.

1 LUNGE

In standing position with hands at sides or on hips, take a slightly exaggerated step forward with one leg (lead leg). The weight of the trail leg can shift to the ball of the foot for stability as the trail knee slightly bends. Once stable, bend lead knee and allow trail knee to bend and drop. Move slowly and with control. Lower until you reach maximum ROM or feel pain. Return to start by focusing weight on lead leg, pushing off lead foot. Repeat as desired. Switch legs and repeat.

PROGRESSION POINTER To increase knee ROM and strength, progress to lowering the trail leg just above the floor. To increase hip ROM, progress to a slightly more exaggerated step forward (watch stability).

KEEP CORE CONTRACTED AND LOOK STRAIGHT AHEAD AS YOU MOVE.

2 CALF RAISE

Standing with hands at sides, slowly lift heels off floor, supporting weight on the balls of feet. Continue raising heels until you reach maximum ROM or feel pain. Return to start by slowly lowering heels to floor. Repeat 10–15 times.

PROGRESSION POINTER Use a step for increased ROM. Lower your heel below the step surface to get a greater stretch.

3 LEG RAISE WITH KNEE EXTENSION

With your hands at sides or on hips, raise your knees toward the ceiling, flexing at the hip and knee (like marching) to a 90-degree angle. Slowly extend leg with toes pointed forward. Then return to the high marching position before placing your foot back on the floor. Repeat 8–10 times. Switch and repeat.

PROGRESSION POINTER Place a dumbbell on thigh of the lifting leg to add resistance.

THIS MOVE IS LIKE A SLOW-MOTION KARATE KICK.

4 SINGLE LEG STEP-UP

Standing with hands at sides, step up lead leg onto a stable surface, such as a stair. Slowly shift weight to lead leg and raise up as you straighten it until you're standing fully erect on surface. Contract your core, stay upright, and look straight ahead as you step. Bring trail leg up to meet lead leg. Stand and relax. Return to start by shifting weight to lead leg and lowering trail leg to floor. Step lead leg down to meet trail leg. Repeat 10–15 times. Switch legs and repeat.

PLACE ENTIRE LEAD FOOT ON SURFACE FOR STABILITY.

- As exercises become less challenging, increase to 10–15 reps for maintenance. Continue beyond 15 reps to improve muscular endurance.
- Start with 1 set (number of times you perform this routine) and build to 3. Continue to increase the number of sets as long as it doesn't cause pain.
- Increase ROM until you feel pain or break proper form.
- Reduce your rest periods between sets for more challenge.
- Hold on to the wall or a chair for balance when you need it.
- If you start to feel intolerable pain, stop and rest until the pain reduces to normal levels.

THIS POWER MOVE WILL UTILIZE ALL THE LOWER-BODY MUSCLES AND BRING EACH OF THE 4 EXERCISES INTO ONE FLUID MOVEMENT.

THE POWER MOVE

5 LUNGE-RAISE-KICK!

Standing with hands on hips, perform the lunge *(A; p. 227)* through the down and up phases. During the upward phase, bring the trail leg forward by swinging it slowly and controlled toward your body. Without touching the floor, continue swinging trail leg past your body to transition into the single leg raise with knee extension exercise *(p. 228)*. Once the trail leg has reached its highest-tolerable point of extension *(B)*, do a calf raise *(p. 227)* with the lead leg (the leg that has been supporting you through this exercise). Return your heel to the floor and place the trail (raised) leg back to the marching position *(C)* before placing it back to the floor to meet the other (lead) leg. Alternate sides for 10–15 reps per leg. Hold on to a wall or chair to maintain balance. You can try the exercise without support when you feel comfortable.

COOLDOWN

March in place at a comfortable pace for 1–5 minutes. Start with a high march and slow it eventually to a heel lift. Stretch lightly: do toe touches, calf stretch, and quad stretch for 30 seconds each.

30-MINUTE WORKOUT
SLEEP BETTER
TONIGHT

Having diabetes is stressful. It can cause both physical and mental problems, which can make you feel exhausted all day. Unfortunately, that stress can follow you into the night.

People with diabetes are more likely to report sleep problems. Sleep disturbances may be brought on by low blood sugar, nocturia (waking up to urinate), anxiety about nighttime glucose management, and more.

It only takes one sleepless night to affect diabetes management. Studies have shown that sleep disturbances can cause physiological stress resulting in a surge of stress hormones (such as epinephrine and cortisol) that circulate in the body. This surge can raise blood glucose levels and worsen insulin resistance. Chronic sleeplessness is also linked to altered eating habits, weight gain, and muscle tension. It's a huge barrier to mental and physical health.

But we have good news: Aerobic training and resistance training can improve mood, sleep quality, and diabetes management. And increasing evidence shows yoga and relaxation exercises are also effective in self-management.

This workout is designed to improve sleep quality by reducing stress and helping you relax before bedtime—or whenever you feel overwhelmed or tight. While each of these exercises can be performed at any time to help you relax, performing them in sequence will provide better results.

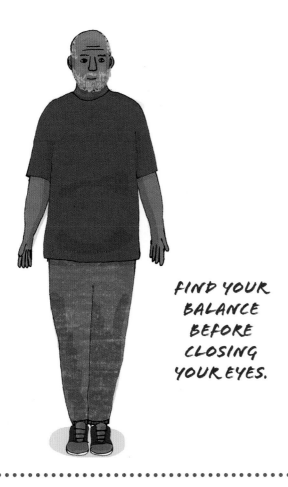

FIND YOUR
BALANCE
BEFORE
CLOSING
YOUR EYES.

1 MOUNTAIN POSE

Stand with feet together and arms at sides. Look ahead. Stand tall with your shoulder blades back, head in line with your pelvis, chin parallel with the floor, and palms open. Maintain your balance by rocking back and forth slightly until you find your center. Close your eyes and focus on your breathing. Inhale and exhale slowly without forcing your breaths. Try to extend your breath duration and deepness over time throughout the pose. Perform 10–30 breaths.

PROGRESSION POINTER When you inhale, your belly should expand rather than suck in.

2 FORWARD FOLD

Stand with feet together and arms at sides. Look ahead. As you exhale, bend forward at your hips (knees slightly bent), lowering hands toward the floor and head down and in toward your torso. Let hands hang as far down legs as possible, allowing your back and the back of your legs to stretch gently. Breathe normally as you focus on expanding your stomach during inhalation and keeping the stretch during exhalation. Hold at least 15 seconds or 10 breaths.

PROGRESSION POINTER Balance issues? A wider stance provides more stability in starting position.

BEND
FORWARD
SLOWLY,
LETTING
ARMS AND
HEAD HANG
NATURALLY.

3 CHILD'S POSE

Kneel on the floor and sit back on your heels (if this is too difficult, rest a pillow between your calves and the back of your thighs). Sit up straight, lengthening your back and opening your chest. As you exhale, slowly bow forward until forehead reaches the floor (or rest it on a pillow). Extend arms out in front of head with palms down, extending through the fingertips and resting palms on the floor. Allow yourself to relax your whole body. With each exhale, relax more and reach your arms out farther if possible for a greater stretch. Hold up to 2 minutes.

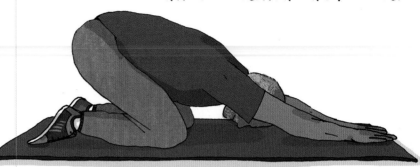

RELAX INTO THE POSE. YOUR FOREHEAD DOESN'T HAVE TO REACH THE FLOOR.

4 COW AND CAT POSES

Begin on your hands and knees with hands directly under shoulders and knees directly under hips.

To perform cow pose, drop your stomach toward the floor as you inhale. Look up while lifting your chin and dropping your shoulder blades.

To transition into cat pose, pull your stomach in as you exhale, arching your back toward the ceiling. Simultaneously drop your head toward the floor, bringing chin in toward chest, and tuck in tailbone. Repeat cow-to-cat sequence 5–20 times.

REST THE TOPS OF YOUR FEET ON THE FLOOR.

THE POWER MOVE

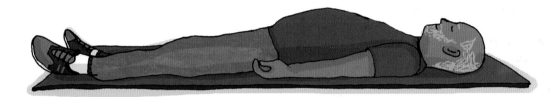

5 CORPSE POSE

This power move is designed to help you relax and fall asleep. Perform this at night prior to bedtime or while lying in bed. Lying on your back, straighten legs and place arms at sides, palms up. Close your eyes and allow your body to completely relax. Focus on progressive muscle relaxation from your toes up through each limb until you reach your head, clearing your mind as you go. Breathe naturally. If you get sidetracked or feel physical tension returning, start over until your entire body is relaxed.

PROGRESSION POINTER Sleep professionals recommend creating a relaxing scene or story to keep your mind from wandering while you concentrate on your breathing pattern.

COOLDOWN
Sit or lie in a comfortable pose after performing the power move. Avoid light aerobic activity; it may counteract the relaxation effects of the regimen.

More than one-third of U.S. adults suffer from reduced quality of life because of inadequate sleep. *Gentle yoga may cut perceived stress in half and improve sleep efficiency by nearly*

40%

HEAD HEALTH
MORE YOGA BENEFITS

According to the *Journal of Diabetes & Metabolism*, yoga's benefits go well beyond the physical.

Studies show that regular yoga practice has a positive effect on mental health, including relaxation, improved breathing, and calm.

The journal further reports that yoga may improve nerve damage and cognitive functions in people with diabetes, which may benefit management of complications.

Yoga may also reverse the negative impact of immune system stress.

The National Institutes of Health lists even more reasons to break out the yoga mat, saying that yoga might improve overall quality of life while relieving tension, anxiety, depression, and insomnia.

30-MINUTE WORKOUT
AT-HOME CIRCUIT *TRAINING*

One of today's most popular workouts is circuit training, which combines aerobic cardio and resistance training so you get the benefits of both forms of exercise in a single session. Circuit training can burn 20–30 percent more calories than cardio or weights alone and provides a multitude of health benefits, including improved blood glucose control, insulin sensitivity, blood pressure, and cholesterol as well as weight loss.

This at-home circuit routine provides those full-body exercise benefits without spending hundreds of dollars on a gym membership. All you need is furniture, some form of weight (light dumbbells, bands, or your own body weight), and a little motivation.

Because it combines cardio exercise with strength and endurance moves, this circuit will work the muscles and joints you use every day, which will noticeably improve your abilities to perform everyday tasks.

And with a little practice and modifications as needed, it's doable for all fitness levels.

According to a study published in *JAMA*, people with diabetes can lower A1C nearly *2 times more with a combination of aerobic and resistance exercises* than with either type alone.

WARM-UP

March in place at a comfortable pace 1–5 minutes. Start by raising heels off the ground and progress to a high march. As you march, raise arms above the head (raise the roof) and extend out in front of you (pushing) for 5 minutes. Do a warm-up set for each exercise by mimicking the movements in a slow, light fashion.

AEROBIC INTERMISSION

Walk in place between each resistance exercise at a light to moderate intensity for 2–3 minutes. Pace yourself.

◄ **1 SQUAT WITH SHOULDER PRESS**

Hold light dumbbells in each hand at shoulders with feet between hip width and shoulder width apart, palms forward, and toes forward or slightly outward. Flexing at hips and knees, lower butt toward floor until thighs are parallel with the floor or as far as your joint mobility allows (when toes raise and back rounds slightly). Keep back neutral or slightly arch the lower back and keep your weight on your heels and knees behind toes. Do not round shoulders or lean forward. Return to standing while raising the weights over your head, keeping elbows in line with ears. Repeat. Perform an aerobic intermission, then move on to Exercise 2. **PROGRESSION POINTER** Squat farther down as you become stronger and more flexible.

2 FORWARD FOLD

◄ Choose a stable chair or low table that can support your body weight. Place hands on the edge, shoulder width apart. Arms extended, walk body out until torso is 3 inches in front of furniture. Keep knees bent at a 90-degree angle, feet flat on floor. Lower until elbows make a 90-degree angle (or as far as you can go). Press down into furniture and extend elbows to return to start. Repeat. Perform aerobic intermission, then move on to Exercise 3. **PROGRESSION POINTER** In starting position, before dipping, kick one leg out by extending the knee; after dip, return foot to floor, extend other leg, and repeat.

KEEP CORE CONTRACTED AND LOOK STRAIGHT AHEAD.

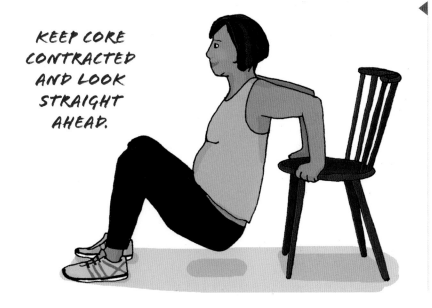

3 STEP-UPS WITH BICEPS CURLS

Stand with weights in hands, palms forward, and arms at sides. Step up onto a step or stool with one foot (lead leg), shifting weight to that leg as you rise, bringing trail leg up to meet lead leg. Simultaneously bend the elbows and curl dumbbells toward your shoulders. Keep arms tight at sides, wrists stiff, and back rigid (don't arch or swing). Stand and relax. Return to the start by lowering trail leg to the floor, followed by lead leg, while slowly lowering dumbbells. Repeat with opposite leg and continue alternating. Perform aerobic intermission, then move on to Exercise 4.

PROGRESSION POINTER Increase the height of your step-up for greater resistance and challenge.

4 CHAIR PULL AND PRESS

Get on your knees facing a stable chair or low table that can support your body weight. Close to the chair, place your hands about shoulder width apart with arms fully extended. Sit back on your heels, stretching your back and arms. This is the starting position. Push into your hands and pull forward to raise your body up and toward the chair. Once you are upright, lean forward and lower your body toward the chair by bending elbows (doing a push-up). Repeat. Perform aerobic intermission, then move on to Exercise 5.

PROGRESSION POINTER In a standing position (on feet, not knees, like a standard push-up position), place yourself on a steeper angle with the chair. You may also use a wall for this.

THE POWER MOVE

THIS MOVE WORKS THE THIGHS, HIPS, ABS, LOWER BACK, AND SHOULDERS.

PROGRESSION

• As exercises become less challenging, increase the number of reps from 8 to 12. To improve muscular endurance, continue beyond 12 reps. If you add weights or bands, do 6–8 reps to improve strength.
• Start with 1 set and build to 3 sets.
• If you can do 2 reps beyond your goal on the last set (2 sets or more), increase resistance (weights or bands). This is called the 2-for-2 rule.
• Speed up walking in place and/or raise legs higher (marching). To involve more muscle groups and rev up your heart rate, add arm movements like "raising the roof," pushing out, and raising arms to sides.

NOTE Master these moves with body weight before progressing to weights or bands. Chronic musculoskeletal conditions may hinder your abilities to perform all movements in this circuit.

5 ARM SWING

Stand with feet flat on floor, hip width to shoulder width apart, toes forward, knees slightly bent. Clasp your hands together and straighten your arms in front of you. Slightly flex hips (not knees) and gently swing your arms back between your legs until torso is parallel to floor. Then swing your arms forward and up toward eye level by extending the hips and knees, elbows extended and back neutral. Use your momentum to swing your arms up. Then swing arms back down. Repeat entire circuit or begin cooldown.

PROGRESSION POINTER Increase your range of motion through the swing as you become stronger and more flexible. Advanced: Grasp a light dumbbell or milk jug in your hands for added resistance.

COOLDOWN

March in place at a comfortable pace for 1–5 minutes. Start with a high march and regress to a heel lift. Stretch lightly; do toe touches, calf stretch, and quad stretch for 30 seconds each. Do static stretches that target the muscles used in the workout, 1–4 sets for each muscle. Stretch until you feel slight discomfort and hold 10–30 seconds.

The American College of Sports Medicine recommends following F.I.T.T. guidelines for this resistance-training program.

F.I.T.T. Goals

FREQUENCY 2–3 times per week on alternate days

INTENSITY 8–12 repetitions (or until you break form); 2–4 sets per exercise

TIME Average 30 minutes. Workout length will depend on the number of sets and rest periods; take a 2–3 minute break between each set.

TYPE Progressive resistance training emphasizing all major muscle groups

SUPPLIES
- Comfortable clothes
- Clock (or something to tell time)
- Resistance: bands, free weights (dumbbells or barbells), light kettle bells

As you progress, you may need
- Heavier resistance equipment
- Greater variety of exercises to avoid additional imbalances

30-MINUTE WORKOUT
BALANCE
YOUR BODY

We constantly aim to find balance in life: work vs. play, social time vs. personal time, wants vs. needs.

When you think about exercise, keep balance in mind, too—muscle balance. It helps your body function better and minimizes the risk for injuries.

Consider how muscles work. When you want to move your body or lift an object, you call upon your muscles to create force to move your bones. When a muscle works to provide movement, that muscle shortens. The primary muscle causing the movement is the *agonist*.

The agonist does the main work; an opposing muscle called the *antagonist* works simultaneously against it to control movement and avoid overstretching.

Muscle imbalance happens if the agonist is much stronger than the antagonist—like a bodily tug-of-war. The stronger muscles pull the attached limbs in their direction, causing an exaggerated stretch on the weaker muscle that over time causes problems like rounded shoulders, a tilting pelvis, and changes in certain movements.

These issues get joints off track and promote chronic pain or impaired movement. In extreme cases, muscle imbalance increases risk of injury.

To prevent imbalance, avoid repetitive positions and moves. Do a variety of aerobic exercises for different muscles and whole-body resistance training for all major muscle groups.

The following workout shows you what we mean. Each exercise gives you two movement patterns that activate both the agonist and antagonist of major muscles.

1 SQUAT
Stand with feet between hip width and shoulder width apart, toes forward or slightly outward. Slowly and controlled, flex at hips and knees and lower body until thighs are parallel with floor (or as far as your joints allow). Keep back neutral or slightly arch lower back. DO NOT round shoulders or lean forward—you should be able to lift your toes. Slowly return to standing. Repeat.
PROGRESSION POINTER Squat farther down as you become stronger and more flexible.

2 PUSH AND PULL
This exercise combo helps achieve an upper-body balance.
A. PUSH-UP Stand arm's length from a wall and place your hands on the wall level with your shoulders, shoulder width apart. Engage core to keep hips from sinking. Bend at elbows and lower your chest toward the wall. Then extend your elbows to starting position to push yourself back out. Repeat.
PROGRESSION POINTER Increase the intensity by walking your feet away from the wall over time. Progress to floor push-ups on your knees.
B. SEATED ROW Sitting, place the middle of a resistance band around the arches of feet, knees slightly bent. Grasp handles or wrap ends around hands, thumbs up, palms facing in. Sit tall with arms extended in front of you. To begin, pull toward your midsection, keeping elbows in tight until the wrists meet the side of your torso. Maintain a rigid, erect posture. Do not lean back as you pull the band. Next, extend arms forward in a controlled movement back to start. Repeat.
PROGRESSION POINTER Increase resistance using the 2-for-2 rule (p. 241).

REST HEELS ON FLOOR AND DON'T LEAN BACK.

A

B

3 CURL AND EXTEND

The push and pull of these exercises helps keep upper-arm balance.

A. BICEPS CURL Stand tall with knees slightly bent, feet shoulder width or hip width apart, and shoulders back. Grab weights or band (anchored under feet), arms at sides, palms forward. Bend elbows and curl weights or band toward the shoulders. Keep arms tight at sides, wrists stiff, and core engaged. All movement should occur at elbows. Slowly lower to starting spot. Repeat.

4 CRUNCH AND FLY

These exercises engage the midsection muscles that both flex and extend the spine.

A. ABDOMINAL CRUNCH Lie on your back with knees bent, feet flat on floor, palms down. Use abs to curl chest toward knees, sliding palms along floor toward heels. Once shoulder blades are completely off the floor or you reach maximum range of motion, slowly lower. Repeat.

PROGRESSION POINTER For added resistance, place hands across chest or extend them above your head.

FOCUS ON USING AB MUSCLES TO LIFT YOURSELF.

B. OVERHEAD TRICEPS EXTENSION Stand tall with knees slightly bent, feet shoulder or hip width apart, and shoulders back. Grab weights or band (anchored under feet). Extend arms over head, aligning elbows with ears. To begin, slowly bend elbows, lowering hands behind head. Keep elbows tight to ears, wrists stiff, shoulders stationary, and core engaged (don't arch back or lean forward). Extend elbows, bringing hands back above your head. Repeat.

B. SUPERMAN Lie on stomach, arms at your sides, palms facing up. Keeping your neck aligned, raise your forehead, shoulders, and chest off the floor toward your butt by curling your lower back muscles. This may be minimal movement. That's OK—just focus on engaging your lower back. Slowly return to the floor. Repeat.
PROGRESSION POINTER For more resistance, extend your arms in front and raise your chest off the floor. Simultaneously raise legs and feet to further engage lower back and glutes.

THE **POWER MOVE**

5 PLANK

Get on hands and knees. Next, rest elbows and forearms on the floor (close to rib cage) to support upper-body weight. Engage core to create a flat back (do not arch, sink, or raise butt). Envision a board lying across your body. Breathe throughout the pose; hold it until you feel form breaking. Rest and repeat.
PROGRESSION POINTER Increase the duration of the pose. When you reach 1-minute holds, make it more challenging by raising knees off the floor and extending arms. Keep straight from head to toe.

▼

COOLDOWN
Include 1–4 sets of static stretching in your cooldown that targets each muscle used in this workout. Stretch until you feel slight discomfort and hold for 10–30 seconds. Stretching daily improves flexibility.

PROGRESSION

- Increase resistance and number of sets as it becomes easier.
- If you can do 2 reps beyond your goal on the last set (2 sets or more), increase resistance (weights or bands). This is called the 2-for-2 rule.
- As exercises become less challenging, increase the number of reps to 8–12. To improve muscular endurance, continue beyond 12 reps. If you add weights or bands, do 6–8 reps to improve strength.
- Start with 1 set (number of times you perform an exercise) and build to 3.

PLANK ENGAGES MANY MAJOR MUSCLES, STIMULATES ALIGNMENT AND POSTURE, AND CAN BE PERFORMED WITH MANY VARIATIONS BASED ON ABILITY.

30-MINUTE WORKOUT

BUILD A STRONGER CORE

"Core." Think about what that word means.

"Core" is synonymous with "center," "foundation," and "hub." Indeed, having a strong midpoint (or core) helps to provide stability with all of a system's working components. Mechanical engineers, for example, design systems to operate with structural integrity and efficiency. That requires a strong infrastructure, or core.

In a similar way, the human body is a mechanical structure that operates only as efficiently as its core. If the core is weak, stability is compromised. Arms and legs have to make up for any lack of central stability, which can lead to increased fatigue, posture problems, or muscle strains. Therefore, we have to engineer our bodies with a strong core to maximize physical functioning for both daily living and recreational activities.

Despite what hyped-up magazine covers may have told you, your core doesn't just consist of abdominals—it includes the lower and middle back, hips, upper thighs, and upper torso. Because your core provides stability for all movements, core exercises should mimic various movement patterns from side to side, front to back, and rotational.

This exercise regimen is a great start toward building an effective and efficient core.

242

KEEP YOUR BODY ALIGNED FROM HEAD THROUGH FEET.

1 BRIDGE
Lie on your back with knees bent and feet flat on floor. Place arms at sides (2–3 inches from hips), palms down. Press down with your midfoot to heel and slowly raise hips toward the ceiling until you feel your shoulder blades lifting off the floor, creating a straight line with your spine and thighs. Focus on engaging your glutes (butt muscles) and hamstrings. Hold this position for 1 or 2 counts. Slowly lower hips back to the floor. Repeat.
PROGRESSION POINTERS Hold the midpoint position for a longer duration. Use one leg to bridge your body.

2 SIDE WALK PLANK
Stand sideways and rest your forearm and palm on a wall. Slowly side-step away from the wall, creating a diagonal line between your arm and feet (you may need to lower your arm position on the wall). Engage your core to keep your body aligned. Don't dip or extend your hips. Hold this position (static) until you begin to struggle to maintain it. Rest and alternate sides.
PROGRESSION POINTER Hold the static position for a longer duration or increase the distance between your feet and the wall to create a greater angle.

3 BIRD DOG

Get on hands and knees with tops of feet resting on the floor and hands directly under shoulders, hips above knees. Use your core to keep your back straight. Extend one leg behind you until it's parallel with the floor (or as high as you can, stopping at or below hip level). Simultaneously raise and extend the opposite arm until it's parallel with the floor at shoulder height. Hold for 1 or 2 counts. Slowly return to start position. Engage abs and lower back to avoid rocking hips and shoulders when you return to start. Repeat on each side.

PROGRESSION POINTER Use ankle or hand weights to increase resistance.

4 DEAD BUG

Lie on your back with arms reaching for the sky and knees bent, creating a 90-degree angle. To start, lower and extend one leg while simultaneously reaching and lowering the opposite arm next to your head (elbow to ear)—each about 1–2 inches from the floor. (For less difficulty, keep your knee slightly bent when lowering to the floor.) Hold for 1 or 2 counts; flex the knee and shoulders to bring limbs back to start. Repeat on each side.

PROGRESSION POINTERS

Hold the midpoint position for a longer duration. Use ankle or hand weights to increase resistance.

REST HEAD ON FLOOR TO AVOID STRESS ON NECK.

THE POWER MOVE

THIS MOVE INVOLVES ALL THE CORE MUSCLES AND ENGAGES THE UPPER AND LOWER BODY.

PROGRESSION

• As exercises become less challenging, increase the number of reps to 8–12. To improve muscular endurance, continue beyond 12 reps.
• To improve muscle endurance and increase intensity, reduce rest periods to 30 seconds or less.
• Increase the number of sets as the exercise becomes easier and you reach the desired reps.
• Use the progression pointers to modify the moves to create a greater challenge.

5 LUNGE WITH ABDOMINAL TWIST

In standing position with hands in front of your abdomen, elbows bent (holding resistance object for added challenge if desired), take a step forward with one leg (lead leg). The weight of the trail leg can shift to the ball of the foot as it slightly bends. Bend lead knee and lower toward floor, allowing trail knee to bend, too. As you lower, twist torso and arms to the same side as the lead leg, reaching for your hip. Lower until you feel pain or reach maximum range of motion (ROM). Return arms and torso to the center and push off the lead foot to return to start. Repeat with each leg. Keep lead knee behind your toes.

PROGRESSION POINTERS Increase your ROM as you become more stable, strong, and flexible. Hold arms out farther in front of you for added resistance.

COOLDOWN

Repeat warm-up for 5–10 minutes. Then stretch the core muscles, holding for 10–30 seconds per stretch: standing side stretches, seated toe touches, and abdominal stretches.

1 in 3

adults age 65 or older suffers from chronic back pain, and people who are obese have roughly a 40% greater risk. *The big culprits: sedentary behavior and weak core muscles*

RECIPE INDEX

On the book spines and covers:
- diabetes what to eat
- diabetes meals by the plate
- diabetic slow cooker
- quick & easy meals
- EAT to BEAT diabetes
- the ultimate diabetes cook book
- Healthy Makeovers for Diabetes

diabetic LIVING **HEALTHY MAKEOVERS** for Diabetes™ SIMPLE WAYS TO TRANSFORM YOUR COOKING

BOOST FIBER INTAKE Swap parsnips for half of the potatoes to help control your blood sugar.

REDUCE CARBS BY HALF Trade traditional pork chop breading for one with nuts.

LOWER SODIUM Replace canned vegetables with fresh for less sodium and more flavor.

ENJOY ALL THE DIABETIC LIVING TITLES

A Better Homes and Gardens Book

Books to Help Everyone

Diabetic Living is your resource for fresh and appealing recipes, as well as lifestyle information, tips and techniques. Relax and enjoy expert information on managing diabetes, planning delicious meals and creating a healthy lifestyle.

Diabetic Living **helps you manage diabetes**

DIABETIC LIVING®